Myth and the Indian Novel in English
A Critical Study

Myth and the Indian Novel in English

A Critical Study

JAYA PRASAD

Prestige Books International
New Delhi

Published by
Prestige Books International
New Delhi 110 060
prestigebooks@gmail.com
Phone: 9818755529

Associate Office
London SW11 6HU

Associate Office
Sydney 2001

ISBN: 81-7851-083-9

Printed in India

Contents

Preface

The present work is devoted to unraveling the mystery and magic of myth and the reciprocal relationship that exists between literature and myth. It discusses in detail the role that myth plays in society and in literature with reference to four novels authored by Indo-Anglian novelists.

In the introductory chapter the different theories related to myth have been discussed. Since myth is a subject common to many disciplines, due cognizance has been taken of the views expressed by experts from fields such as anthropology, psychology, sociology besides literature. Thereafter the relationship between myth and literature has been examined. The contribution that myth makes to literature, the techniques used to incorporate myth in literary works, the sources of myth, the different types of myth and the female perspective on myth are some of the issues that have been raised and discussed in the introductory chapter.

The second chapter is *The Bengal Peasant Life*: *Myths as Celebration of Collectivity and Connectivity.* It presents a comprehensive study of Lal Bihari Day's artifice vis-à-vis the myth in his novel *The Bengal Peasant Life* (1874). In this novel, myth exemplifies Bronislaw Malinowski's functionalism. At the same time Northrop Frye's four mythos corresponding to the four seasons become evident in the narrative structure. In this masterpiece of Day, one comes face to face with the socio-religious utility of myth in the lives of the peasantry of Bengal. The novel brings to the fore the reality that religious myth is permeated with the spirit of sustainable development. It is devoted to maintaining ecological balance and protecting the environment. Evan though this novel was commissioned by a benevolent zamindar, Day has not hesitated in highlighting the tyranny of this class and how the hapless peasantry suffered at its hands. On the whole, Day emerges as a neutral analyst of rural life in which myth is seen to play a positive as well as negative role. Day does not assume the mantle of the judge. He simply narrates, without bias and prejudice, the socio-religious life of the Hindu peasantry as it was during the late 19ths century.

In sharp contrast to Day's work is the second novel that has been studied in the third chapter *The Big Heart: A Discordant Note*. This chapter presents the socialist perspective of its writer Mulk Raj Anand and its protagonist Ananta on the matter of myth. Anand was a rebel so far as religion and religious values are concerned. Consequently, he created heroes with a similar mentality. Anand always protested against the rigidities of primitive myth and religion because he found them regressive and repressive. As a natural corollary he attacked and rejected mythic archetypes, patterns and values that overtly or covertly promote rejection and repression of men and women on the basis of caste, class and gender. Surprisingly, however, none of his protagonists including Ananta are militant in their opposition to mythic ideology. Rather the orthodox elements of his novels are aggressive, violent and inhuman while advocating regressive traditions. In *The Big Heart* (1945), Anand brings to the fore the elements of barbarity and irrationality latent in the myths and in those who believe in them. His heroes like Ananta, Bakha or Munoo—are, on the other hand, reasonable individuals who rarely allow emotions to overpower them.

Thus, one comes face-to-face with two authors who use myth differently. While Day is subtle in highlighting the manipulation of myth by vested interests, Anand does not mince his words in exposing the subversion of human rights in the name of myth. Well before independence the conflict between traditional viewpoint and modern ideology had already begun in the pages of Indian English literature. The two novels show that Indian English novelists have, since the early days, fearlessly articulated opinion on even delicate issues such as religion and myth at a time when both traditional power holders and alien rulers often worked in tandem to harass ordinary Indians.

The fourth chapter of the book is a study of Raja Rao's masterpiece *The Serpent and the Rope* (1960). Unlike Day and Anand, Rao emerges strongly in favour of the myth both in life as well as in literature. His novel is permeated with the mythic world view. The work tries to highlight the contribution that myth makes in the emotional well-being of man. Rao is at pains to convince that myth is not a liability but an asset for humanity. He digresses to epics such as the *Ramayana* or refers to Hindu and Greek mythic figures to explain certain key concepts like *dharma* or to resolve the emotional problems of his characters. It is almost a religious novel that is strangely secular too.

The fifth chapter focusing on Githa Hariharan's award winning novel *The Thousand Faces of Night* (1992) brings to the fore the contemporary female perspective on myth. This novel reveals the duality inherent to the myth and the ambivalence of women towards it. The leading lady of this novel ultimately realizes the need for the constant reinterpretation of myth. She also becomes conscious of the exploitation integral to the 'myth' of the 'modern/liberated' woman. She finally musters the courage required for the total rejection of the old as well as the new myth so as to create a value system that would do justice to her and all other women.

The concluding chapter compares and contrasts the novels selected for study and the role of myth in each of them. It incorporates the views of eminent critics and writers to stress the fact that myth continues to be useful and dynamic because whether a writer loves the myth or hates it, he continues to create interesting works because of it.

The book includes relevant appendices that together illustrate the inter-relationship of myth and literature.

Patna 2021 **Jaya Prasad**

Acknowledgements

Myth is a fascinating and intriguing subject, very challenging and demanding. Many people were witness to my effort and endeavour to make sense of it.

First and foremost, I thank Prof. Shaileshwar Sati Prasad, a renowned academician and intellectual of Bihar, for his guidance and constructive criticism. I wish to thank all my teachers of Department of English, Patna University, and Department of English, Magadh Mahila College, Patna. I would especially like to mention Prof. S.M. Ashok, Prof. Shankar Dutta, Prof. Muniba Sami, Prof. Shiv Jatan Thakur, Prof. Suman Prabha and Prof. Zaira Kalim. I fondly recall all my colleagues and staff at YSNM College, Daltonganj, who have tried their best to be supportive to me. I am equally thankful to my present place of work B.S. College, Danapur. The college has treated me like family.

I have been blessed with an exceptional family. My mother Smt. Kusum Verma Prasad has nurtured me most lovingly and has been a great motivating force. My elder brother Dr Sangeet Kumar, my sisters Divya Prasad and Pratima Prasad have been my strongest supporters and most vigilant critics! My husband Manteswari Charan has also been there for me. Shashwat, our parents' first grandchild, this book is for you too as the younger generation has to carry the cultural legacy forward.

The competence and efficiency of my late father Radha Mohan Prasad, a retired administrator, still inspires me. I seek his blessings every day.

JAYA PRASAD

Introduction

Myth has always been engaging and engrossing. It has enchanted and intrigued many since centuries. While laymen have been wonderstruck by these marvellous stories, trying to imbibe certain values from them; literary critics have devoted themselves to unravelling the magic and mystery of myth.

Two important questions have always raised the hackles of the littérateurs: 'what is myth'? and 'what has myth got to do with literature'? Northrop Frye replies: "Myth is and always has been an integral element of literature, the interest of poets in myth and mythology having been remarkable and constant since Homer's time." (349)

It is clear from Frye's assertion that the nexus of myth and literature is of antiquity. Contemporary writers too reiterate rather than refute Frye's claims. Sri Lankan novelist Romesh Gunesekera says that "novels feed on everything that has gone before" thereby including myth as one of the formative influences on literature. He further makes clear: "a novel has to create a world and cannot simply rely on the real place to provide sustenance. Sometimes it is the real place that gains sustenance from the fictional." Thus, myth both as a figment of imagination or as a fact finds legitimacy in literature.

The term myth has numerous connotations to it depending upon the context in which it is used and the perspective from which it is viewed. It is actually a subject common to a number of disciplines, literature being just one of them. However, a vital difference between literature and anthropology, sociology or psychology is that while literature uses myth, the other disciplines study it.

Myth, in general opinion, is something opposed to reality. It is the antithesis of that which is actual and factual. In other words, myth implies that which is false, imaginary or fictitious. It is that which is not real or true. Etymologically, however, the term is derived from the Greek word 'mythos' that means story. Story in turn can imply either a recounting of past events, incidents, narration of the invented or imagined; plot of book or play; report in a newspaper or untrue statement and description.

Myth, thus, as a synonym of story can imply an account of real as well as imaginary events. It all depends on one's point of view. If Ram is myth for the present generation, then, say a thousand years later, Mahatma Gandhi may appear the same to the humanity of the time.

One often hears statements like "wealth is myth" or that money is an 'illusion,' a 'maya' or a 'mirage' while real happiness lies in contentment. Thus, myth is a term that can imply not just falsehood but also illusion and delusion. It is, in fact, a subjective term explaining different psychological states of man that are related to his sense of sadness and jubilation, failure and success, material achievement or penury. Philosophers and saints use the term 'myth' so as to teach people the value of equanimity in life. According to them, success and failure are fleeting phases of life. These are 'myth,' that is, an illusion. What ultimately matters is man's integrity—his ability to remain firmly grounded in right values all through his life. Visionaries, in this context, use the term myth both to highlight the transitory nature of human feelings as also to exemplify through stories the values and virtues that they want to instill in their disciples and devotees.

Myth, however, is more than mere story. Primitive myth, in particular, seems to be the product of a time when, as Nietzsche has observed: "man's religious, aesthetic, and moral perceptions were at one" (Qtd. Daiches and Thorlby 61). This is probably why the litterateurs look back to it. The relationship between literature and myth is two way. On the one hand, there is a compelling urge in writers and artists to re-tell myth. On the other hand, there is an equally strong tendency towards demythologization as evident in feminist writings. The two trends have their own justifications but what is undeniably true about both is that the two are invariably dealing with the same subject—myth. Thus, myth continues to survive even in those texts that are anti-myth.

Mythology is at the genesis of many of the ideologies and movements. They have emerged partly in reaction to ancient mythic values. Myth, therefore, can be credited with contributing to modern dialectics and discourse. In reaction to the ideology of the ancients, have arisen the doctrine of democracy, Marxism, feminism etc. Myth, thus, has political, economic and gender connotations to it too. The contradictions and anomalies inherent to myth have given rise to a number of schools of thought.

Another vital dimension of myth is that it has, since times immemorial, catered to man's recreational needs. It also answers to man's innate inquisitiveness. Human beings have always been eager to know about the other. At the same time, mankind has been jealously eager to preserve all that it knows or wants to tell. This urge to preserve, tell, know and even share manifests itself best in 'myth.' The question whether myth is true or false is irrelevant. It needs to be taken as a point of view with which we are free to agree or disagree.

Myth is both a way of 'association' and 'disassociation.' It is a way of maintaining our cultural identity. "The social memory, myths, folklore, legends and proverbs are essential links with . . . culture and . . . can be overlooked only with the inevitable result of highbrowism and alienation" (Sati Prasad 1995: 94). Moreover, myth caters to the human eagerness to make ourselves distinct from the rest. At the same time, it is a way of identifying and uniting with our own. In fact, myth is often used by writers and artists to establish their ethnic or national identity in works of art. This is especially true in the context of Asian and African writers who use English as a medium of expression:

> The English language could not be abandoned if the country and its

> people were to avail of the opportunities it provided worldwide. Nor could the cultural/ethnic identity be martyred at the altar of Westernization or Americanization. A way out of the problem was to infuse the English language itself with ethnic cultures.
>
> It was with this end in view that native myths and legends began to be used in English language texts. This was not creolization as had happened in the Caribbean. Rather the method was translation. Authors such as Tagore, Aurobindo and Raja Rao translated and incorporated Indian myths and legends in their works to give them a touch of the varied Indian ethnicity. In recent times, African writers and poets such as Dennis Brutus and Ezepiel Maphahule of South Africa, Wole Soyinka, Chinua Achebe and Christopher Okigbo of Nigeria have done the same.
>
> The insistence of Asian and African writers to include indigenous myths and legends in English language texts shows their commitment to their own ethnic identities. This is not surprising in view of the spell of colonization and the consequent denigration of native ethnic culture that their people have had to put up with. It is as if by reinstating ethnic identities in English language texts, the Empire is striking back. (Jaya Prasad 2002: 30)

Myth is also a way of living, loving and learning. It is a way of life. It tries to channelize human energy, focus human attention, govern human relationship and coordinate human interaction, that is, guide human life in general. Myth, in reality, is actually a part of culture and cultural ethos. In fact, "myth not only responds to physical reality but also tries to go beyond it and comprehend the metaphysical basis of existence" (Ila Sinha iv). Myth is the verbal and literal expression of culture. The best way, therefore, to comprehend the culture of a country, community or society, to understand its ethos, is to go through its myths and legends. What is acceptable and unacceptable in a particular society? What is permissible? What is not permissible? How to dress, talk and interact? What to expect or not to expect? What to say or not to say? Who and what are important? What is sacred and what is profane and why? These are some of the queries that myths attempt to answer. "Any body of myths tries to give a comprehensive account of the world and of the people to whom it belongs" (Wiegel 10). In other words, myths describe "the political organization . . . codes of laws . . . high ethical code, and above all . . . conceptions of God, the soul, and the universe" (Mackenzie v) of a society.

Primitive myth belongs to the time when man possessed a unified sensibility and a unified vision. Consequently, myth of the time is story as well as song, fiction as well as fact. It is instruction as well as entertainment. It is art as well as science. Myth, in reality, has "more than one function" (Daiches and Thorlby 70). It would be wrong to dismiss myths as merely hypothetical stories about gods, goddesses, kings, queens, witches, demons, ghosts or fairies. These personages are merely an excuse or a medium of explaining, in an interesting and engrossing manner, certain vital truths about human life or the guiding principles of a society. The fact that myths are stories about celestial and royal beings is only half the truth. Myth actually tries to make people understand not just the human world but the world of nature as well. It connects not just man to man but man to nature as well. Myth, in fact, is deeply steeped with the spirit of sustainable development:

> It is through myths that people are taught how to relate to their natural environment. In India many tribal and Hindu myths render sacred a host of plants, trees, birds and animals such as the Tulsi, the Peepal tree, the owl, the cow, the tiger etc. The plants and trees, it has been found, have therapeutic value while the birds and animals are crucial for ecological balance and for tribal and rural economy. Hence the notion that all myths are unscientific or the imaginary creations of an illiterate and primitive people is itself a myth. Myths seem to be the storehouse or the wealth of knowledge accumulated by our ancestors about the natural as well as human phenomena. Perhaps the myths were given the status of 'dharma' or 'religion' in each ethnic group only to ensure the preservation of the knowledge which the ancestors had painstakingly collected. (Jaya Prasad 2002: 31)

"Myths of ancient people that have come down to us" are thus "of great scientific value in this respect" (Panoy 137). The knowledge latent in the myths, legends and folktales have created a new science called 'geomythology'. This new discipline is dedicated to the analysis of previous natural disasters so as to gauge, guess and escape impending natural calamities by decoding the myths. "Myth can tell us a great deal about what happened in the past and are important in establishing what happened here 300 years ago" said Brian Atwater, of the U.S. Geological Survey in Seattle. What this new discipline called geomythology does is to combine earth science studies and the analysis of ancient myths and legends to make a historical and geographical account of natural occurrences. The purpose is to see if there is any pattern or link between past and present events in the world of nature and if predictions can be made on the basis of it. Geologists have found that Middle Eastern flooding myths, including the story of Noah, could be traced to the sudden inundation of the Black Sea 7,600 years ago. Ruth Ludwin, a seismologist in Seattle, discovered tales of villages being washed away and of whales and thunderbirds locked in fights. These stories were a key influence on Mr. Atwater, who started to study the 680-mile-long Cascadian subduction zone fault along the coast. What he found provided a shock. Long stretches had suffered sudden inundation relatively recently. The study of tree stumps in this drowned landscape indicates that there had been a huge earthquake and a tsunami between 1680 and 1720. Later research on tree rings put the date at between 1699 and 1700. Local legends proved helpful. Japanese researchers studied their records and traced an orphan tsunami—a giant wave not linked to a local earthquake—that destroyed several villages on January 27, 1700. The December 25, 2004 tsunami was also triggered by a strong earthquake. The Moken or sea gypsies of Thailand have a tradition which warns that when tides recede far and fast, now known as a precursor of a tsunami, then a man-eating wave will soon head their way; so, they should run far and fast. On 26 December, 2004, they did exactly this and survived.

Thus, it is wrong to dismiss 'myths' as myth. What needs to be done is to decode the myths and tap the knowledge and experience of our ancestors about the natural and human phenomena and benefit from it. Hence anthropologists like Bronislaw Malinowski are slightly off the mark when they assert: "Myth is not a piece of primitive science" (210). Myths and legends may not explain the exact causes of natural calamities but they at least contain a record of such occurrences as also ways to gauge the coming of such disasters and how to escape them unhurt. The aboriginal population of Andaman and Nicobar Islands suffered minimum casualties on 26 December 2004 because of their folk-knowledge. On the other hand, modernized tribal population that had forgotten its cultural past was unable to cope with the tsunami. It is for this reason that the science of Geomythology has begun to discover geographical and environmental evidences of events mentioned in myths.

Mythology is generally believed to be a source of knowing one's cultural and social history. There has been a growing tendency to take recourse to myths "for making the people aware of their heritage and history" (Sati Prasad 1995: 51). History often provides themes and topics and subjects for story-making or myth making. Literature, by borrowing from mythology and history, helps keep alive our socio-political and religious heritage. Shashi Deshpande observed in *The Stone Women*: "The *Mahabharata* . . . is getting less and less known." Culturally conscious writers like the authoress herself, however, incorporate the myths of the *Ramayana* and the *Mahabharata* and other cultural stories in their narratives, thereby, keeping them alive in the memory of the people. A classic example of this is Shashi Tharoor's political satire *The Great Indian Novel* (1989). In this book Tharoor mixes contemporary and mythic history and exposes each in the context of the other. This tactic brings to light the unspoken, hushed or hidden frailties of divine, seemingly divine or legendary personages in a humorous manner that amuses rather than offends. He caricatures both myth and history producing ripples of laughter instead of arousing anger and resentment.

Thus, literature is an area wherein myth and history can

mingle. The three can be fruitfully and fabulously fused together. It is clear that events or incidents are often labeled 'mythic' when it is hard to prove that they actually happened. History alludes to 'reality' or 'fact.' It deals with events that actually took place. History, in fact, begins from where myth ends. Myth is often a story without dates. History, on the other hand, is full of dates and factual evidences. Myth is more or less a matter of 'belief' and 'faith' and also 'lifestyle.' History is something undeniable. For example, "the white man's burden" is a myth but Nazism is not. It is an undeniable fact which no one can refute because it did happen. People experienced it. History, thus, has a persuasive power which myth lacks. The powers of myth are largely psychological rather than factual. It is largely subjective. History is accurate and objective. That which cannot be verified is myth while that which can be verified is history. Presumption is myth. History, on the other hand, is not presumed but it is a record of events and activities that actually took place at some point of time in the past.

As already pointed out, literature makes use of both myth and history. Both provide themes and ideas to literature. Since literature is primarily concerned with society whereas myth and history deal with the lives of people in the past or present, the three are mutually inclusive. Literature too comes handy to the historian in order to study the social life of the people of a particular period. Thus, the three subjects—literature, myth and history—replenish each other. The renowned Swiss psychologist C.G. Jung believed that "history and mythology are sometimes . . . the material with which . . . poets" work.

An important reality of myth is that it is fundamentally 'inclusive. It first binds man to man and then the whole of humanity to the world of nature and vice-versa. It promotes cohesion and group activity. It is to be noted that in traditional myth-believing societies joint family is commonly found while the nuclear family system is not so popular. "Myths are by nature collective and communal; they bind a tribe or a nation together in common psychological and spiritual activities" (Guerian 161).

Since myth is tied to religion, it is a 'living' force and not something dead and distant. It is not merely a story to be heard. Rather, myth in many societies is also practiced and observed as rituals. In Hindu society and tribal societies myth is almost a way of life. Myth gets manifested in the behaviour of the people also, in their day-to-day activities. It almost manages the life of man from dawn to dusk. Mythic beliefs and practices have been so well internalized by the people that even the most educated and ultra-modern of men and women unconsciously retain myth ordained behavioural patterns in spite of their apparent detachment from indigenous ideology. Sometimes psychological problems grip people primarily because the innate desire to get grounded in mythically acclaimed social institutions like family or marriage refuses to die down despite the fast life and upward mobility. Myth, thus, is not a system that aims to contain, restrain or constrict man. Rather myth is devoted towards fulfilling the essential or fundamental physical, psychological and social requirements of man. This is the reason why myth refuses to become redundant. People may reject one body of myths but only to embrace another. The Greek myths are today merely stories primarily because the Greek got another collection of myths to feel anchored—the Christian myth. Religious conversions are, thus, just a rejection of a particular set of myths in favour of another.

Myths, in every society, are basically the projection of people's hopes, desires, requirements, values, fears and joys as man is biologically and psychologically the same everywhere in spite of racial differences. Hence almost all myths deal invariably with the similar issues—birth, death, marriage, management of life in general, does and don't etc. The purpose too is the same—to channelize human activity and shape "the mind and character of people" (Guerin 161). Thus, in spite of apparent differences, different mythologies have a lot in common.

James Frazer (1854-1941), Sigmund Freud (1856-1939) Bronislaw Malinowski (1884-1942), Richard V. Chase (1904-1988), Claude Levi-Strauss (1908-2000) and Northrop Frye

(1912-1991) are some of the prominent social scientists and literary critics who made significant contributions towards unraveling the mystery of the myths. Each of the experts named above represent a different approach towards myth. Their views are divergent and they have directly and boldly questioned each other's standpoint. The discourse has created an interesting body of work on myths, legends and folktales.

Canadian critic Northrop Frye was basically a man of literature. He studied myths from a literary point of view. He co-related literature, myth and the world of nature. According to Frye, myth provides archetypes to literature. The mythic archetypes are based on the seasonal cycle. Frye did not deny that myth would have *something* to do with other branches of knowledges: "Myth is a conception which runs through many areas of contemporary thought: anthropology, psychology, comparative religion, sociology, and several others" (349). However, he firmly believed that myth's most "common and easily recognized form" is "as a work of literature" (349). He asserted:

> By myth . . . I mean primarily a certain type of story. It is a story in which some of the chief characters are gods or other kings larger in power than humanity. Very seldom is it located in history: its action takes place in a world above or prior to ordinary time. Hence like the folk tale, it is an abstract story-pattern. The characters can do what they like, which means what the story-teller likes: there is no need to be plausible or logical in motivation. The things that happen in myth are things that happen only in stories; they are in a self-contained literary world. (360)

In his definition of myth Frye has underlined the unrestrained expression of imagination in myths. He has highlighted the immense freedom that the writers of myths have enjoyed while creating their weird, wild, magical, mysterious and mesmerizing tales. At the same he claims that in spite of apparent incongruity and illogicality, myths as stories do have a 'pattern.' Frye further says that "as a type of story, myth is a form of verbal art, and belongs to the world of art" (360). In the context of art, the critic opines: "The total form of art, so to speak, is a world whose content is nature but whose form is human, hence when it 'imitates' nature, it assimilates nature to human forms" (360-61). According to him myth, as a natural corollary, too attempts to see nature in human shape. Frye postulates: "Myth seizes on the fundamental element of design offered by nature—the cycles, as we have it daily in the sun and yearly in the seasons—and assimilates it to the human cycle of life, death, and (analogy again) rebirth" (361). Frye then goes on to explicate his famous theory about myths as analogous and identical to the seasonal cycle:

> The absorption of the natural cycle into mythology provides myth with two of these structures; the raising movement which we find in the myths of spring or the dawn, of birth, marriage and resurrection, and the falling movement in myths of death, metamorphosis or sacrifice. These movements reappear as the structural principles of comedy and tragedy in literature. (362)

In his acclaimed book *Anatomy of Criticism* (1957) Frye indicates the correspondent genres for the four seasons as follows:

1. The mythos of spring: comedy
2. The mythos of summer: romance
3. The mythos of fall: tragedy
4. The mythos of winter: irony

Thus, according to Frye, myth is the structural organizing principle of literary form. In *The Stubborn Structure* (1970), he claims that "mythology as a whole provides a kind of diagram or blueprint of what literature as a whole is all about, an imaginative survey of the human situation from the beginning to the end, from the heights to the depths, of what is imaginatively conceivable" (Guerin). Frye firmly believes that in spite of the apparent disorder, there is a kind of 'order' in the myths that corresponds strongly to the cycle of both human life and natural world. Myths reflect the major divisions or phases in the life of man and nature.

Psychoanalysts, however, presented an entirely different and radical interpretation of myth. Sigmund Freud (1856-1939), the

Austrian founding father of psychoanalysis, postulated in *The Interpretation of Dreams* (1899) and later in *Totem and Taboo* (1913) that myth is the distorted wish-dreams of entire peoples. He studied Sophocles' fifth century Athenian drama Oedipus Rex to arrive at the conclusion that myths are basically a manifestation of repressed desires. These suppressed sexual fantasies, in Freud's opinion, got expressed not just in myth but also in dreams, fairy tales, folktales and even jokes.

Freud's one-time protégé and later rival, Carl Gustave Jung (1875-1861) rejected not just his mentor's ideas but also those of Frye's. He gave two key concepts called the 'collective unconscious' and 'archetypes' so as to explain the 'content' and 'meaning' of myth. By 'collective unconscious' he meant racial or primeval memory. 'Archetypes,' on the other hand, were universal motifs that come from the collective unconscious and are the basic content of myth, fairy tales and dreams. Myth, therefore, is not dependent on external factors such as seasonal or solar cycle. On the contrary, myth is the projection of the innate psychic phenomena.

Myth is the means by which archetypes, that is, the collective unconscious become manifest and articulate to the conscious mind. Jung developed these ideas in works like *The Psychology of the Unconscious* (1912) later revised as *Symbols of Transformation* (1967) and *The Archetypes and the Collective Unconscious* (1959) to detect an intimate relationship between dreams, myth and art. According to him, the three serve as media through which archetypes become accessible to the consciousness. In *Modern Man in Search of a Soul* (1933), Jung observed that a great artist is a person who possesses the primordial vision, a special sensibility to archetypal patterns and a gift for speaking in primordial images that enable him/her to transmit experiences of the inner world through art.

The Polish born British anthropologist Bronislaw Malinowski differs from the likes of Northrop Frye and Sigmund Freud. In *Sex, Culture, and Myth* (1963), Malinowski observes: "Myth must be studied in its social, ritual and ethical effects rather than as an imaginative and pseudo-scientific tale" (246). According to Malinowski myth is central to religion and thereby has a crucial role to play in the matter of ethics and the structure of society. In other words, he lays more stress on the practical aspect of myth. Co-relating myth and religion, he opines "since myth is an inevitable background of faith, its very backbone indeed, we have to study myth as it affects the life of people" (249). Defining the term 'myth,' Malinowski says:

> It is a story which is told in order to establish a belief, to serve as a precedent in ceremony or ritual, or to rank as a pattern of moral or religious conduct. Mythology, therefore, or the sacred tradition of society, is a body of narrative woven into their culture, dictating their belief, defining their ritual, acting as the chart of their social order and the pattern of their moral behaviour. Every myth has naturally a literary content, since it is always a narrative, but this narrative is not merely a piece of entertaining fiction or explanatory statement to the believer. It is a true account of sensational events which have shaped the constitution of the world, the essence of moral conduct, and determines the ritual contact between man and his maker, or the powers that be. (249)

Thus, in the above excerpt the Polish anthropologist adopts a functionalist approach to myth. What is the utility of myth? How and what is it contributing to human society? Malinowski does not deny that myth is yet another type of literature but he refuses to dismiss it as something recreational. He calls myth "the sacred tradition of society" (249) and asserts repeatedly in *Sex, Culture, and Myth*: "It is maintained here that myth is an intrinsic part in the make-up of any religion, more precisely that it supplies the charter for belief, moral conduct and social organization" (210). He further states: "This implies that myth is not a piece of primitive science, not yet a primeval philosophic allegory of a semi-poetic, rhapsodic nature, not yet a strangely garbled historic account. Hence the primary function of myth is neither to explain, nor to recount past historical events, nor to express the fantasies or crystallized day-dreams of a community" (210).

Malinowski does not just present his views on the matter but analyses all that has already been said by other critics on myth. He scrutinizes the psychoanalytical, functional and social approach to myth. He strongly supports utilitarian/ functional dimension of myth. He seems to have been influenced by fellow anthropologists and sociologists like Robertson Smith, Durkheim, Hubert Morse and Radcliff Brown who made a comprehensive study of religion. Since myth is part of religion, Malinowski believes that "its fundamental function is . . . essentially a precedent in support of religion and magical belief, or in support of social and moral order" (292). He opines "myth is in a way a mere unfolding of dogma even a cursory glance at any religion would show" (248).

Another aspect of myth that Malinowski has harped on is the 'ritual.' According to him ritual is the actual or practical manifestation of myth. Ritual is the behavioural aspect of myth. In the Indian context let's consider the dogma of 'pativrata nari.' The story of Sita and Savitri are the myths that contain this dogma. The tendency of Hindu women to touch the feet of their husbands is the ritual manifestation of this dogma and the myth related to it. "The actual sociological function of mythology . . . the main object of the sacred tradition . . . is to lay down the effective precedent of a glorified past for repetitive actions in the present" (251). Influenced strongly by the views of sociologist Robertson Smith who believed that a religious myth must have ritual expression else it is not at all sacred, Malinowski asserted emphatically: "I would say that a myth that is not expressed in ritual is not a myth but merely an old wives' or an old men's tale" (254).

Smith and Malinowski have rightly highlighted the nexus between religion, myth, ritual and dogma. Indeed, myth has some or the other role to play in all of these. Religion makes use of myth to elaborate its basic ideas. For example, the notion of 'pativrata nari' is central to the Hindu religion. Hence there are a host of stories and mythic heroines like Sita, Savitri, Sati or Mata Anasuya whose life histories explain what 'satitva' is all about or what kind of a life a pativrata nari leads. D.D. Kosambi rightly observes: "religion clothes some myth in dogma" (237) or as Malinowski repeats again and again "most dogmas have their foundation in myth" (254). Myths have been used to illustrate the dogma. In other words, dogma originates from myth.

Richard Chase, the American literary critic, sought to distance myth from dogma. He was more interested in the 'literariness' of myth. To him myth was another manifestation of art or of man's aesthetic and creative impulses and urges. Hence there is always a recreational angle to myth and it is not without purpose. Malinowski always sought to play down or negate the recreational aspect of myth. Chase, however, asserted that myth, as a kind of poetry, performs "the same cathartic function" (Wimsatt & Brooks 712) that Aristotle has talked about in his 'Poetics.' Consequently, even when taken solely as poetry or art, myth does not become useless or valueless. Rather it contributes to the psychological well-being of man. First of all, the process of myth making allows man to give free play to his imagination, to express his aesthetic and creative potentialities. Secondly, as a recipient/ hearer/ participant/ actor/ dancer of myth it allows man to give vent to his suppressed emotions and unexpressed feelings or acknowledge the hidden psychological upheavals caused by conflicts (such as between 'duty' and 'desire')

The arguments of Chase and Malinowski make clear that whether one takes myth as literature or myth as dogma and religion, it cannot be equated with the 'fairy tale' or the 'legend.' There is a general tendency to group them together as stories. The three categories namely myth, fairytale and legend are indeed 'stories' basically but there exists an important difference of 'degree' between them if not of 'kind':

> There is a class of stories which might be called fairy-tales or folk-tales. . . . They are told entirely for entertainment. Their subject matter consists of grotesque, miraculous, and often bawdy events which appear in the same light to the natives [and non-natives]. . . . These stories definitely form what may be called . . . tales told for mere

> entertainment—and they do not convey any important truths, moral percepts, or ritual directions.
>
> A second class . . . consists of historical legends believed to be true and usually told to enhance or define the status of a community, clan, or family. These stories as a rule contain little or nothing that is actually miraculous or extravagant, although they are not always free from exaggerations in the heroic line.
>
> There is a third class of story, told for a very serious purpose, and connected with religious belief, social order, or moral issues, and last but not the least with ritual. These stories, like the fairy tales, have a strong tinge of the supernatural. But here the supernatural is not a mere trick of fancy, not an idle satisfaction of day-dreaming, but a miracle which is firmly believed in, a miracle, moreover, which, is as likely as not, will be re-enacted in a partial and modified form through the ritual of native magic and religion.
>
> Thus, there exists a special class of story regarded as sacred, embodied in ritual, morals and social organisation. (304)

The "third class of story" is the myth. While Malinowski values these stories for their social and functional contribution in the life of man, Chase appreciates them for the psychological reprieve that they offer to humanity as a work of art and literature. In other words, both Malinowski and Chase make myth crucial for man's well-being. They seem to disagree only over the way in which myth performs this role: as art or as religion and dogma?

A pertinent point in this context is that why is it considered necessary to cloth dogma in myth or myth in dogma? In other words, why is myth considered an appropriate vehicle for propagating dogmatic or religious ideas? Is theoretical or prosaic religion inadequate to create the impact that myth can manage? Does myth make both religion and its dogmas attractive, interesting or easy to imbibe? Kosaṁbi replied "A myth may grip us by its imagery" (37). This brings us to the aesthetic of myth.

Frye in his study of myths has stated that myths are based on the seasonal cycle. Consequently, the world of myth is as varied in colour and tone as nature herself. Secondly, language is the vehicle of myth. Hence, myth, as narrative, includes almost all the tricks, techniques or ornaments of language. Even Malinowski, who strongly opposes Frye's analysis, admits the literary content of myths and the consequent enjoyment that can be derived from them: "Every myth has naturally a literary content, since it is always a narrative" (249).

Chase is much enamoured of myth as a narrative art. In fact, the ideas of Chase or Frye are not wholly new: "The Neapolitan scholar Giambaltista Vico had elaborated the theory that myth was a kind of poetic language, the only language that man was capable of in his primitive stage of development, and yet, for all that, a genuine language with its own principle of structure and its own logic" (Wimsatt & Brooks 700).

Taking the cue from Vico, Chase propounded famously in *The Quest for Myth* that "myth . . . is only art" (*Ibid.* 711). He was not favourably disposed to the Malinowskian idea of myth as dogma or dogma as myth. He rather chose to believe that myths constitute, from primeval times, man's "most vital experiences" (Jung 182). Instead of co-relating myth with dogma or religion, he saw strong resemblance between poetry and myth: "Poetry and myth, he argues, arise out of the same human needs, represent the same kind of symbolic structure, succeed in investing experience with the same kind of awe and magical wonder, and perform the same cathartic function" (Wimsatt & Brooks 711).

Almost all the critics, however, are unanimous over the fact at least that myths express man's primordial experiences. Hence in spite of geographical, racial or climatic differences mythologies of different societies or cultures are found to have common themes, topics or issues. The personages or characters too are invariably of the same type. In the mythologies of all cultures the principal characters are gods, goddesses, devils, witches, kings, queens, super heroes and the like. SIMILARLY, the themes are also common. Anthropologist Clyde Kluc Khohn in his article 'Recurrent Themes in Myth and Mythmaking' writes: "Five themes occur in the myth and folktales of all societies: catastrophe, generally through floods; the slaying of monsters; incests;

sibling rivalry, generally between brothers; and castration, sometimes actual but more commonly symbolic." The myths of almost all societies "tell us how the world was created, what powers rule it, why men must behave in certain ways, and why they must die" (Thorlby 70).

British anthropologist Sir James G. Frazer (1854-1941) observed "the essential similarity of man's chief wants everywhere and at all times" (Guerin 168). Hence the symbols used in myths represent the fundamental needs and feelings that are almost similar across the ancient mythologies. These 'common' symbols found in different mythologies are what Jung called 'archetypes.' Some of such symbols and images are the 'sky father' and 'earth mother,' 'light,' 'blood,' 'the axis of a wheel,' 'water,' etc. Almost all of these have similar connotations in societies that have no history of cultural exchange. Hence the only explanation for similar symbols and images for primordial experiences is that man is biologically and psychological the same everywhere. "Similar motifs or themes may be found among many different mythologies, and certain images that recur in the myths of people widely separated in time and place tend to have a common meaning or, more accurately, tend to elicit comparable psychological responses and to serve similar cultural functions. Such motifs and images are called archetypes. Stated simply, archetypes are universal symbols" (Guerin 161).

These archetypes embody not just man's collective, unconscious experiences but also bring forth the inherited response-patterns of the human race. The mythologies of antiquity are "a relic of such experiences" (Jung 183) and a museum of such symbols and archetypes that do not require explanation or classification in societies where myth continues to be a living force. "It is therefore to be expected of the poet that he will resort to mythology in order to give his experience its most fitting expression" (*Ibid.*) and get/ make the desired reaction/ effect from his readers/audience. "It would be a serious mistake to suppose that he works with materials received at second-hand. The primordial experience is the source of his creativeness; it cannot be fathomed, and therefore requires mythological imagery to give it form" (*Ibid.*). Often a person's experiences or feelings are complex, his visions multiple. Hence he must have "at his disposal a huge store of materials if he is to communicate even a few of his intimations. . . . What is more he must resort to an imagery that is difficult to handle and full of contradictions in order to express the weird paradoxicality of his visions" (*Ibid.*). Such scope only the myth can offer. Mythic imagery has multiple meanings and is, as a result, full of unlimited "narrative potentialities" (Sati Prasad 1995: 54).

Meenakshi Mukherjee in her book *The Twice Born Fiction* discusses the multiple ways in which the 'narrative potential of myths has become evident in the works of Indian English writers: "There seems to be two distinct ways in which myths have been used in Indo-Anglian novels: as part of a digressional technique . . . and as structural parallels, where a mythical situation underlies the whole or part of a novel" (136). The 'digressional technique' implies "weaving in stories within a story or pausing to narrate a parable to drive home a point" (138). Mukherjee says that "the digressional method of story-telling is perhaps the oldest device in narrative literature . . . characteristic . . . of the Panchatantra, the Vishnu Purana and other Sanskrit narrative treatises, and of the *Mahabharata* and the *Ramayana* as well" (138). 'Structural parallel,' on the other hand, requires some similarity between the myth and the story being written by a writer. "A mythic parallel becomes significant only when a human situation is primarily and recognizably human and real. A concrete and particular situation gains an extension into infinity by being absorbed into a corresponding situation in mythology" (149).

Besides the digressional technique and the structural parallel, there exists yet another method. This too requires establishing an essential analogy between the myth and the story being written. Thereafter, says Mukherjee, the writer "changes it totally, intending perhaps to indicate that the same ending is no longer possible (or desirable) for our times" (137).

While Raja Rao and Sudhir Ghose, believes Mukherjee, are the chief exponents of the digressional as well as the structural technique, it is Mulk Raj Anand, the rationalist, who has used the third method. He establishes a parallel between his character and the mythic story only to turn it upside down. In his novels, role reversals are also possible as evident in 'The Big Heart.' In his works, the 'bad' personages of the myth become 'good' and the 'good' are shown as 'bad' in reality.

This bifurcation into good/ bad, virtuous/evil is, according to French anthropologist Claude Levi-Strauss, the essential purpose of myth. "Levi-Strauss puts a focal emphasis on binary oppositions and appears to see the function of myths as essentially that of mediating or resolving structural oppositions that are evident in the natural and cultural world, as well as reconciling contradictions between mythical and experimental knowledge" (Morris 287). According to Levi-Strauss, it is a universal characteristic of human thinking to categorize the world of our experience into pairs of opposites. Some of these are 'given,' and nobody would question their universality: hot/cold, above/below, right/left, for example. Even with these simple pairs, examples may be found which do not fall clearly on one or other side of the line. "Myth is concerned with more troubling ambiguities. The distinction between nature and culture is one: man is an animal, part of nature, but by possessing culture he is apart from the rest of nature. Myths in which animals behave like humans refer to this ambiguity" (Mair).

Levi-Strauss presented a voluminous study of South and North American myths in the four volumes of *Mythologiques* (1964-1971). On the basis of his analysis, he rejected Cassirer's arguments that primitive thought, as evident in myth, is determined by emotional or mystical experiences. He also did not agree with the Jungian idea of archetypal patterns. Jung (1909-1946), in turn, was in disagreement with Bronislaw Malinowski for whom myth is something essentially cultural.

"Jung, on the contrary, regarded myths not as indices of or

charters for cultural institutions but as psychological realities", as expressions of the "archetypes" or "primordial images" of the "collective unconscious" (*International Encyclopedia of Social Sciences* 578). Thus, in Jung's view myths are first and foremost psychic manifestations that represent the nature of the psyche. All the myths concerned with occurrences of nature, such as summer and winter, the phases of the moon, and the rainy seasons, are definitely not allegories of these objective experiences, nor are they to be understood as explanations of the sunrise, the sunset, and other natural phenomena. "Rather they are symbolic expressions of the inner and unconscious psychic drama that becomes accessible to human consciousness by projection—that is, by being mirrored in the events of nature" (*Ibid.*).

For Levi-Strauss, however, myth is "one mode of human communication" (Kirk 43) that gives "access to the mechanism of thought." Myth is a key to understand human perception. Myth and other forms of primitive religious phenomena help us understand how man makes sense of human and natural world. According to Strauss it is with the help of 'metaphor,' the logic of binary oppositions and correlations, exclusions and inclusions, compatibilities and incompatibilities that man makes sense of the world around him. This is essentially how myths are made and indeed the whole of man's intellect. Thus, according to Strauss, the elements of myth (mythemes) like the elements of human language (phonemes) can become meaningful only in relation to other elements.

Noted literary critic P. Lal believes that like each mytheme, contemporary literature too cannot have its significance alone. Contemporary literature can become meaningful work of art only when it relates itself somehow with the primitive myths and legends. "What should an Indian writer in English, or a creative writer in any language, be writing about if not love, and hate, and war, and pride, and peace? And where will he find the complexities of these feelings and activities if not in the myth-world? The gods and goddesses are not out there, separated permanently from us; nor are the anti-gods and rakshasas. They populate the earth: to know them is to really know ourselves" (Lal 17-18).

Thus, the tendency to use archetypal characters, patterns and symbols (through the digressional technique or the structural pattern) is not as some critics allege an endorsement of dogmatic ideas. Rather it is an attempt to understand "the complexities" of human "feelings and activities." It is actually an endeavour "to really know ourselves" (Lal 18). It is an effort to express the inexpressible or the unexplainable. Last but not the least, mythic symbols help the writer to make clear what is permissible or not permissible in human relationships and societies?

In this context it would be worthwhile to recall what Malinowski said in *Sex, Culture, and Myth.* According to him myths can be 'major' as well as 'minor.' In other words, even among the myths there are some that define or illustrate the "fundamental tenants" of native belief and hence are more important. On the other hand, there are less important or "local minor myths" that have "only local currency . . . telling the story of an occurrence . . . a recent event" (307). Even Raja Rao in his *Preface* to *Kanthapura* observed that each place has its own 'sthala purana' or local myths, legends and folktales to boast of.

The 'major' and 'minor' myths that Malinowski has talk about in *'Sex, Culture, And Myth* are actually, according to American anthropologist Robert Redfield (1897-1958) the 'great' and 'little' traditions of every civilization. Redfield proposed the concepts in his book *Peasant Society and Culture (1956).* According to him the customs, beliefs, behavioural pattern, rites and rituals, festivals etc. of the elite/ educated/ thinking class of the population, that is, of the *great community*, are the *great traditions* of society. On the other hand, the uneducated rural peasants and tribals form the *little community* of each civilization and their life styles, beliefs, practices, food habits, dress code etc. are the *little traditions*. It is from these 'great traditions' and 'little traditions', 'great communities' and 'little communities' that 'major' and 'minor' myths are drawn:

Great Community	Little Community
↓	↓
Great Tradition	Little Tradition
↓	↓
Major Myths	Minor Myths

Nadeem Hasnain writes in his book *Indian Anthropology*: "Great Traditions are usually mentioned in original religious epics. Their range is very wide, usually national in nature. These are related with elite, thinking, reflective few of the urban class. Moreover, they are usually organized and norms, rituals etc. are largely clear cut and unambiguous. The great traditions are transmitted from one generation to the other through texts; sometimes these are referred to as 'elite' tradition" (174).

Little traditions, on the other hand, are according to Hasnain: "Mostly oral and are followed by mere beliefs not based on rationality; these are mostly localized and related with rural, unlettered, folk, tribal or peasantry. These are believed to be usually unorganized, haphazard and ambiguous, transmitted orally, through oral literature" (173).

In the Indian context, the 'great traditions' of the Hindus are embodied in the *Mahabharata*, the *Ramayana,* the *Gita,* the *Durga Saptashati,* the *Vishnu Purana* etc. On the other hand, "the folklore, religio-magical practices, customs and rituals whose references are not found in religious epics and which are transmitted orally constitute Little Traditions" (Hasnain 173) of the Hindus.

The *Vedas* and the *Puranas* form the earliest sources of the 'great tradition' of the Hindu community. It is in the *Vedas*, especially the *Rig Veda* (1200 B.C.) that gods/ goddesses have been introduced. "The gods . . . represent the chief powers of nature, such as fire, sun and thunderstorm" (Brockington 10). Hymns or highly refined poetry are addressed to these 'devas' to worship them "Myth are frequently alluded to, but not recounted in extenso, and only the hieratic views are given more prominence" (*Ibid.* 8).

It was only in the Gupta Period that the myths referred to in the *Rig Veda* were elaborated to form the epics. This was the age of the decline of Buddhism and the rise of a reformed Brahmanism. Long poems called the Puranas (old tales) were created. In these poems some of the ancient myths about the gods were preserved and new myths were formulated. Theoretically there are eighteen major Puranas and the same number of minor ones. The extant *Puranas* were compiled between fourth and twelfth centuries while the later ones date between fourth to sixth centuries. Each *Purana* covers five topics: the emanation of the universe, its destruction and re-emanation, the reigns and periods of the *Manus*, the genealogies of the gods and sages and the genealogy of the solar and lunar dynasties to which all dynasties of kings trace their ancestry. The main purpose of these poems was to make *Hinduism* more accessible to the people. Its motive was to bring about a compromise between the beliefs and practices of the hieratic *Vedas* and *Upanishads*. The *Puranas* have a definite *Vaishnava* or *Saiva* orientation. Yet they remain the first expression of the synthesizing strand, concentrating on simple rituals rather than exact doctrines. *Hinduism* that prevails today can trace its root to the Gupta period and label itself Puranic Hinduism. "The Puranas are even better known as the great storehouses of Hindu mythology, from which are derived other narrations of the luxuriant myths that form so large a part of traditional Hinduism" (*Ibid.* 195).

The myths of Europe, on the other hand, date back to 1900 B.C. onwards. The following illustration demonstrates the growth of Western myth over the centuries:

1900—c.1100: Mycenean Age (Bronze Age): The pre-historical time to which many legends date back (e.g., the Trojan War, King Midas on Crete, Theseus and Heracles. . .)

c. 750-500: Archaic Age

Poets Homer, Hesiod, lyric poets like Sappho, Pindar, and

Bacchylides; Homeric Hymns
499-338: Classical Age
Dramatists Aeschylus, Euripides, Sophocles,
Historians Harodotus and Thucydides
Philosophers Socrates, Plato, Aristotle
Alexandrian Age: 338 BC-146 BC
Apollonius of Rhodes: The Argonautica
Callimachus: Aetia
Nicander, Boios, Antoninus Liberalis . . .
Roman Era:
Romans: Catullus, Ovid, and many, many more
Greeks: Pausanias (Mythographer), Plutarch, etc.
Christian Era: Euhemerus

Indian English writers have drawn myths not just from the 'great tradition' but also from the 'little tradition'. Moreover, they have been rather eclectic in their selection. Not just the native great and little traditions but also the alien ones have been used without hesitation. Like T.S. Eliot, Indian writers like Raja Rao have shown great "artistic virtuosity, and . . . cultural relativity" (Jaya Prasad 34) in the matter. Myths, folktales and legends from the Indian to the English, Greek and Chinese can be found in their works.

Radcliffe-Brown's categorization of myths and other cultural elements on the basis of urbanity and rurality etc. has been further bifurcated by Indian sociologist S.C. Dube. If one accepts Dube's arguments then myths can be classified on the basis of the classical tradition, the regional, local, western, emergent national tradition and the sub-cultural tradition of special groups, it must also be borne in mind that myths are not always primitive and mythology a static or stagnant subject. New myths and mythologies get created with the passage of time. While primitive archetypal symbols get demythologized, contemporary personalities and events get mythologized. Laurence Coupe points out in the book *Myth*: "not all myths are linked with ritual, not all myths are about God and not all myths concern a time outside of historical time." Comic strip, characters such as 'superman,' 'spiderman,' 'phantom' 'mogly' etc. are myths of the contemporary era enjoying global currency. Mythology, in fact, is alive and kicking in the modern age through urban legends, scientific mythology and comic characters. Roland Barthes (1915-1980) published a series of essays examining modern myths and the process of their creation in his book Mythologies (1957).

Writers and artists, thus, have at their disposal not just modern myth or story cycles to inspire them but also a large collection of primitive mythology to add 'colour' and 'content' to their contemporary works of art. Frye, however, states that mythic symbols and patterns need not always be inherited. Every poet or person or artist or any individual for that matter can have his own private mythology, his own spectroscopic band or peculiar formation of symbols of which he may or may not be conscious. Myth, thus, is not always the creation of a whole community. Nor is it common. It is not always culturally inherited or a relic from the past. Mythic symbols can be personal and private. People are free to create their own unique mythology. Poets and writers, in particular, are seen to create their own symbols and imagery apart from using inherited mythic elements. "A good example of a poet who has 'invented' a mythology akin to the traditional kind is William Blake. He said that he felt obliged to create a system: otherwise he would be enslaved by someone else's" (Cuddon).

William Blake's sentiment on the matter of myth is shared by many. It has introduced an element of innovation and dynamism to the field of myth and mythology. Writers and artists have been freely experimenting with myth and mythic symbols re-creating/ re-moulding/ re-arranging or questioning old ones and re-placing them with new ones. The most prominent of such innovative and argumentative writers/artists have been the women. The democratic spirit of the modern era gave further impetus to this tendency. The clarion call for liberty, equality, fraternity emboldened women to demand parity. Karl Marx (1818-1883) made their task easier by exposing how religious dogma is used to exploit the working class in particular and the female population in general. Hence, they boldly began to question mythic values of yore in letter as well as in spirit.

In the context of Indian English literature, Mulk Raj Anand was the first to strike a similar note. Influenced by Marxist ideology he attacked caste and gender discriminations that have their roots in myth and mythology. He pinned great faith on humanism and believed that no one should be "enslaved by someone else's" mythology or ideology. This is the reason why in some of his novels like *The Old Woman and the Cow*, Anand followed the Sita "myth upto a . . . point and then suddenly reversed" (164), thereby, implying that old values and parameters will no longer work. Time has come to re-write the rules and change the equation of society.

Anand found a kindred spirit in the women writers of Indian English literature. The crusade that he started against the hegemony of mythic values on human life was let fire and brimstone by the women writers. They have found mythic values inexcusable and inexpedient as far as women issues are concerned. Their anger against the myth has been inexhaustible and their contribution to female emancipation as a result of it inestimable. Their questions have made the sacred myths fallible. Women writers have made it possible to talk about myth and mythology without the fear of the inferno.

Women and 'myth' have, in fact, been like two sides of a coin. It is impossible to talk about 'myth' without reference to women. Women are the 'subject' as well as the 'object' of myth. They are at its 'centre' as well as at the 'periphery'. Since centuries they have been the chief 'preservers' and 'narrators' of myth. Women have been its 'victims' as well as 'votaries.' Today, however, women are also its most vociferous critics and ardent admirers.

Since the advent of the 20th century, women and some men all over the world have been struggling to convince society not to treat women as 'myth' but as 'reality.' Myth is not 'women' and women are not 'myth.' The struggle has been long and hard but the tide is slowly turning. There is a growing realization that women are not an extension of 'myth' and 'myth' not a manifestation of women. Slowly but surely society is learning to talk about women without the baggage of 'myth.'

Thanks largely to social reformers, activists, writers, policy makers, liberal political ideologies and lenient families as also the socio-economic compulsions that have necessitated 'employed' and 'earning' women; women are gradually gaining ground as 'humans' parallel to the men. Neither inferior like 'slaves' nor superior like 'goddesses' but as 'natural' and 'normal' as the men with 'human' strengths and weaknesses, 'human' problems and predicaments, 'human' needs and aspirations that need 'human' redressal and support rather than the divine or the mythic.

A.S. Altekar in *The Position of Women in Hindu Civilization* observes: "one of the best ways to understand the spirit of a civilization and to appreciate its excellences and realize its limitations is to study the history of the position and status of women in it" (1). He further opines "how far a religion stands for justice and fair play and how far it has succeeded in exploding prejudices and shibboleths of a primitive age can be seen from the position it assigns to women in its ritual and theology" (2). Myth, thus, as part of religion and theology assumes significance vis-à-vis the women.

Myth, in fact, has always been a potent force in shaping the destiny of women. It continues to remain so even now. Not just Hindu myths but the myths of all societies have been both a 'boon' and a 'bane' for women. It is 'myth' that has shaped people's attitude towards women both for the better and worse. It is for this reason that not just fiery feminists but also historians, anthropologists, sociologist, psychologists, political activists, philosophers and the literati look back (in anger as well as in admiration!) to 'myth' to find out the root of either women's 'magnification' as 'devi' or 'marginalization' as 'dasi.' It is to be noted that in both positions women are denied normal human claims and entitlements.

The Brahmanical tradition categorizes women with shudras, animals, illiterates and rural people who need to be held on a tight leash least they go astray. Tulsi Das writes in *Shri Ramcharita Manas*: "Dhol gavar shudra pashu nari Sakal taaran ke adhikari" (736). Implicit in this categorization is the negation of women as human beings comparable to men. The motive is to marginalize this gender so that they do not assert themselves too much and demand political, economic, social or sexual rights thereby challenging the authority/monopoly of the men and complicate matters for them.

The battle being waged today by women and their male sympathizers is not to supersede the men and establish matriarchy all over the world. They are also not shedding crocodile tears to extract unjustified social, legal and financial concessions for women. The fight is on to get women recognized as 'human beings' first and foremost. The struggle is to safeguard their lives, their rights and their property as such. The motive is not to create a social system and style of living in which men nor women would be oppressed or depressed by the other. For these purposes, if religion, theology, mythology and indeed the 'constitution' of different countries and cultures need to be revised, reformed or re-written, then so it be.

In fact, it is to correct the negative tilt in people's attitude, thanks largely to religious and mythic values, that welfare nation /states have begun making so many legal provisions and concessions for the female folks. The effort is to convince people neither to 'deify' women nor to 'denigrate' them but to recognize them as human beings and give them their due as such. Governments are encouraging people not to look upon this gender as a social and financial liability or as a pain in the neck. Crusade has been launched against female infanticide, dowry-deaths, mental and physical harassment of women. There is, in fact, an over-all focus to minimize the demographic, social, political and educational marginalization of the fair sex. The effort is to turn the 'myth' of Kali, Lakshmi and Saraswati into a 'reality' so that each woman and girl child combines in herself all the three abilities—strength, prosperity and learning so as to survive with dignity in life. Neither denying her 'natural' duties nor perishing as a result of it but getting ample opportunities for individual growth as well if she so desires.

There has also been a growing consciousness that women must also not be treated as 'silent' recipients of mercy. Rather women must be allowed and encouraged to 'ask' as well as 'talk' not just about their children, husbands or parents but also about 'themselves.' Raja Rao writes in *The Serpent and the Rope:* "A woman must grumble—it's her biological defence against the strength of man" (260) and against everything else that might be hurting her or her gender.

Since the emotional and physical well-being of humanity is dependent on women, the opinion of this gender is as important as of the men. The world will not progress if women and their viewpoints are neglected. Women must be encouraged to 'talk' so that the world gets to know their perspective. The "consent and willingness" of women is crucial not only to "continue with age old systems" (Pratima Prasad) but also to initiate change. Hence, an effort must be made to know what they 'want' or 'do not want.' After all the hands that rock the cradle also shake the world.

In fact, this urge to 'talk' and 'tell' is inherent to women. It is almost their incorrigible habit. In the *Mahabharata* when *Yudhistra* got to know that Karna too was his brother and that his mother Kunti had hid this fact all along, he cursed that henceforth womenfolk will never be able to conceal any secret. Since then, it is alleged, the 'talkativeness' of women has been proverbial. The gender is prone to gossiping over mundane issues and also incessantly. At the same time, however, they are also "natural storytellers" (Iyengar 435) and story-weavers.

Since times immemorial women have been not only 'narrating' the 'stories' of others but also 'creating' some of their own. The oral tradition of folktales and songs (that often includes the mythic as well) has survived thanks largely to the women. In the *Vedic* age there was no dearth of women teachers, writers, poets and narrators who not only 'learned,' 'told' and 'taught' what already existed but 'created' new knowledge and narratives as well. "According to the orthodox tradition itself as recorded in the Sarvanukramanika," there were as many as twenty "women among the 'seers' or authors of Rigveda" (Altekar 10). There has been, thus, in the Indian culture a healthy tradition of the female perspective on graver issues too apart from the mundane. The various vernacular languages too boast of a rich collection of women's writing on all matters of social, religious or aesthetic import.

As far as Indian English literature is concerned, Toru Dutt, an Indian Christian girl, was one of the pioneers. She was the one who initiated Indian women in the genre of Indian English poetry. It was in her hands that Indian English poetry as a whole came of age, graduating from "imitation to authenticity" (Naik 1992: 37). Not only did she read the scriptures of her native religion but also learned the ancient Sanskrit language to come to terms with the indigenous cultural ethos of her motherland and communicate the same in her work. She was much influenced by English and French cultures but through the study of Sanskrit and the epics such as the *Ramayana*, the *Mahabharata*, the *Vishnu Purana* and the *Bhagavad Gita,* regained her Indian consciousness and expressed them brilliantly in *Ancient Ballads and Legends of Hindustan* (1882). She was the first female writer to talk about Sita, Savitri and Goddess Uma in English language. It was Toru who introduced these mythic and marvellous Indian women to the English-speaking world. Despite her conversion to Christianity, the poetess was not shy of acknowledging her literary and cultural heritage. She was not ashamed of singing about strange women who 'chased' death, or 'courted fire' or 'danced' in the battlefield with ten hands:

> Absurd may be the tale I tell,
> Ill-suited to the marching times,
> I loved the lips from which it fell,
> So let it stand among my rhymes.

Toru died young but the flame of poetry written by women in Indian English literature remained ablaze. From Sarojini Naidu to Kamala Das, from Shreela Ray (The Passion of Draupadi) to Lalitha Venkateswaran (Rocking Horse; Tree Bird) and many more, Indian women have been using the English language to talk about past (mythic) and present (real) world as they see or understand. The tones may be soft or steely, but the determination to 'express' women's perspective is strong in all. Women are shedding not just mental, physical and social inhibitions but inhibitions of the language too. Their expressions are amazingly candid, confident, critical and cantankerous.

In the genre of fiction too, Indian women were quick to register their presence and express views akin to the poetesses. Raj Lakshmi Debi published her novel *The Hindu Wife or The Enchanted Fruit* as early as 1876. In 1894 and 1895 were published *Kamala: A Story of Hindu Life* and *Saguna* written by Mrs. Krupbai Satthianadhan. The titles of these early novels suggest that the primary concern of the women novelists was women's life and lot in Hindu society.

The trend started by these early poetesses and authoresses has gathered strength with passing time. Today there are so many women writing poetry, prose, drama novel and short—stories in Indian English that a separate 'women's literature' can easily be carved out of the large canon of Indian English literature: "Today, women writers work in a variety of literary genres—short story, drama, poetry, essay, life story /testimony, and the novel—that are often inspired by and rooted in a writer's own indigenous oral and folk traditions (as in Africa and the Caribbean), as well as literary traditions in other languages (in India). . . . Women writers share specific gender concerns in terms of how social and cultural factors appear from a female point of view. Their literary works imaginatively explore several conflicts between tradition (social, custom, religion) and modernization" (Katrak 232).

However, it was not until India's independence and a few years after, that women's writing in Indian English literature became numerous and noticeable. This is especially true in the context of the 'novel.' From the late 1950s onwards Kamala Markandaya, Ruth Prawer Jhabvala and Anita Desai began publishing one novel after another concentrating on the social, economic and domestic position of women caught in the flux of a society neither totally traditional nor completely modern. Though the pull of nostalgia was strong, the sympathy of these women writers was tilted in favour of 'liberal' values rather than the religious or the 'mythic.' Hence, they set down to 'demystify' women. Their creative concerns ran contrary to mythic representations of women as either 'exotic,' 'erotic' or 'ethereal.' Though the aesthetic attraction of 'myth' remained, there was also an equally strong determination to show Indian women as they 'are' and not as they 'should be.'

In fact, in India "issues relating to women are quite vast and of bewildering complexity" because of "variations between different regions, between rural and urban areas, between classes and also between different religions, ethnic and caste groups" (Singh v) Indian women writers, however, have more than met the challenge. They have been sharp enough to grasp the complex ground realities and communicate and articulate the same in their works. Far from being evasive or cursory, the women writers have analyzed the caste, community, class, rural and urban angles in the lives of women threadbare. Not only have they alluded to the predicaments of conventional life but also to the problems inherent in unconventional solutions to tide over crises.

Succeeding generations of women novelists writing after and

along with this forceful female trinity of authoresses—Markandaya, Jhabvala and Desai—share and express the same 'concerns' albeit more uninhibitedly. There is no relationship that they have not analyzed threadbare, no pain that they have not hinted and howled at in their narratives, no experience or feeling that they have not described graphically. Today there are no taboo topics and hushed issues in women's novels. Nothing is left to imagination, speculation or conjecture so much so that some readers often feel shy and uncomfortable at acknowledging the they have 'read' or 'liked' a 'certain' book by this or that female novelist. They either keep their mouths shut or skirt the issue as intelligently and swiftly as possible despite even academic compulsions. The readers are often at loss as to how to react but definitely not the defiant and irreverent authoresses of contemporary times. Shashi Deshpande, Shobha De, Gita Mehta, Bharati Mukherjee, Arundhati Roy, Rina Sibal, Dina Mehta, Sara Banerjee, Jhumpa Lahiri, Leena Dhingra or Namita Gokhale—all have written frankly, fearlessly and feverishly about women in families, in marriages, at home and outside, in legitimate and illegitimate relationships, in 'myth' and in 'reality' in a manner that would put to shame almost everyone and put in the dock almost everything.

Shashi Deshpande, who has concentrated on mythical women in her novella *The Stone Women* agrees that "myths have given us a moral framework by which we live" (4). She acknowledges the fact that "they have shaped our ideas for a great many years, they embody our dreams" (94). Yet she also asserts the right to reinterpret the myths and retain only those beliefs that are "relevant to our lives today" and "suit the needs of the modern women" (94).

The Sita, Savitri, Sati, Saraswati models are, consequently, under attack by women who want to live normal lives with normal human demands and duties. "Nari Dharma as understood in traditional Indian society or the concept of pativrata nari" (Jaya Prasad 2005: 63) is not being rejected outright by the female writers. What they are asking for is to "lessen the rigidity of these notions so that women could breathe more easily and feely" (*Ibid.*). The women writers, activists and reformers are also asking for parity as far as 'duties' and 'expectations' are concerned from the two genders. They contend that there must not be separate set of rules for men and women. If chastity and fidelity is crucial for women, why don't the men also fall in line? Why the burden of 'mythic' values only on women?

In their fiction women show how their gender is made to bear not just the 'burden' but also the 'brunt' of myths. Is preserving the moral fibre of society the sole responsibility of women? Moreover, the women writers highlight how even the so called 'traditional' women are denied happiness and honour due to them from family and society. Their devotion is taken for granted not just by their husbands or parents but even by their children. This is the reason why women novelists tend to 'demystify' 'marriage' as well as 'family.' Shashi Deshpande asserts: "Being mother, daughter, wife is important for a woman but that is not the be all and end all of her existence" (qtd. Sahi in Mohan 22). Women writers like Anita Desai, Githa Hariharan Arundhati Roy and their fictional characters seem to believe in what Deshpande has brilliantly expressed: "We don't reject the ideals, but we know we can't approximate to these pictures of ideal womanhood. And we will not bear any guilt that we cannot do so" (2000: 94).

It is not that these women writers have reacted against only the 'pious' and 'pure' mythic model of Sita and Savitri. The myths of the 'Pancha Kanyas' too have been analyzed carefully and deeply by women in fiction as well as in poetry. The stories of the 'Pancha Kanyas'—Ahilya, Tara, Kunti, Draupadi and Mandodari—allow fidelity as well as sexual license and liberty all justified by queer dharmic logic that are highly questionable and offensive. These unhappy and unfortunate women suffered immensely and disproportionately because of men's fancies and their own follies. Not just the women but even the men agree that the 'Pancha Kanyas' are the most pitiable victims of patriarchy. The multitude of the Hindu population still shudders at the memory of these heroic women. They are quietly revered for their struggle to live with dignity but daughters are never or rarely named after them. The literati, however, keep recalling these mythic women. Writers like Shashi Deshpande in *The Stone Women*, Arundhati Roy in *The God of Small Things* and Githa Hariharan in *The Thousand Faces of Night* have highlighted the pain, problem and protest of the 'Pancha Kanyas' as also of other mythic heroines like Amba and Gandhari who too were denied what they desired or deserved.

Last but not the least, these novelists have also presented a critique of the mother myth. In Shashi Deshpande's *The Dark Holds No Terrors*, Githa Hariharan's *Thousand Faces of Night* and Arundhati Roy's *God of Small Things*, the reader comes face-to-face with mother figures who are "not the matriarchs to be glorified but the suffocative and authoritative figures to be disdained" (Deshpande 2000: 94). Saru in *The Dark Holds No Terrors* and Ammu in *The God of Small Things* are at the receiving end of their mother's gender bias. In *The Thousand Faces of Night* Sita does not suffer from this malady but gives Devi little scope to decide things for herself. She thrusts her opinions and decisions on not just Mahadevan but also on Devi.

In all cultures 'mother' is a respected figure but "the apotheosis of the mother has reached a greater height in India than anywhere else" (qtd. Sahi in Mohan 20). It is believed by Indians that "there is no shelter like the mother; there is no refuge like her; there is no better defence than her . . . in the person of the father is a combination of all gods; but in the person of the mother, however, is a combination of all gods and also all humanity" (Prabhu 253). The novelists, however, show that, in reality, all such assumptions and presumptions are 'myth' and that mother and mothers-in-law in Indian homes are often very tough and tyrannical towards daughters and daughters—in—law. They see to it that girls 'remember' their 'secondary' position in society and in family. They are the ones who push "myths that socialize and contain the Indian women" (Iyer 43) down the throats of daughters and daughters-in-law.

Women writers, thus, have gone back to the 'myth' not just to protest against the 'magnification' as well as the 'marginalization' of women but also to pull women out of 'illusion.'

There is another category of 'myths' that feed the female imagination with rosy romanticism about men, marriage, domesticity and love. Commercial cinema, serials, advertisement, even certain types of literature (Mills & Boon variety) encourage girls and women to build castles in the air. Though the Indian society is more liberal and tolerant today, it has not yet reached the stage when every boy would go down on his knees to propose to a girl or every husband would be as worthy as Kamadeva, Dushyanta or Nala. Expectations are rocket-high and they come crashing down when Indian women meet very down to earth, practical, matter of fact men for whom 'marriage' is a task to 'get done and over with.' In Western society couples are 'lovers' before they get married. Hence there already exists an understanding and awareness about each other. In India 'romance' is supposed to start after 'marriage' but the most common complain of Indian women is that this rarely happens. In many novels written by Shashi Deshpande, Anita Desai, Githa Hariharan, Namita Gokhale and others, this is a major grudge of the female protagonists. Fed on 'romantic' myths of all types—romantic novels, songs and cinema—Indian women seem to be ill-equipped to handle the stark realities. Devi in *The Thousand Faces of Night* recalls, with ironic nostalgia, the myth of Nala and Damayanti that granny Pati had narrated to her in childhood. The contrast between Damayanti's swayamwara and her own marriage negotiations is stark.

Thus, there are a variety of 'myths' that Indian English women novelists have reacted against. Some of the myths are not 'sacred' but also 'secular.' Though 'modernity' is seen and perceived as a panacea for all the 'ills' of 'tradition, in the cases of certain women even 'modernity' turns out to be a 'myth.' This is amply brought out in Gita Hariharan's novel *The Thousand* Faces of Night. Devi's mother Sita and husband Mahesh are 'modern' myths. Their fetish for 'perfection' is in reality, a version of mythical 'idealism.' In their opinion women's education and cultured grooming means that they play the traditional roles with greater sophistication and finesse. The serials being telecast on different television channels too bear testimony to this new trend and tyranny. In the novel Devi realizes that the liberal attitude of her mother and her husband Mahesh is just a façade. Their modernity is superficial, a myth, a farce while their mentality is mythical. It is to reach the mythical goal of 'perfection'; it is in the chase of 'mythic' models that they have become practical and matter of fact. Unlike granny Pati or her professor father-in-law who were unashamedly traditional but at least sympathetic and sensitive; *Sita* and *Mahesh* are clinical in the execution of their plans thereby making themselves all the more crude and cruel. In comparison to the so called liberal and modern *Sita* and her chosen son-in-law Mahesh; both Pati, Devi's father-in-law and even father Mahadevan appear as better human beings—traditional but at least gentle, lovable, caring and receptive to Devi's feelings.

It is in reaction to too much 'practicality,' 'reality' or modern 'matter-of-factness' that a pro-myth wave is discernable in literature written by both men and women. This is not a new phenomenon but can be traced back to the nineteenth century when Indian English literature was in its infancy. Another equally compelling reason that has made myth useful to writers is the need for an artistic or aesthetic framework authentic to their country. Just like the male writers, the female writers have engaged themselves with 'myth' in these ways too.

In the fiction of novelists like Kamala Markandaya and Anita Desai, both types of attitudes are discernible. They are conscious of the fact that myth is a 'strategy of containment' as far as women are concerned. Yet Markandaya also seems to realize that "mythic attitude is needed to survive the tremendous hardships of life faced by the common peasant in rural India" (Khan 103). In the novels of Desai, on the other hand, some of her middle-class protagonists "tend to choose the mythic over the realistic mode primarily because they are women and, as such, have too much responsibility and very little liberty within the realist mode of life" (Khan 62). In novels like *Where Shall We Go This Summer* and *Fire on the Mountain*, Anita Desai explores the theme of mythic escapism verses social responsibility or reality. In recent years novelists, like Githa Hariharan have used myth both as a strategy of 'containment' as well as 'liberation' in their works. Others like Namita Gokhale in her novel *Shakuntala* have used myth to primarily and specifically explore female sexuality.

Shashi Deshpande, in fact asserts that whether women novelists abhor or embrace the myth they are doing a great service to the cultural heritage of the country by keeping them alive in the memory of the people. She pointed out in *The Stone Women*: "the *Mahabharata* stories have an important place in our lives, but it is getting less and less known" (4). By writing about Kunti, Sita, Amba, Draupadi Gandhari, Radha or Shakuntala women novelists are making an attempt to understand the strings that bind the Indian women. At the same time, through the technique of intertextuality, the women are also playing their traditional role of 'story-telling' that is so natural and spontaneous to them. The racial memory of the Indian people, their collective consciousness is, thus, being innovatively preserved by women. They are not reducing the magic or mystery of the myths but only clearing the ambiguities so as to arrive at a better understanding of those extraordinary times and lives in the context of our own.

It may safely be concluded that the female novelists are well aware of the beauty, burden and necessity of 'myth.' There is no aspect of 'myth that they have not revealed in their narratives. There is no colour of these cultural stories that they have not shown. The female writers are apologetic neither in their 'attack' on the myths nor in their 'admiration' of them. The 'ambivalent' character of the cultural narratives that is both "beautiful and . . . sinister" (Khan 92) is fully understood and revealed by the writers. They are also aware of the necessity to preserve myth for posterity. Their work on myth today is no longer merely 'criticism.' Motivated by "the concept of human rights" which is "inextricably linked with the concept of human dignity" what women writers have done is to present a critique of myth so as to pave way for the "optimum growth" and realization of women's "personality and potentials" (Kumar 15)

Women writers have, thus, emerged as one of strongest voices on the subject of myth and mythology. Any discussion of myth and mythology would be incomplete without taking cognizance of what women writers, critics or women in general have to say on the matter. This book, however, is not devoted entirely to the views of the feminine gender.

The present study is devoted primarily to bring forth the narrative potential of myth as evident in the works of Indian English writers such as Lal Bihari Day, Mulk Raj Anand, Raja Rao and Githa Hariharan. The selected authors belong to different epochs. An attempt has been made to see if there is any attitudinal change vis-à-vis the myth in different periods of history—from the pre-independence era to the contemporary times. Another motive is to reveal the gender perspective on myth. Do men and women writers treat myth differently? How do their characters react to myth in the novels? Have divergent views on the matter been given space in the works? Have the political/ philosophical ideologies of the writers influenced their attitude towards myth? Attention has also been paid to the source of myths selected by the writers. Are the myths local in origin, regional, pan-Indian, alien, from the oral tradition or the scriptural? These are some of the issues explored in the book.

Lal Bihari Day's *Bengal Peasant Life*: Myths as Celebration of Collectivity and Connectivity

Lal Bihari Day's *Bengal Peasant Life* (1874) is an authentic and ethnic work of art, very real and true to life as lived in Indian villages. It had to be, for, the manifest purpose of writing this novel was to illustrate "the social and domestic life of the rural population and working classes of Bengal." As a natural corollary of the thematic focus, myths and legends could not be left out of the narrative as mythology is and has always been a potent force in Hindu Indian society. Any work of art purporting to be a realistic portrayal of the domestic life of the Indian people will have to take into account the myths, legends, customs and beliefs on which they pin their hope and seek solace as well as solution.

Myths and rituals are the living traditions of India. In fact, "India is one of the last civilizations left that continues to sustain and cherish the pagan world view" (Lal 15). No description of Indian life would be complete without some reference to them. In the novels written before independence, the inclusion of myths and the description of rituals were both a necessity and a compulsion. The pressure at that time was not only to produce works realistic but also typically Indian. Hence, in the pursuit of realism and authenticity many writers incorporated myths and legends in their fiction because Indian life, especially Hindu life, as emphasized earlier, is essentially mythical. The habits, the behaviour, the custom of the people—all have one or the other myth operating behind them. Any writer or poet, aiming to write about the Indian men and women must know the "myth-values and structures" of these people. He must not, as P. Lal has observed, be "ignorant of

. . . little things like, for instance, why the Indian male will not, as a rule hold his wife, or indeed any girl, by the hand and escort her across the street; or why the beloved in Indian painting and sculpture, always sits on the left of her lover, never on his right; or why a girl stands with lowered eyes in front of males; or why a wife will not address her husband by his first name. And big things like what is the difference between dharma and svadharma, the difference between avatara and incarnation, the varieties of karma, the nature of moksha" (17).

Bengal Peasant Life is a narrative which describes the ups and downs, the highs and lows in the life of Badan and his kith and kin in the village of Kanchanpura. This is a joint family comprising Badan, his mother Alanga, his wife Sundari, daughter Malti, son Govinda, two younger brothers and a sister-in-law Aduri. All of them live under the same roof, have one kitchen and till the same piece of land for livelihood. The women, however, stay at home and run the household. The affairs of the outside world are managed by the eldest son Badan and his younger brothers Kalamanik and Jayaram in consultation with the matriarch Alanga.

The novel is a journey from the birth to the death of Badan's son Govinda. In the course of these two events is shown the daily routine of peasants in Indian villages. It is in this context that Day incorporates myths and folktales as each auspicious and inauspicious event in the life of Badan and his family invariably involves the performance of some religious ceremony at the core of which rests some myth and its related ritual.

Bengal Peasant Life, beginning on a note of optimism and joy, gradually turns sombre and ultimately ends on a gloomy note. It is a meticulous work of art covering every aspect of village life—social, economic, political and religious. It mirrors both communal and personal life with equal ease. The novel, in spite of being primarily the story of a family's fortune, is actually a documentary of an Indian village. The work is an absorbing blend of the personal and the social. It provides a mine of information about the kind of life that the rural Indian people led before independence.

Some of Day's descriptions, however, are valid even today bearing testimony to India's undying traditions that have faced many onslaughts and yet retained their essence and presence.

At a time when Anglophiles prided in their "borrowed plumes" (Anand 1935: 178), Lal Bihari Day, a Christian convert, was painstakingly jotting down all the important customs, rites, rituals, myths and legends of his original religion. Unlike other new converts who are always at the forefront in criticizing and ridiculing their native faith, Day is surprisingly very balanced in his observations. He describes the Hindu way of life "with an observing and understanding eye" ignoring neither its "romance and routine" nor the "current abuses" (Iyengar 528) that have crept into it. The writer has dealt with the indigenous culture of his birth not tendentiously but judiciously.

The novel is dedicated to a jamindar Baboo Joy Kissen Mookerjea. In the *Preface*, Day discloses that the novel was written in response to a competition organized by Baboo Mookerjea. In 1871 the *jamindar* had announced that he would award fifty dollars to any novel, written either in Bengali or English, that reflected best "the social and domestic life of the rural population and working classes of Bengal" (vii). Day's novel was adjudged the best entry and till date it remains one of the most accurate and graphic descriptions of Indian village life in the whole realm of Indian English fiction.

It must be noted that Baboo Mookerjea's patronage did not make Day blind to the tyranny of the jamindars. In his novel he has described graphically the torture inflicted on the peasantry by the landed aristocracy. After getting the award Day added three more chapters to the manuscript. It was published in two volumes with the title *Govinda Samanta*, in 1874. Two years later in 1876 the novel was re-printed with a new title the *Bengal Peasant Life*.

The novel opens with a 'Prefatory' in which Day discloses "what the reader is to expect, and what he is not to expect, in this authentic history" (1). On the whole the chapter is a disclaimer. The writer says that the reader must not expect "anything marvelous or wonderful in this little book" (2). "The age of marvels has gone by; giants do not pay now-a-days; scepticism is the order of the day; and the veriest stripling, whose throat is still full of his mother's milk, says to his father, when a story is told him: "Papa, is it true?" (2-3)

The writer makes it clear that he is not going to talk about gods or kings. He rules out other themes as well. His novel is not to be a romance full of "intricate evolutions of plot" (4). It is also not going to show love scenes. Last but not the least, the reader must not come to the book expecting "big words" (4). Day says: "Big thinkers may require. . . big words; but we, plain country folk, talking of fields, of paddy, of the plough and the harrow, have no sublime thoughts, and do not, therefore, require sublime words" (4). Day rounds off the 'Prefatory' with the modest observation that the *Bengal Peasant Life* is an "unvarnished tale of a plain peasant, living in this plain country of Bengal . . . bold in a plain manner" (4).

Though Day had cautioned the readers against expecting mythic and marvellous tales and fables in *Bengal Peasant Life*, the novel is a much about rural men and women as it is about gods, goddesses, ghosts and witches. Myths and folk beliefs are profusely mentioned in the novel especially in the first half. A string of auspicious and inauspicious events dominates the narrative beginning with Govinda's birth. Each occasion has a myth and a ritual according to which it is celebrated or observed. Consequently, in *Bengal Peasant Life* one comes across exactly those entities about whom Day had claimed he has not written about.

The different gods, goddesses and supernatural elements mentioned are Goddess *Nisi; Vidhata Purusha*; Goddess *Shashth*i; Goddess *Saraswati*; Lord *Shiva*; Ghosts; *Sati*; *Hanuman* and Lord *Ram*; Goddess *Durga*; Jesus Christ; Goddess *Lakshmi* and God *Agni*; Lord *Krishna* and *Vishnu*; Lord *Jagannath*; *Mritanjaya; Nava Krishna; Ganesh, Lakshmi* & *Vishnu* and last but not the last Lord *Visvakarma*. Thus, all the important gods, goddesses and important beliefs of the Hindu people have been given a place in the narrative.

However, the villagers are more reverent towards deities responsible for ensuring fecundity, longevity and prosperity. Rural folk, especially the peasant community make obeisance to the divine not for valour or vanquish of enemies. They do not seek scholarly wisdom. Their demands and dreams are basic and rooted in the soil. A good monsoon, good crops, hale and hearty spouse and progeny, who often double as work-force in the fields, proper tools and a good cattle-stock are some of the fundamental requirements of the peasantry. Hence, it is not gods of valour, wisdom or scholarship that are worshipped by the cultivator's community. Rather it is Goddess *Shashthi*, *Vidhata Purusha, Shiva, Sati, Lakshmi, Visvakarma* and the like who receive deferential treatment.

The novel is, in fact, a chronicle of the Hindu way of life which is fundamentally the same throughout the country. The ceremonies and the rituals that are observed by Badan's family and most of the related myths are pan-Indian in nature. *Durga Puja*, Jagannath *Rath Yatra* and *Makara Sankranti* are occasions of communal celebration. Each Indian village, as Raja Rao has rightly observed, has its own "*sthala purana*" (5), yet these are some religious festivals celebrated by almost the whole of Hindu community.

However, *Bengal Peasant Life* is not just pan Indian in the matter of myth but also region specific. As mentioned earlier it has included myths and festivals common to all Hindus. At the same time, it has its own share of "sthala purana" peculiar to the region of Bengal. One such myth is related to Goddess *Nisi*. Just as Shakespeare's *Macbeth* begins with the three witches, this novel has a malevolent Goddess in the very first chapter. Day writes: "It is the invariable custom of the rural population of Bengal never to respond to a call at night especially after midnight, till it is repeated three times. It is believed that Nisi, that is night personified, has often stood at the doors of simple folk, called them out of their beds, and decoyed them to pools and tanks, where they were drowned. The sable goddess never calls, it is believed, more than three times; and in order to be sure that it is the voice of a human being, and not of Nisi, no answer is given till after the fourth time" (6).

This myth is narrated in the context of Badan's younger brother Kalamanik's visit to fetch Rupa's mother, the village midwife, at night. He stands before the door of Rupa and her mother and calls out four times to convince them that he is not Goddess Nisi but genuinely Kalamanik desperate to fetch help for his pregnant sister-in-law, that is, Badan's wife. Predictably, only after the fourth shout, Rupa and her mother respond to the urgent summon.

The birth of the child Govind Samant ushers in festivities in which the midwife and the paternal grandmother play prominent role. Number of rituals is observed and obeisance is paid to the deity of fecundity Goddess Shasthi, who is also the protectress of children, and Vidhata Purusha, whom the midwife claims to have seen writing the destiny of the newborn child. Her claims are testimony not just to her fertile imagination, her garrulity but also the gullibility of the rural folks:

> "After two praharas of the night were over," said Rupa's mother. . . "I heard the sound of footsteps at the door. Immediately after I heard a sound similar to that which is made by a man when writing, but I saw no figure. Shortly after I heard the sound of retreating footsteps, and I rushed towards the door and said, "Thakur! I hope you have written favourably. The god knew me well, as he has often seen me, and told me what he had written on the forehead of the child, but on the condition of strictest secrecy. I dare not disclose it to you, for if I disclose it to you, Vidhata will be angry with me, and mother Alanga, rejoice, for your grandchild's Kapala is very good." (38)

Goddess Shashthi, as already mentioned earlier, is considered the protectress of children. The Divine Mother is also worshipped for fecundity by women. Day writes:

> As the importer of fecundity to women, as the protectress of children, and the patroness of domestic happiness, Mother Shashthi, as she is generally called, is universally regarded, especially by women, with feelings not only of the deepest reverence, but of the

warmest affection. (46)

Sundari, Govinda's mother, like other village women, was devoted to Mother Shasthi. It was quite natural that she would observe and perform carefully all the rituals related to Shasthi at the birth of her son. Badan too participated in the rituals presenting the Goddess with offerings and prayers. In fact, both the mother and the father of Govinda manifested the greatest delight in the worship of the Divine Mother to whose kindness they attributed all their domestic and marital happiness.

In the novel, Day makes explicit an important co-relation between custom, myth and superstition. It can be inferred from his observations that whenever man is unable to decipher the reason or cause of a certain natural or unnatural occurrence, he concocts a myth (story) attributing a supernatural entity with the power of having accomplished the unexplained happening.

The customs and myth, with the passage of time, become established superstitions. Sometimes science unravels the mystery, yet so deeply entrenched are the beliefs of the people, that the superstition lives on and so does the myth and the custom.

The novel opens with the birth of the hero Govinda and ends with his death. The whole cycle of his life is presented to us with the hero serving as a symbol/ representative of the rural peasantry and his life as a reflection of rural life. This provides the author innumerable opportunities to mention different customs observed and ceremonies performed by the rural peasantry. The myths mentioned in the novel help in unraveling the logic behind the conduct of the people of the village Kanchanpura.

Though there are occasional celebrations in the family, a string of unhappy events take place that leave a lasting impact on Badan's family. Earlier engrossed in worshipping the Goddess of fertility, the family is shown gradually realizing and acknowledging the presence of malevolent powers, both divine and human, who cause upheavals in their placid existence changing the very course of their life permanently.

The first such incident to cause anxiety to Badan's clan and to call for obeisance to a mercurial deity was an attack of convulsions to Govinda. Alanga attributes the problem to 'Pencho'—an incarnation of Lord *Shiva*:

> Alanga, observing Govinda's convulsions, and the contortions which his body was undergoing, at once inferred the cause, and weeping said: "Oh, mother, my child is possessed by Pencho. . . . Alanga concluded in her mind that Govinda must have that day, while playing with other cow-boys at the Panchanantala (that is, the foot of Panchanana's tree), touched the divinity, or unwittingly shown some disrespect to him; and that therefore the God, by way of punishment, had taken possession of him." (62-63)

In order to pacify the angry God, *puja* is at once arranged.

Thus, the rural population is shown to be completely in the grip of mythology. The joy and sorrow that they experience in their life, they attribute them fully to the divine and supernatural forces. Each problem, each achievement is the outcome of either a divinity's wrath or kindness. More often than not, these divine forces are symbolized by inanimate objects of nature or by plants and animals. Moreover, the process of appeasement is always a community affair involving not just the affected family but almost the whole village. It is to be noted that every religious ceremony in Hindu families is invariably accompanied by folk songs sung by a couple of women. In other words, almost all Hindu religious ceremonies are events of communal participation. They are rarely carried out in closet. The rituals are performed in the midst of people who directly or indirectly participate. In fact, in certain ceremonies, it is mandatory to have at least five married men & women as participants.

It is clear that belief in myths and legends has promoted a whole way of life that is social and communal rather than personal and private. The influence of mythology has necessitated an inter-relation between, not just man and man, but between man and his natural environment. Myths have tied the Hindu people with plants, animals, water, stone and soil in a bond that is far deeper than just need based on consumption. The tie is psychological.

Man has learned to see nature as the symbol of those divine forces that guide and decide the destiny of people. Hence, he interacts with nature not with insouciance but with care and circumspection. Hindu myths and folktales, in fact, go a long way in serving the cause of environmental protection and sustainable development.

Hindu religion accords great prestige and power to the female goddesses. They are not subservient to the male gods but considered superior to them because they are not just females or wives of gods but 'mother figures' combining in themselves power to protect as well punish, construct as well as destruct. Before them even *Brahma*, *Vishnu* and *Mahesh* take a back seat because *Saraswati*, *Lakshmi* and *Durga* are the source of all the *shakti* or energy in the universe. According to the holy book *Durga Saptashati*, Goddess *Durga* is the embodiment of the collective strength of all the male gods including the Trinity. She is a mother figure not just for mortals but the immortals as well. It is to her that the gods appeal for help. It is goddess *Durga* who defends the kingdom of *Indra* by defeating the demon kings *Shumbha* and *Nishumbha*. It is the Supreme Mother who initiates as well as ends the human world. She combines in herself the ability to be merciful as well as merciless simultaneously.

Goddess *Durga* is believed to be the wife of Lord *Shiva*. She is also the mother of *Ganesh* and *Kartikeya*. She was born twice. First as *Sati* and then as *Parvati*. In both incarnations she was married to *Shiva*. As *Sati*, she had jumped into the *yagya* fire when she could no longer put up with the insult of her husband *Shiva* at the hands of her haughty father. Born again as *Parvati*, she pleased Lord *Shiva* with her *bhakti* and married him again. *Sati* and *Parvati* are considered epitomes of marital fidelity. They are looked up by mortal women as ideal wives and are worshipped for conjugal bliss as well as fecundity.

Like *Sati* and *Parvati*, *Sita*, *Savitri*, *Anasuya* and *Damayanti* too are considered epitomes of the *pativrata dharma* in which the wife is chaste and does not think of any other man even in dream.

Even in the most pressing of circumstances and most tempting of situations, their devotion to their respective husbands remains resolute. They accompany their husbands in every quest and *Savitri,* in particular, followed her husband *Satyavana* even to death till *Yama* was persuaded by her to give back his life.

Though the power and prestige accorded to these divine female deities is a matter of pride for all Hindus, it has not made life easier for lesser women dwelling on earth. Mortal women do not enjoy the same honour and importance. On the contrary, the examples set by the divine goddesses has made life all the more difficult and miserable for the common Indian women bogged and beleaguered as they are by expectations not humanly possible to meet. Society expects them to toe the line of *Sati, Savitri* and *Parvati* to prove their devotion, duty, purity and perfection. The possibility that it may cost the women their lives, does not rattle the conscience of the people. A brutal custom emanating from undue expectations is that of *sati*.

Named after the first wife of Lord *Shiva*, *sati* is a *pratha (custom)* in which the wife of a dead man allows herself to be cremated along with the corpse of her husband. The woman takes this extreme step, ostensibly, out of love for her husband. In reality, however, the myth of *Sati, Savitri, Sita* and *Parvati*, is used expediently by the society to get rid of unwanted widows who are brainwashed and pushed towards committing *sati*. The status of women has, in fact, always been a contentious issue in Indian society. They been sold, shared and abandoned at the flimsiest of grounds. Men have always lacked the courage to stand by their women who have had to make immense sacrifices at the altar of tradition. Though most of the traditions seem to originate from mythology and theology, social and economic reasons are at the root of most of them.

During the Mughal period, Hindu women used to commit *sati* to avoid dishonour at the hands of Muslim conquerors. However, with the passage of time women began to be pushed towards *sati* as their kith and kin were unwilling to support widows. Who would feed them and provide social security lifelong? These questions loomed large and the best solution which people could find was either to push the husbandless women towards *sati* or banish them to places like Vrindavan to lead a destitute life.

It was only after Raja Rammohun Roy took up the cause of these hapless women that consensus began to build up against the inhuman practice of sati. It was declared unlawful by William Bentinck in 1829. It is not that the *pratha* is restricted to weaker sections of the society. A famous incident that took place in the pre-independence era is related to poet Rabindranath Tagore's family. His sister-in-law, that is, brother's wife, was saved only at the eleventh hour after the intervention of the poet himself. It is to be noted that the Tagore clan was one of the most illustrious, prosperous and eminent families of the pre-independence era Bengal. The ban imposed by Bentinck continues but stray incidents are not unheard of even today. The most famous case being of the 1980s in which a young, beautiful and educated girl called Roop Kanwar was forced to commit sati in Rajasthan at the premature death of her husband. In other words, modern age too has not remained immune from such ancient social malice.

In *Bengal Peasant Life,* the reader comes across six widows—*Alanga, Aduri, Malti, Sundari, Sudhamuki* and *Kadambini*. All of them are related to Badan either directly or indirectly. They belong to one of the peasant castes, quite low in the caste hierarchy, yet, remarkably none of these women commit *sati*. Neither they nor their family members contemplate about it. However, it is Ram Dhan Misra, a *Brahmin*, whose old mother is shown committing *sati*. Neither is she a young lady who needs to be protected nor does she belong to a poor family. Yet she is not stopped from this sort of religious suicide. On the contrary, her family turns the occasion into an event of pomp and show, in the din of which the hapless woman's howls are drowned. What was intended as suicide, turned into gruesome murder as the burning woman was not allowed to change her mind and escape:

> But lo! The *sati* has disengaged herself from the ropes by which she

> had been tied. She sites up. She stretches out her hands imploringly. She screams. She attempts to escape. The intoxication of superstition had hitherto kept her up, but she now gives way to nature. But in vain. The drums are now beat at their loudest; deafening shouts of Hari bol! Hari bol! pierce the skies; and by means of two bamboos, which were kept in readiness, the *sati* is prevented from getting down. It is all over with her. She has fallen a victim to grim superstition. More faggots and ghee were had in requisition till the bodies were quite consumed. (121)

Day describes in detail the whole procedure of *sati* before the final burning—the routine of the consenting woman and the behaviour of the people around her who do not stop but aid and abet in the act considering it their good fortune to witness and help a *sati*. The woman does not behave like a widow, that is, cry or weep. Rather she is decorated like a bride and adorned with new clothes and jewellery. Thereafter, she proceeds to the cremation ground to join the corpse of her husband: all the while she is accorded veneration fit for a goddess:

> There was not a single person in the village, male or female, who did not look upon her with the utmost reverence. They called her *sati*, or the Chaste One, by way of eminence, as her conjugal fidelity was such that she was following her husband into the invisible world. They compared her to Savitri—the ideal of a Hindu wife, and praised her for her extra ordinary piety, her conjugal faithfulness, and her heroic fortitude. (119-20)

Ramdhan Misra's mother is forced to continue with divine pretensions. The crowd, on its part, does not even realize that it is being cruel or callous. The inherent inhumanity in the whole proceeding is not recognized or acknowledged. It simply does not enter their mind that they are actually aiding and abetting a heinous crime. On the contrary, they consider it their religious duty to assist in *sati*. They look upon themselves as being extremely fortunate in getting an opportunity to lend a helping hand in the apotheosis of an ordinary woman:

> There was not a single man or woman in all Kanchanpur who felt

> that there was anything wrong in that dreadful act of self-murder; on the contrary, all regarded it as an act of the highest piety, and looked upon the unfortunate victim of Brahmanical superstition as an especial favourite of Heaven. (121-22)

The *Ramayana* and the *Mahabharata* are two epics with pan Indian appeal permeating "the collective unconscious of the whole nation" (Mukherjee 135). The two epics tie the people of the country, in spite of linguistic, caste, class and geographical disparity, into a common bond of belief. The two myths together "give a comprehensive account of the world and the people" (Weigel 10) of India. They satisfy the urge of the people "to be aware of," their "roots. . . gods, kings and heroes. . .and the values by which" (*Ibid.* 13, 14) they have to live. Hence the two epics have survived in the memory of the people. If the *Ramayana* is eulogized for its idealism, the *Mahabharat* is valued for its realism and for the panoramic view of human fallacies.

Lal Bihari Day, however, has surprisingly not given the two epics much space in his narrative. In Bengal, which is practically a matriarchal society, it is the cult of the Mother Goddess, in all its forms, that dominates the region. The *Ramayana* and the *Mahabharata*, on the other hand, highlight male prowess while showing the best and the worst of a patriarchal society. This probably is the reason why the villagers of Kanchanpura, living practically in a matriarchal society, do not refer to the epics in their day-to-day activities. Rather it is the Mother Goddess, who is the presiding deity of their life. This is not to say that the people are irreverent towards Ram or Krishna. Neither are they ignorant of them. It is just that they pin their hopes more on the mother figure than on the father figure. Hence, it is the Mother Goddesses—*Durga, Kali, Parvati, Shashthi, Sati, Savitri and Nishi*—who call the shots in the life of the Bengali people.

The writer, however, hints clearly that both he and his fictional characters are aware of the story and struggle of *Shri Ram* and the *Pandavas*. A reference is made to the characters of t*he Ramayana* by Govinda and his friends while grazing the cows.

The monkeys, playing on the trees, are called *Hanuman*. Lord *Hanuman* is the monkey-faced devotee of Shri Ram and is an important character in the *Ramayana*. The friend of Govinda is fearful of the apes but Govinda tries to allay his fears by drawing parallels between Lord *Hanuman* and the local monkeys hanging on the trees above their heads:

> Third Lad: Very likely. Look! The Hanuman has gone up the tree. I hope the fellow will not pelt our heads.
> Govinda: If he did you should be thankful, as Hanuman was Rama's beloved servant and devoted disciple. Your head would be sanctified. (144)

This is the only instance in the narrative where Day has made a reference to the myth of the *Ramayana*. While the custom and rituals associated with the Mother Goddesses are interwoven in the day-to-day life of the village folks, the same is not the case with the gods, goddesses, heroes, heroines, demons and witches associated with the two greatest religious epics of the Hindu community-the *Ramayana* and the *Mahabharata*.

It is while discussing the friend circle of Govinda that Day refers to the *Dussehra* festival celebrated with great pomp in Bengal. Govinda has six close friends each of whom belongs to a different caste and consequently to a different profession. One of his friends is Kapila. Kapila is the son of the village carpenter Sagara Mistri. Mistri specializes in making bedsteads, stools, wooden boxes and palanquins of exquisite beauty. However, his forte lies not in the making of the village furniture but in the making of clay idols especially of Goddess *Durga*:

> But that in which he chiefly excelled was the making of earthen images of the Hindu gods. . . . His skill was every year called forth, especially at the time of the Durga Puja, the image of which goddess he made almost to perfection. . . . All the inhabitants of the village used to be in raptures with the image of Durga and her group which Sagara made for the zamindar of Kanchanpura. (152)

Thus, while discussing the friend circle of Govinda, Day

introduces to the readers the chief female goddess of the Hindus and the presiding deity of the Bengala people—Goddess *Durga*. According to the holy narrative *Devi Mahatmya* or *Durga Saptshati,* when the demon *Mahishasur* "installed himself in Heaven as the successor of *Indra*" (Knappert 84), by defeating and humiliating the gods, the fury of the Trinity (*Brahma, Vishnu and Mahesh*) knew no bounds. The energy produced by their combined anger took the shape of *shakti* or divine power. "The goddess already existed as a deity. . . as *Maya*, but now the gods" gave her "a share of their tremendous energy so that she became perceptible matter" (*Ibid.* 84). Jan Knappert says: "*Devi* is the goddess of defence and warfare like Athena-Minervas and like her she is also the goddess of wisdom and knowledge. Both goddesses inspire terror (Athena by means of the lethal Medusa head on her shield) and are at the same time faithful helpers of their worshippers, giving rich boons to devout supplicants" (85).

Bengal being a matriarchal society for all practical purposes, Goddess *Durga*, along with her seventh incarnation *Kali*, is the presiding deity of the region. The *Dussehra Puja*, hence, is celebrated with great pomp by the Bangla people.

As mentioned earlier, *Kali* is a very important incarnation of *Devi Durga* and worshipped devoutly by all Bengalese. Yet another important incarnation of the Supreme Mother is Lak*shmi* whose worship is not limited or restricted to any particular region of the country. Since *Lakshmi*, the wife of *Vishnu*, is also *viridhi*, that is, the goddess of growth, she is worshipped by every Hindu and in every Hindu household. She guarantees growth in finance, in family (progeny), in fortune, in fame, that is, in all worldly matters. Hence, before the commencement of any important work *Lakshmi* is worshipped along with her godson *Ganesh,* the deity responsible for removing obstacles in the path of progress. Together they are assumed to ensure unhindered and successful completion of any task along with the assurance of divine help in future as well. Jan Knappert says: "She was born from the waters when the gods churned the World Ocean. She is also depicted as reclining on her husband Vishnu's chest, while he is seated on Shesha. Lakshmi gives children and harvest, she protects the granary. Lakshmi is also . . . associated with cow dung . . . which is used as fertilizer and as fuel for cooking the family meal. Thus, Lakshmi lives in the homes of people as *Vridhi*, the goddess of growth, as *Matrirupa*, the mother of all living things. . . . She is the goddess of fruits (*Ambika,* the mango goddess) and of all food" (143).

It is not surprising, therefore, that Badan and the other peasantry would be shown submitting themselves before this Goddess who is also called *Shri*, the provider of prosperity, wealth, majesty, splendour, fortune and intellect. If *Durga* or *Kali* is prayed to destroy evil, *Lakshmi* is appeased to 'provide': "Every day loads of sugar-cane are given away to children and Brahmans; but the peasants give them away with cheerful hearts, believing that Mother Lakshmi will bless them the coming year with a more abundant crop" (227).

Day writes that after Badan and other farmers have cut the sugar-cane crop and are ready to extract its juice and prepare jaggery, that is, "*gud* or molasses," they pray to Goddess *Lakshmi*:

> I may state here that certain religious ceremonies are always gone through when Hindu raiyats set up the boiling housing. At the setting up of Badan's press, his family priest Ram Dhan Misra, consecrated it. Prayers were offered chiefly to the two divinities—Lakshmi, the Indian Demeter; and Agni, the god of fire. The first was not so much thanked for past favours as prayed to for future ones; and the second was earnestly besought to preserve the sugar-cane house from fire. 9226)

Among the divinities of the Hindu pantheon, there are certain gods and goddesses closely associated with specific functions, activities or phenomena of nature. Chief among such minor deities are "*Indra*—the rain and thunder king, the overlord of gods, *Agni*—the Fire God, *Vayu*—the Wind God . . . all efficient, decent specialist" (Zimmer 186). *Agni*, the fire god, is closely associated with *Indra*, and is sometimes called his twin brother. The two were "the most prominent deities in *Vedic* times; about 250 hymns are addressed to *Indra* and over 200 to *Agni*" (Mackenzie 79). *Agni* is believed to manifest himself in lightening, in celestial sun flames, in the sacred blaze rising from the altar and in homely household fire. When pleased the fire god was "the greatest bestower" (*Ibid.* 23) but when angry, he could reduce everything to naught.

No wonder Badan and other village folks considered it necessary to worship not just Goddess *Lakshmi* but also God *Agni* whose wrath had the potential to reduce months of labour to ash. Hence, before starting with the making of jaggery the family priest is called and prayers are offered to the God of blazes. Little does Badan know at that time that the God is going to spare his sugarcane crop only to inflict a heavier damage on his family in the time to come, crippling them forever.

In the time to come, fire reduces to ash not only Govinda's hut and the belongings of the family but also "those receipts which the zamindar had given him on payments of rents" (361). Govinda, now, has no proof that he has already paid the debts. Thus, the zamindar Jay Chand, through his conspiracy, not only destroys Govinda's property but also forces him to repay the old debts twice. The ruin of the hero is complete and the Fire God proves to be a co-conspirator, a perpetrator of the end of Badan's family.

Hence, in the life of Badan and his family, the mythic forces, Hindu gods and goddesses play positive as well as negative role. If at the start of the narrative Goddess *Shashthi* gives fecundity ensuring growth then around the end of the novel, the God of Fire destroys the family almost completely. God *Agni*, thus, plays a far more pivotal role in the novel though it seems initially as if the female goddesses are more in command. It is he, the *Agni* God, who seals the fate of the family. Govinda is unable to recover from the aftermath of the fire that consumes his hut. One hardship after another hits him till he dies as a labourer far away from home. The fire incident is the beginning of the end of the *Samanta* family. Both Badan and Govinda die as men broken both in mind and body.

It is to be noted that the worship of Goddess *Lakshmi* and God *Agni* almost marks the end of that part of the narrative in which the matriarchal forces or the feminine principle dominate. In fact, the change of guard takes place at exactly the middle of the novel. Subtitled *Navanna*, it is devoted entirely to the activities of men who spend the day in leisure after putting in months of hard labour in the fields. *Navanna* is the festival of offering rice from the first crop of paddy cultivated primarily for the purpose. It is a religious occasion on which all creatures—celestial as well as terrestrial—are offered the new rice by the family priest. The role of the women is restricted merely to prepare the dishes for worship and for the community feast that commences after an offering is made to the whole cosmos:

> Ram Dhan Chakravartti, the family priest . . . mixes the new rice with milk . . . and offers the agreeable viands to the invisible deities. . . . The five elements, the great progenitors of mankind, the Munis and Rishis of the golden age, and Badan's forefathers, next come in for their share. . . . The cows and bullock are presented with the rice. The other beasts of the field, like the jackal, sacred to the God Mahadeva, and even the birds of the air, must not go without their portion. . . . A small quantity is thrown into the tank near the house for the fishes, and another small quantity is put near a hole in the corner of a wall for rats, mice, ants, and all creatures that creep on the ground. When the Gods of every description—celestial, terrestrial, and infernal—and living creatures of every species, have been thus feasted, Badan, Kalamanik, and Govinda squat on the floor, and partake with thankful hearts of the bounty of providence; and woman, the creator's last and best workmanship, comes in finally for her share. The religious part of the festival is now over. (205-6)

Day describes how the men and young boys relax after having a sumptuous meal. While the men sit under the tree and relax, the younger generation becomes engrossed in a number of folk games—*danda-guli, hadu-dudu* and last but not the least wrestling. Thus, after months of living under the shadow of the mother figure and after ceaselessly toiling in the fields, the masculine principle comes out of hibernation. It shows the transition from female dominance to male dominance. Previously the women were in command and at the forefront as domestic issues dominated the narrative. However, with the crops ready in the field, it seems as if maternal cares and control is no longer needed. The period of nurturing is over and hence the men gear up to take charge of life while the women take a back seat.

As mentioned earlier, the worship of the Mother goddess or *Matri Bhakti* is a cult which wields considerable influence in Bengal. However, it must also be kept in mind that the worship of the female Goddess is not the only cult in Bengal or in the whole of India.

Vishnu Bhakti, Shiva Bhakti and *Nirguna* (formless) *Bhakti* are the other major cults, besides the *Shakti* cult, that have enjoyed eminence in different parts of the country since ages and continue to do so even now. According to the *Sources of Indian Tradition*: "Beside the great intellectual and artistic achievements of Indian culture . . . is another aspect of the Indian tradition that many argue reflects more truly its aspirations and its vitality. This is *bhakti*, the devotional religion that spread throughout India and expressed itself in the regional languages of the whole subcontinent. It began as early as the fourth century B.C. in Tamil Nadu, in South India (under the Pallava rulers of Kanchi) but flourished from the twelfth to the eighteenth century in all regions and languages" (Embree 342).

Lal Bihari Day in his novel *Bengal Peasant Life* has mentioned the *bhakti* traditions relevant in the context of Bengal. Apart from the Mother Goddess or *Shakta* cult, another equally strong religious current is that of *Vaishnav dharma*, that is, *Vishnu* or *Krishna* cult. An adherent of this cult named *Prema Bhakta Vairagi* is a regular visitor to the Badan household coming off and on for alms and to bless the family on auspicious occasions like marriages. Later on, events take such a turn that the widowed daughter-in-law of the family *Aduri* too joins the *Vishnu* cult and become a *Vaishnava*.

A trait common to all the adherents of the *bhakti* tradition is the complete "disregard for social conventions, including family life, religious rituals, and normal economic and political values." This is not to say that the *bhakti* cults have no human concerns. On the contrary "the *bhakti* tradition as it developed in the different geographical regions in India" helped provide "an outlet for economic and social discontent as well as for religious aspirations. . . . Unlike the protest movements in other civilizations . . . *bhakti* did not deny the underlying assumptions of society. It was a protest that in the end . . . emphasized the unreality of existing social bonds, not their injustice" (*Ibid.*). This is especially true in the context of the *Nirguna* tradition whose chief proponents were harbingers of social change in medieval *India. Nirguna* saints such as *Kabir* and Guru Nanak challenged both *Brahmanism* and casteism paving the way for a more egalitarian and tolerant Indian society. Cross fertilization with the Sufi movement of Islam laid the seed of the secular spirit, and the creation of the *Ganga-Jamuni sanskriti*. Thus, in spite of remaining detached from the mainstream socio-economic concerns of the Hindu society, the different bhakti movements played a vital role in its amelioration.

Yet another fundamental trait of these *bhakti* streams is "the expression of an intense and passionate relation with the divine" (342-43). All the cults direct their devotion to a particular deity after whom they are named. The Shaktas worship Shakti or Goddess Durga (also Kali), the Vaishanavs worship Lord Krishna or Vishnu and the Shaivites have Lord Shiva as their principal deity. The Nirguna cult, on the other hand, eulogizes the divine "as formless and without attributes" (342).

All the *bhakti* cults played a very crucial role in nurturing the literary tradition of the vernacular languages. The *bhakti* cults were propagated and promoted primarily by saints with the gift of gab. "The *bhakti* tradition found expression through devotees, often referred to in the west as poet-saints, who went about singing songs in the vernacular languages of their region" (343). The songs and limericks composed by Tulsi Das, Kabir, Surdas, Meera, Basavanna, Purandaradasa, Ramprasad and the like are remarkable not only for their devotional fervor but also for their literary merit. These poet-saints are big names not only of religion but also of the world of art and music. Purandaradasa (1480-1564), a Vishnu bhakt, for example, laid the foundation of the modern Karnataka music.

Music, thus, was integral to all the bhakti cults both as a medium of devotional expression and as a vehicle for propagation. In *Bengal Peasant Life*, Day describes how the Bengali *Vaishnavas* use music and dance to express both their deep devotion but also their excitement:

> Vaishnavas had flocked thither from all parts of the country. Vairagis, Bauls, Nagas, Nedas, and Nedis, in their grotesque habiliments, were all there. The music of the khol or mridanga and of the karatala were heard day and night. They sang the praises of Gopinath in merry groups through the village. They danced with excitement . . . many mridangas and karatals were broken through violence of striking. (231-32)

The *Shakta*, hence, is not the only popular cult of Bengal. As Day has observed "the Hindu population of Bengal may be ranged under two classes, the *Saktas* and the *Vaishnavas*: the worshippers of *Sakti* or the Divine Female Principle, and the worshippers of *Vishnu*, or rather of *Krishna*" (228).

Day goes on to describe in detail the beliefs of the Bengali *Vaishnavas*, their main pilgrim centres and the "institution of the repetition of the name of *Hari*" (229) at least hundred and eight times by the devotees. Day says "the chief divinity of the Bengali *Vaishnavas* is *Krishna*, the cow-herd of *Vrindavan* near *Mathura* (*Muthra*); and his mistress *Radha*, the principal *gopi* (cowherdess) amongst sixteen hundred women of the same occupation, receives equal adoration to himself. The sports and amours of *Radha* and *Krishna* form the subject of the *Vaishnava* daily meditation" (229).

It is apparent that in this cult the divine duo of *Radha-Krishna* occupies the same exalted position which the heavenly pair of *Shiva-Parvati* enjoys in the *Shiva bhakti* tradition. However, one major difference between the two pairs is that while *Shiva* and *Parvati* are a married couple, the relation between *Krishna* and *Radha* is that of a lover and his paramour who is wedded to someone else.

Consequently, in the *Vaishnava* cult promiscuous conduct of male and female *vairagis* is not looked down upon. Rather it is an accepted form of interaction, a re-enactment of the *Radha-Krishna* relationship. "They shouted the names of *Radha-Krishna* till their throats became hoarse; . . . men and women danced together promiscuously, the latter excelling the former in the violence of their gestures" (232). Marriage is not allowed in the cult but unlike other monastic orders, the men and women are not debarred from each other's company. Entry of young women is always looked forward to and even encouraged.

Prem Bhakta Vairagi comes across Alanga and Aduri in Agradvipa during the great *Vaishnava Mahotsava*. Fully aware of the fact that Aduri was a young widow at the moment with only her old mother-in-law by her side, he lost no time in trapping her for the cult:

> He was singing, dancing and shouting at a tremendous rate; . . . As he was going through all this buffoonery . . . his eyes met those of Aduri. Suddenly he fell down on the ground as if perfectly senseless. . . . Alanga and Aduri at once recognized him to be Prem Bhakta Vairagi. . . . Being in a state of dasa, he was asked what he had seen. He said he had a sight of Gopinathji who revealed to him the interesting fact that there was one woman there . . . who was destined to be one of the most glorious of mendicant *Vaishnavas* . . . the woman in question was a young widow . . . and who was at the moment standing under a tree. . . . All eyes were turned to the foot of the tree and sure enough four women were standing there, one of whom, Aduri was a young widow. (233-34)

Thus, by making a mixture of myth and fact, Prem Bhakta Vairagi lays a trap for Aduri. Perhaps he always had an eye on Aduri but got an opportune moment only now when she was a widow and without any male escort of her wedded family. Alone and vulnerable, both Aduri and Alanga succumb to pressure exerted on them in the name of *Gopinath*, that is, *Lord Krishan*:

> The leader of the *Vaishnava* group went up to Aduri, acquainted her with the subject-matter of the revelation vouchsafed to Prem Bhakta, congratulated her on her singular good fortune, and added that, under the circumstances, it was her duty to take *bhek*, that is, put on the grab of a mendicant nun and to join the Vairagi order. Alanga did not know what to make of the affair. The idea never occurred to her simple soul that any imposture was practised. (234)

The aforementioned incident makes clear how the different religious cults broke the strong hold of orthodox religion on the lives of people only to trap and exploit them in other ways. The *bhakti* cults challenged the supremacy of the priestly order and questioned the practice of umpteen rituals. They also questioned the monopoly of the priests over sacred texts. They argued for equal rights and access to all religious texts and sacred places of worship. These were some of the positive contributions that the *bhakti* cults made to society.

However, the flip side of the story is that they freed the people form orthodoxy and ignorance only to envelope them into another sort of orthodoxy and ignorance—the cultic one—in which reasoning was drowned by frenzy and haste. The cults had exposed the exploitation of religious myths by *Brahmans* for financial and social gains. With the passage of time some of the cults succumbed to the same malice. Myths and legends began to be used expediently even by them:

> As religious bigotry allows of no delay in swallowing its victims, Aduri was there and then made to go through the ceremonies, and admitted into the order. *Vairagis*, as men who are destitute of passion—for that is the meaning of the term—of course never marry; neither are female *Vairagis* given in marriage, they being like the angels in heaven; yet a pious *Vairagi* has a religious female companion, who is to him a sort of helpmate, and an invaluable auxiliary in devotional exercises. For this holy purpose Aduri was entrusted to the care of Prem Bhakta who was the instrument of her

> conversion. (234)

Aduri's conversion to the cult and her subsequent separation or rather alienation from the family hurt Alanga, the mother-in-law, a lot. She loved her youngest daughter-in-law, but was powerless to protect her from the enticement of the *Vaishnavas*. Her own gullibility further weakened whatever little hold she had on Aduri. She had to let go believing it to be God *Krishna's* divine wish even though she was most unwilling. Alanga ended her pilgrimage abruptly and returned home with a heavy heart:
She had scarcely reached the door of her house at Kanchanpur when she set up a loud cry lamenting the loss of Aduri" (234).

Disheartened though Alanga was over the Aduri episode yet she was not disillusioned with the idea of pilgrimage. It was not long before the old temptation returned. She had returned home without visiting Puri—the most hallowed of all *Vaishnava* pilgrim centres. Hence, the craving to go there this time with the help of a *Sethuya*, or pilgrim guide, who left no stone unturned to convince the old lady about the benefits of paying obeisance at Puri. Little did Alanga realize then that the *Sethuya* was to be her nemesis just like Prem Bhakta Vairagi was for Aduri:

> Yes, indeed, it is a sort of religious madness which takes possession of old Hindu women, impelling them to go on distant pilgrimages, utterly regardless of the pains and troubles connected with the journey. The *Sethuya*, or the pilgrim-guide, had for many days past been visiting Alanga, describing to her the glories of the temples of Jagannath at Puri in Orissa, and expatiating on the ineffable merit of visiting those holy shrines. Alanga's imagination was set on fire. She made up her mind to go. In her dreams every night she saw the armless deity in all his glory nothing would dissuade her from going. (237)

Both her sons oppose her decision. The family had not yet recovered from Aduri's estrangement. It was still fresh in their memory. Badan is extremely apprehensive fearing that he might lose his mother forever. Kalamanik offers to accompany her so that he can look after her and bring her back safely. All such suggestions and reasoning are turned down by an adamant Alanga.

Her grandson Govinda too joins his father and uncle in convincing the old lady against falling prey to the temptations of the pilgrim-guide. The grandson offers a very reasonable and practical advice to his grandmother: "But, grandma, what is the use of your going at all? You can worship *Jagannath* here in the house. Everyman's mind is a temple of worship. I do not see the use of going to distant places to worship God. God can be worshipped in the mind" (236).

The wisdom and practicality inherent in the philosophy of Govinda, however, is not fully comprehended by Alanga. The wise counsel of her grandson only amuses her but does not alter her mind. She lacks the confidence to take an independent stand like Govinda in the matter of religion. She joins the flock of sheep that is heading towards Puri in the search of *Jagannath* who, as Govinda had claimed, "can be worshipped in the mind" (236). Though Govinda does not succeed in dissuading his grandmother from undertaking the perilous journey, he emerges as a spokesperson of the new generation that is gifted with a great clarity of mind and the confidence to speak out.

For the first time in the novel, Day brings face to face three generations of the family and shows the gradual evolution of their personality as they grapple with life. While Alanga emerges as a symbol of orthodoxy, Badan is more in the grip of emotion, Kalamanik is sentimental as well as sensitive. It is Govinda who emerges as the most balanced personality—philosophical as well as practical, sensible as well as sensitive. His observations about God places him in the category of a visionary and seer. It is as if Lord *Jagannath* himself was speaking through him and trying to dissuade Alanga from a journey that was going to be ill-fated.

However, Alanga failed to realize that God often speaks through the mouths of the young too. She had pinned all her faith on the priestly class and accepted the *pandits*, the *vairagis*, the *sadhus* and the pilgrim-guides as the only mediators between the God and the common man. She did not see that for most of them religion was a profession through which they earned their bread and butter. Hence, most of what they said was not the result of divine direction but dictated by their basic need to provide for themselves and their families. Overriding the objections of her family, Alanga starts off for Puri to pay obeisance to Lord *Jagannath.*

Jagannath, it is believed, is "an appearance of *Vishnu*" but some scholars maintain "*Jagannath* was *Buddha*, others that he was really *Krishna*" (Knappert 125), who is himself an incarnation of Lord *Vishnu.* Day narrates in detail the whole story about the genesis of Lord *Jagannath* and introduces the reader to the first among the divine trinity—*Brahma.*

Brahma is "the God-Creator of the Universe" (Zimmer 67). He is four-faced and "seated in the centre of the golden lotus, which expands and is radiant with the glowing energy of creation" (*Ibid.*). Heinrich Zimmer makes a very pertinent observation about *Brahma.* He says: "in Hindu mythology *Brahma* personifies exclusively the positive aspect of the life-process of the universe, and is never represented as destroying what he has produced. He symbolizes . . . merely the creative phase, pure spirituality. . . .*Vishnu* and *Shiva*, on the other hand, as well as the Goddess Mother of the World, are strongly visualized as terrible and creative and destructive, hideous and comely" (*Ibid.* 124). No wonder it is Lord *Brahma* who officiates the deification of the image made by Lord *Visvakarma.* Lord *Jagannath* becomes a force, a power only after *Brahma* plays his creative and constructive part.

It is to be noted, however, that Day has not made a direct discussion of *Brahma.* It is only in the context of Lord *Jagannath* that the first of the Divine Trinity is mentioned by the author. Yet another noteworthy point is that except *Brahma*, the two other Gods—*Vishnu* and *Mahesh*—have been mentioned but only in their incarnated forms. The reader is introduced to *Mahesh* not in his principal form as *Shiva* but as Pencho. Similarly, one comes across not Lord *Vishnu* himself but his various incarnations—*Ram, Krishna* and *Jaganath.* It is only *Brahma* whom one finds in the narrative as himself and not his shadow or incarnation.

Similar is the case with *shakti*. It is her sixth incarnation as *Shashthi* who is highlighted in the narrative. Her more powerful and fearsome incarnations like *Kali* and *Durga* (the all-encompassing goddess) are mentioned only in passing. Both as *Kali* and as the all-powerful *Durga,* the Divine Mother exercises immense destructive power. *Bengal Peasant Life,* on the other hand, is a domestic and social tale. Perhaps this is the reason why Day avoided giving prominence to *Kali* and *Durga.* The peasants need seed, soil, water, healthy cattle and man-power for good harvest. All of these are related to fecundity and fertility—both of man as well as nature, which in turn, according to mythology, is promised by goddess *Shashthi*. Hence, in the life of Bengali peasants, the sixth incarnation of *shakti* assumes great significance.

As mentioned earlier, Alanga wanted to visit Puri primarily to pray to Lord *Jagannath* and to participate in the annual *Rath Yatra*. The *Rath Yatra* begins every year on the *dweetiya teethe, shukla paksha* of *ashadha maas*. On this day the idol of *Shri Jagannath* along with elder brother *Balram* and their sister *Subhadra* is taken out of the temple in three different chariots.

The characterization of Alanga makes it clear that Day has included each and every character in the novel with a definite purpose. When the story opens, Alanga appears to be nothing more than an indulgent grandmother, a fussing mother and mother-in-law, a lady fully in control of the Samanta household. Little does the reader realize that through her the writer would bring a crucial turn in the narrative. As Alanga proceeds towards Puri to meet her *nirvana*, domesticity recedes to the background. What seeps in is both detachment and disintegration in the family of Badan. Moreover, there is shift of focus from the personal to the public, from domestic problems to more serious issues involving the law-enforcing agencies of the British *Raj*.

Alanga's obsessive desire to go on pilgrimage gave Day the opportunity to describe in detail an event of great religious and social import—the *Jagannath Rath Yatra*. Moreover, the writer also got the chance to describe the different branches of the Hindu religion, that is, the different cults. Both the characters of Alanga as well as Aduri facilitate a deeper study of Hindu religion, mythology and society.

It is apparent from the narrative that each and every auspicious and inauspicious event and occurrence in the life of Badan's family has given Day an opportunity to introduce to the reader supernatural forces deeply revered by the people. He has used the different occasions to communicate the deep-rooted faiths and beliefs of the people which not only order and organize their world but also give it meaning and method. The myths and legends, kings, queens, gods and goddesses are not just sources of fun, fear and furore. The exceptional characters and mythical stories provide to the people emotional succour, support, security, mental strength and stability to carry on with life in spite of all upheavals, to maintain equanimity even in moments of extreme joy or ecstasy.

By the time Govinda comes off age, Day has already described a number of festivals, religious functions and occasions. All the major gods and goddess—the Divine Trinity of *Brahma*, *Vishnu* and *Mahesh* as also the Supreme Mother *Shashthi*, Goddess *Nishi*, *Saraswati*, *Lakshmi* and *Pencho* along with the ghosts and witches—exercise some degree of influence on the live of the peasantry. Last but not the least of them is *Visvakarma*. He has already been mentioned by Day while describing Alanga's visit to Puri to witness the *Jagannath Rath Yatra*.

Every year in the month of *Chaitra* (half of March and half of April) the peasantry worship *Visvakarma*. The image of the *Visvakarma* is seldom made for worship at home. Rather the implements are regarded as symbols of the god and hence on the auspicious day the tools are set apart and worshipped. Day observes: "The celebration, like all Hindu *pujas*, was partly religious and partly social" (352).

After the religious part of the ceremony is over, the day is spent in festivities and "the blacksmith, the carpenter, the weaver, the barber, the husbandman, eat better dinners than perhaps on any other day in the year" (353). However, this wining and dining is restricted not just to the family members. Invitations are sent to fellow artisans and colleagues also. The more affluent an artisan, the more elaborate are the arrangements made and the longer is the list of invitees. Once the feasting is over, the professional class spends the remaining hours of the day in recreational activities. They amuse themselves by indulging in a number of folk games.

Thus, Hindu mythology has made even the tools and implements sacred along with the whole of the natural world. The rat, the fish, the tortoise, the bear—all are creatures not to be abhorred but valued for the role they play on this earth. Hinduism, in fact, promotes a way of life which is nature friendly. Even the smallest of creature or object, even a lifeless stone is worthy of veneration if it directly or indirectly contributes to the good of all.

Every living and non-living thing is believed to be a manifestation of *Brahma* himself. Each combines in itself the dual energies—of creation as well as destruction. Their due must be given to them and hence a sense of gratitude is evident. The harm their non-cooperation can inflict on humanity evokes fear as well. Cooperation by these creatures in human endeavour implies that these creatures, objects or forces of nature will do nothing to harm the interest of their devotees. It also implies that each creature will simply follow its own nature. The eagle must eat the snake, the snake in turn must swallow the rats, the rats, on the other hand, must eat the rotten edibles, the birds must feed on the insects. In this way each must live according to its nature so as to ensure check and balance in the universe. This probably is the reason why the Hindu religion, through the stories of various incarnations of gods/goddess as plants and animals, tries to impress upon its adherents the significance of every bit of this diverse universe. Even the tools with the help of which they till the land, grind the grains, make the furniture as well as make the idols of gods/ goddess/ animal/ bird/ human forms are objects worthy of worship.

It must be recalled here that in *Bengal Peasant Life*, the family of Badan is shown worshipping not just gods such as *Pencho* or *Krishna* and goddesses such as *Shashthi* or *Saraswati* but even that rats, the crows and the cows who are offered obeisance during the *Navanna* (new rice) festival.

It is true that "every mythology has its obscurities, inconsistencies, and absurdities," but, as the myths and legends used by Day in *Bengal Peasant Life* show, mythologies also "offer a way of apprehending reality, of making sense of nature and human life, no matter how irrational they might appear to us" (Wiegel 10). Hindu mythology, in particular, is steeped with the spirit of sustainability, closely co-relating the well-being of man with the well-being of flora and fauna. This probably is the reason why many believe that myths "in their vital stage, when they are accepted as truth . . . represent the learning of a society, its accumulated knowledge and wisdom" (*Ibid.*). They "give a comprehensive account of the world and of the people to whom" (*Ibid.*) they belong.

It is, therefore, necessary for the realistic description of Indian society to take cognizance of the myths and legends it believes in. It is the mythological tales and poetries which provide a key to the understanding of a society's "political organizations . . . codes of laws . . . ethical code, and above all" its "conceptions of God, the soul and the Universe" (Mackenzie vi). Myths explain why people of different cultures behave the way they do. Hence a reference to myths and legends becomes a necessity in order to understand the whys and wherefores behind various socio-cultural activities. Religion, with its bundle of mythic tales, rituals and superstitions, co-ordinates all these activities. This is the reason why Lal Bihari Day, while presenting a socio-religious account of the Bengal peasantry, has including many mythic stories in the narrative process, so as to paint a 'realistic' picture of how they live and die, celebrate and mourn, crumble or cope with the pressures of human life.

Mulk Raj Anand's *The Big Heart:* A Discordant Note

It is surprising that a leftist writer should make use of myths and legends even though Karl Marx had made it clear that religion and its other concomitants are opium of the masses. Mulk Raj Anand makes use of mythology in his narratives and with great aplomb. *The Old Woman and the Cow* (1960), *The Road* (1961) and *Death of a Hero* (1963) are three of his novels well known for their mythic suggestions. However even in an early novel like *The Big Heart* (1945), he makes use of mythic figures and no less significantly.

Anand is a novelist of the subalterns in the sense that most of his novels deal not with the *haut monde* but with the lowest rungs of the Hindu society depicting all the violence and vulgarity without any attempt at sophistication or subtlety. This is especially true in the context of novels such as the *Untouchable* (1933) and *The Big Heart*. Neither pleasure and pain nor poignancy is couched in polite terms. Everything is communicated with so much ribaldry that one is left shell shocked both at the author's temerity and the vulgar reality of the Indian society.

It is in the midst of this degradation, deprivation and obscenity that Anand makes use of myths and legends in these novels without allowing the ruggedness of the milieu to ruin the dignity of the mythic suggestions. The mythic figures remain untouched by the squalor around them. There is no blasphemy either by the author or the hard-pressed riff-raff characters who live on the fringes. This is perhaps Anand's greatest achievement. The characters do not challenge the gods. Rather they challenge the forces that wield authority in the name of gods. Marxism may have taught Anand to doubt and dismiss religion but, in his narratives, at least, sacred myths and legends are dealt with due deference.

Like the *Untouchable*, *The Big Heart* deals with the life of one of the low castes—the coppersmiths. The focus, however, is different. The emphasis is not on the social but the economic. Like Dickens' *Hard Times* (1854), the novel is about capitalism and industrialism. However, unlike *Hard Times* wherein the 'isms' were well established and flourishing, crushing the working and the non-working classes alike; in *The Big Heart* the battle between traditional and modern systems has just begun. The dispute is also about as to how this battle has to be waged. The problems seem to lie less in the preceding or succeeding systems of work than in the flawed perceptions of the issues. It is with this 'flawed perception' that the hero of the novel grapples with and ultimately dies for.

The novel is overshadowed by a foreboding sense of gloom and doom. The reader finds the hero banging his head against the walls of rugged, rustic, egoist individuals whose empty stomachs do not make them pliable but all the more obstinate, arrogant and angry. That the hero is destined to fail is clear from the very beginning, for it is not myths of fertility and fun that are roped in the narrative, rather of death, chaos and angst—*Kali, Yama, Ravan and the Devil*.

The mythic figure that keeps recurring in the novel is that of Goddess *Kali*. Her name is the feminine form of the word *'Kala'* meaning Time—the all producing, all annihilating principle. *Kali* is the consort of *Shiva*. As *Shakti* she preserves and as *Kali* she destroys:

> The Goddess represents clearly enough by her feminine nature the life-bearing, life-nourishing, maternal principles. . . . But the counter-balancing negative aspect, her ever-destructive function, which takes back and swallows again the creatures brought forth, requires a shock of vivid horror. . . . To this end she is represented as *Kali,* the Black One. (Zimmer 211)

It is in the second chapter that Ananta first recalls his dream about the goddess. He shudders but does not realize that it was going to be ominous, and that time was baying for his blood or that the inevitable change will want the sacrifice of his life:

> And they were following him, while he had run, their hands dripping with blood. He had been frightened and had tried to run faster, but behind him there was a voice calling, I am hungry, I want blood, and he had felt almost overpowered. . . . He had looked back and found a black woman with a trident in her hand standing on the cremation ground, stamping upon corpses and dancing as she shrieked again and again, I am hungry! I want blood! And he could hear the dead moaning under the feet of the woman, whom he soon recognized as the Goddess *Kali*, for her tongue was bulging.

The vision visits him again when he has reached almost the end of his life. It is only then that he begins to read the hidden, sinister meaning of the dream. Yet, true to his name he does not give up: "Ananta fairly ran across. . . . He would try this last chance."

Ananta is the main character, the protagonist of *The Big Heart*. He and other coppersmiths such as Ralia, Viroo, Dina, Bati, Banta, Mela, Bihari, Mukund have been rendered jobless because Lala Murli Dhar, the Chaudhury of their caste, and Lala Gokul Chand, the headman of the Kaseras have set up a factory. Now everything is made by machines. Without work, the coppersmiths face starvation. Ananta, who has the experience of workers' union in Bombay, advises the same course of action to his brethren. He advocates the path of negotiation with the factory owners. Satyapal, the radical, representing the younger generation, dismisses the idea of negotiations and incites the unemployed workers to immediate action. Hans Raj, on the other hand, states that salvation lies in religion. These are the conflicting ideologies and options before the workers.

Ananta, a representative of socialism, is pitted against all. His task is complicated further by the fact that he lacks credibility amongst his fellowmen because of his liaison with Janaki, his widow mistress. Yet he is not cowed down and resolves to somehow convince the coppersmiths to see reason. He understands the whole situation with all its complexity. He knows where the solution lies.

However, driven to hunger and anger, the disgruntled lot, represented by Ralia, has little patience for Ananta's words of wisdom. Ralia gets incited by Satypal's rabble rousing. He breaks into the factory damaging the machines and killing Ananta. In the penultimate pages Ralia shouts:

> I am the destroyer. . . . Come, brother,
> I am *Shiva.*

Ralia gets caught up in his own frenzy and becomes uncontrollable like *Rudra*, the destructive *Shiva*—a personification of *tamas*—the quality or principle of darkness, obstruction, anger, dullness and sorrow.

Thus, a novel that began with the chase of *Kali* ends with the dance of *Shiva*, her consort. In between is spent the life of the hero Ananta. *Kali*, as already pointed out, is the destructive form of *Parvati*, or *Durga.* Her name means black thereby suggesting her ferocious and terrifying nature. She is depicted as a black woman of voluptuous appearance but with blazing bloodthirsty eyes, from which human blood drips, and with her long tongue hanging out, ready to lick up her victim's blood. Human skulls hang on strings around her body, snakes writhe around her neck and there are weapons in each of her ten hands. She is painted dancing on her husband *Shiva*'s body.

The point is who is *Kali* in this novel? What is the significance of the dream about her in the narrative? It cannot merely be aesthetic. Of course, Anand uses her to set the tone of the novel, to accentuate the sense of doom and gloom. Apart from this aesthetic appeal, Anand found something more useful in the *Kali* myth. It is also to be noted that Ralia is a representation of not just *Kali* but also of *Shiva* in his *tandava nritya*. In Ralia the two mythic images of the ravaging *Kali* and of the ferociously dancing *Shiva* coalesce.

In *Durga Saptshati*, the wife of *Shiva*, Goddess *Parvati*, assumes the form of *Kali* to annihilate the demons who had captured *Indra Lok* and were tormenting the whole universe:

> *Shiva's* complex character is reflected in the various forms assumed by his bride. As the Destroyer he is associated with *Durga*, who has great beauty and is also a war goddess. As *Kali* she is the black earth—mother, and as *Jagadgauri,* the yellow woman, the harvest bride. Armed with celestial weapons, *Durga* is a renowned slayer of demons.
>
> In her *Kali* form she is of hideous aspect. Sculptors and painters have depicted her standing on the prostrate form of *Shiva* and grinning with outstretched tongue. Her body is smeared with blood because she has waged a ferocious and successful war against the giants.
>
> Like *Shiva,* she has a flaming third eye on her foreheads. Her body is naked save for a girdle of giants' hand suspended from her waist; round her neck she wears a long necklace of giants' skulls: like the Egyptian Isis, *Kali* can conceal herself in her long and abundant hair. She has four arms: in one she holds a weapon, and in another the dripping head of a giant; two empty hands are raised to bless her worshippers. Like the Egyptian Hathor or Sekhet, the "Eye of Ra," she goes forth to slay the enemies of the gods, rejoicing in slaughter. Like Hathor, too, she is asked to desist, but heeds not. Then *Shiva* approaches her and lies down among her victims. *Kali* dances over the battlefield and leaps over her husband's body. When she observes, however, what she has done, she ejects her tongue with shame. (Mackenzie 149-50)

A careful comparison of the excerpt quoted above about Kali and the situation created by Anand in the novel shows striking similarity but with some serious jarring notes. The mythic image is imitated but later inverted. Ralia is *Kali* and Ananta is *Shiva*. However, Ralia is also *Shiva* with Ananta being the suffering creativity reeling under his dance of destruction, the *tandava nritya*. On yet another level Ralia is not *Kali* but plain devil, a mere personification of destruction. One is forced to wonder if the real *Kali* is Janaki, the mistress of Ananta? It is only after Ananta's return from Bombay with her that he sees Goddess *Kali* in his dreams. Is her association, a relationship without the label of marriage on it, inauspicious for him?

Ananta is not a very religious man. He is actually a maverick. He enters into a love relationship with Janaki without the fear of either divine retribution or social ridicule. Religious rules and social codes bother him less and human inequities and injustices more. In personal life he is a radical but in the social sphere he seeks rational and peaceful solutions. He does not depend on Gods to find out what is right. He trusts the mind of man more but only to his own nemesis.

It is clear that to a certain extent the image of *Kali* is used also to symbolically represent Ananta's mental state, his fears and worries lurking in his mind in spite of the external show of optimism and reason. He is a human being after all and 'socialism' does not make him immune to either mythic or man-made fears. He is tormented by 'angry' deities who visit him in dreams and try to weaken his resolve. So do his compatriots who fail to understand him and treat him like an enemy.

Though apparently free from the shackles of religion, Ananta's unconscious mind reverberates with mythic images. A man unorthodox in his views is drawn involuntarily into the vortex of religious mythology. Thus, psychologically Ananta does not seem to be as distanced from religion and mythology as he apparently seems to be. His innermost fears and doubts are communicated by his mind through the mythic symbols and images that are familiar to him and also comprehensible. Dangers slowly gather around him. By bringing Janaki home, Ananta has already made his reputation questionable. His 'socialist' stand further accentuates the irritation that some people feel for him. His alien 'ways' of living with a woman without wedding her and his alien 'ideas' about work and livelihood issues make him a misfit. The image of

Kali haunts him in dream because his unconscious mind senses the impending dangers and tries to warn him.

Ananta was well acquainted with Hindu myths and legends. All Indians, even the most illiterate and poor, have a sound knowledge of the mythic figures. No education is required to know who *Ram, Ravan, Sita, Savitri, Parvati, Shiva* and *Kali* are. Their symbolic significance too is known to every child. Hence the recurrent dream about *Kali* sends a shiver down Ananta's spin. He knows what *Kali* stands for. Her symbolic significance is clear to him. She inspires and generates fear but as slayer of demons she also annihilates fear. She is the loving wife of *Shiva* shamed by her recklessness in not heeding to her husband's plea to stop the dance of death. Multiple meanings abound about her. What is Ananta to make of the dream? Apprehensions drown him and he breaks into cold sweat: "He had looked back and found a black woman standing on the cremation ground, stamping upon corpses and dancing as she shrieked again and again, 'I am hungry! I want blood."

In Hindu mythology *Kali* is an ambivalent character. She undoubtedly symbolizes destruction. However, this destruction is not merely for destruction's sake. She kills but only to create a better and healthier world. Hence even in the most ferocious of her forms she is revered.

Anand's selection of the mythic figure of *Kali*, thus, serves multiple purposes. *Kali* helps him to create a foreboding environment, heavily loaded with a sense of gloom and doom. The dream envelops Ananta, the chief character, with a seriousness that rarely leaves him. The author drives home the message that destruction and creation go hand in hand. *Kali* kills only to create. 'Time' or *Kali* demands sacrifice. Those who seek change must be ready for the upheavals that it will unleash. The world is freed from demonic forces only after *Kali* dances. Death is the ultimate reply of evil. Death is also the supreme effort or offering by the pious so that the riot of demonic forces is controlled. Nature, that is the gods and goddesses, tolerate evil only to a certain limit. Thereafter they become unstoppable. Nature begins to take her own revenge till order is restored and sense prevails. In *The Big Heart*, however, Kali is not the mythic goddess of destruction who liberates the world from demonic forces. She is a manifestation of the irrational and evil powers that try to dominate and destroy man. Ralia is *Kali* while Ananta is the *Shiva* lying at the Divine Mother's feet trying to stop her fearsome dance. Ralia is a representation of the evil that attempts to annihilate the good. It is to be noted that the colour black represents evil, gloom and doom.

True to his ideological belief, Mulk Raj Anand uses mythic elements in his novel only to subvert them. In mythology *Kali* kills to create. She eliminates the evil forces. In *The Big Heart*, however, it is the evil that triumphs, Ralia kills Ananta and not the other way round. Thus, myth in Anand's work is used for aesthetic and antithetical purposes. He seems to acknowledge myths and legends as literary works or as works of art that can be used to add colour or tone to any other creative work. He is willing to concern himself, to a certain extent, with their 'form' but as far as 'content' is concerned, he backs out. "Anand follows the mythical design to a certain point and then changes it totally, intending perhaps to indicate that the same ending is no longer possible (or desirable) in our times" (Mukherjee 137).

Intoxicated by his own false sense of 'power,' carried away or consumed by his own anger, Ralia claims: "I am the destroyer. . . . Come, brother, I am Shiva." He then kills Ananta, the symbol of humanism in the novel. In this context too Anand seems to invert the mythic pattern. In mythology, *Shiva* is also the lord of dances, that is, *Nataraja*. "*Shiva*, by his dance, destroys the creation to make room for new things, just as fire destroys the corpses on the shamshana, the cremation-field."[5] However here Ralia ends the life of Ananta not to create but obstruct the inevitable flow of time which invariably brings in change. Ralia refuses to acknowledge the advent of new ideas. Neither is he able to stomach the factory system nor Ananta's tactics of adjustment with the changing work culture. Anger and hunger make him clamour for the 'past,' the 'status quo' of yester years in which he felt safe, secure and satiated. He resents change and that is why resents both capitalism and socialism. Both have pushed him to the brink of hunger and hence he sees no merit in them. He seeks out to destroy both—the factory as well as Ananta. His 'dance' is not the dance of *Shiva* that paves way for a fresh round of creativity. To make space for the 'new.' Rather he hankers for the past which at least provided him with two squares of meal every day. Hence, he yells out "I am the destroyer." Ralia's motive is to destroy both the factory owners and Ananta. He hates the factory owners who have snatched his livelihood by the use of machines and he hates Ananta too because Ananta is open to change and conciliatory towards it. Ralia sees it as betrayal. Hence, he harms both the machines and Ananta. In his perception, he is not the devil or the elephant demon whom *Shiva* killed by making the animal dance endlessly. Rather it is the factory and Ananta who are the real culprits and need to be destroyed. The perception of 'what is right' and 'what is wrong' differs greatly and Ananta pays heavily for it. Ananta's *Shiva* is Ralia's 'demon' while Ralia's *Shiva* is Ananta's 'devil.'

In the portrayal of Ananta's mistress Janaki, Anand again breaks the mythic mould. She reminds of Goddess *Sita*, the epitome of marital devotion. In fact, the word 'Janaki' is one of the names of Sita. Sita was the daughter of King Janak who ruled over Mithila. Hence, she was also called Janaki or Mithilesh Kumari. In the epic the *Ramayana*, Sita is abducted by Ravan, the king of Lanka. Ram, her husband, rescues her. Just as Sita is an ideal woman or wife, Ram is an ideal husband. He is devoted to Sita and steadfast in his decision to refrain from re-marrying. In fact, the immediate provocation of Sita's abduction was Ram and Lakshman's rude and humiliating refusal to marry Suparnakha, the sister of Ravan who had fallen in love with Ram. Infuriated by the physical injuries and insult inflicted on his dear sister, Ravan stole

Sita away so that he could make her another of his wives. Though confined, Sita refused. She was finally rescued by Ram, her husband, who put an end to the demonic reign of Ravan in Lanka.

This mythic story is reversed by Mulk Raj Anand in *The Big Heart*. In the original epic the abductor is the devil, the bad man who forcibly carries away another's wife inflicting mental and physical discomfort on her. In the novel, however, the bad man is not the abductor but the husband and his family. Firstly, Janaki's marriage was incompatible. Secondly, she was widowed young and forced to remain clinging to his memory in the hostile and insensitive company of her in-laws who did not believe in giving the young widowed woman a second chance. Ultimately it is left to Ananta to rescue Janaki from this hapless situation. He elopes with her, that is, he abducts her. He returns to his native place with her and begins to live with the young widow as man and wife. Janaki begins to live a fairly better life with Ananta. His love does much to assuage Janaki's problems. He is the buffer between her and the insensitive and unsympathetic society but their live-in-relationship also makes Ananta socially weak His credibility gets eroded even if, from humanitarian point of view, his support to Janaki is not wrong.

Thus, the abductor in this case is not 'bad' but 'good.' Unlike *Ravan* in the *Ramayana*, he does not abduct the woman to torment her. Rather he takes her away to give reprieve. Ananta rescues Janaki from a callous situation. Hence in *The Big Heart* the marital home is *Lanka* for Janaki. The abductor is not *Ravan* but *Ram*. The role of *Ram* and *Ravan* is reversed. *Ram* becomes *Ravan* and *Ravan* is *Ram*. Marital tie is not blissful for her. On the contrary it becomes like a nose around her neck slowly tightening itself till she dies. It is Ananta, the abductor, the *Ravan*, who rescues her. He breaks her from bondage to a dead man's memory and takes her away as the mistress of his life and home. Even if illegitimate, their relationship is far more livable for Janaki than her life as a wife and widow. What is present as a kernel in this novel later develops into a full-fledged technique in Anand's later novel *The Old Woman and the Cow* (1960). Meenakshi Mukherjee writes:

> It is part of Anand's technique that in his novel a myth should be pursued up to a certain point and then suddenly reversed. This contains an implicit comment on the values of the past, and reveals Anand's rejection of the ideal represented in the particular, myth. *The Old Woman and The Cow* is not a particularly successful novel, but Anand's negative use of myth is worth special mention, because this novel is unique among Indian novels in rejecting rather than extolling the time-honoured womanly virtues of patience and submission. (164)

The time-honoured womanly virtues of patience and submission as symbolized by mythical women is again knocked down by Anand in his presentation of Gauri, the wife of Ralia. Ralia and Gauri are a married couple while Ananta and Janaki are not. In Hindu mythology all married pairs right from Ram and Sita to Parvati and Shiva, Savitri and Satyavan, Krishna and Rukmini, Vishnu and Lakshmi—are shown leading fairly peaceful lives with lot of love for each other. They conduct themselves with each other with great deal of care, courtesy and decency. Both the husband and wife are an epitome of grace. The wives worship their husbands. They hover around their husbands in awe and acquiescence. The husbands, on the other hand, smile smugly and knowledgeably. Their opinion is that their wives enjoy being lorded over. This blissful, ideal, idyllic and romantic setting is not to Anand's liking and in his view very far from reality. Ralia's wife Gauri is a faithful and devoted wife but also a fiercely independent individual with a keen sense of pride. She does not try to appease her husband. She never tolerates any of his insults. On the contrary she retaliates in the same coin. She has her own vocabulary of 'abuses' to match those of Ralia's. The decorum and decency depicted between the mythical couples is thrown to the winds by Anand in the context of Ralia and Gauri. The married life of this real couple is devoid of rosy romanticism. They live together and yet fight like cats and dogs.

It is clear that in the context of women, whether mythical or real, Anand's approach is different. Directly or indirectly, he extols not submissive, delicate and feminine females, but strong and bold women who reveal the courage to make choices and take decisions. He seems to dislike submissive and soft women like Sita. Rather he appreciates women who take the responsibility of their lives in their own hands. Of all the mythical goddesses, it is the ferocious Kali that Anand selects for his narrative. Kali is dark, black, ugly and fearsome. Just the opposite of the other bright, beautiful, merciful goddesses like Lakshmi or Saraswati or Sati and Savitri. It is the feminine principle in its fiercest form that Mulk Raj Anand depicts in his narrative. He has no use of beautiful and benign goddesses like Lakshmi, Saraswati or Sita in his novels. Nor does he become weak before the bewitching beauty of nymphs like Menaka or Shakuntala. He likes Kali, the black but the powerful, who makes even her husband, Lord Shiva, lie prostrate before her. He prefers women like the Black Divine Mother who, when required, can be kind as well as cruel. Likewise, he makes his mortal women strong. Janaki cooperates with Ananta when he comes to rescue her. Gauri too is as rude and raucous as her husband. He negates the Sita myth and tries to establish women who have traces of Kali in them—the ability to react and hit back.

Mulk Raj Anand, thus, possesses an innovative attitude towards mythical values. Myth is, traditionally, a charter of conduct. Anand has always reacted against this notion. He does not believe in carrying on the baggage of the past if it proves to be an impediment in the way of human happiness. Change is inevitable. Each moment a new reality is born which requires to be comprehended and assimilated with an objective mindset. Hence not only does he reject old 'ideals' but also searches for 'new' ones. His eulogy of Gandhi and socialism, Marxism and humanism are actually an attempt to find 'new' gods and 'mantras,' that is, a new mythology to guide and govern humanity. In the dedication to *Morning Face*, Anand says to Lord *Krishna*: "You are really not the *Krishna* of the age of gods. You cannot be."

Jan Knappert in his book *Indian Mythology* opines that myths motivate "the people to perform certain special ceremonies, daily or annually, as their lives more through the cycle of seasons." It is this overt and covert pressure of myths that Anand resents. He is of the opinion that much of world's misery is rooted in the manner in which religious values (as epitomized by mythic gods, goddesses, heroes and heroines) have structured our society and conditioned our minds. Though he has never directly addressed religious issues, his study of Indian social life reveals how religious beliefs, myths, dogmas and superstitions have coalesced to dehumanize the people. They have categorized people and given them both—a false sense of superiority and a false sense of inferiority—on the basis of caste, class and gender. People are no longer just 'humans.' Rather they are either 'greater' humans or 'lesser' humans depending upon their birth, lineage and sex. Whoever gains the upper hand unleashes a reign of terror to settle scores. Better sense prevails only after a lot of damage is done and after the sacrifice of good people like the protagonist Ananta. Leaders like Mahatma Gandhi too did not deserve to die the way they did. They struggled for political, social and financial justice to all only to be denied justice themselves —the justice to live a normal life and die a natural death. This is the reason why Mulk Raj Anand tries to install political, social and economic reformers like Karl Marx and Mahatma Gandhi as the 'new gods' and ideologies like humanism, capitalism and socialism as the 'new religions' of the modern era. His novels begin with the exposure of old suppressive systems and then move towards welcoming new ideologies and icons.

His very first novel *Untouchable* is a scathing attack on the caste system and its concomitant 'untouchability' that is central to the Hindu religion. The caste system, originally designed as *varna vyavastha,* to ensure division of labour became hereditary later with a rigid code of prohibitions and inhibitions. A person of the upper caste could not interact with those of the lower. Intermarriage was, of course, out of question when even minimum of social etiquette and cordiality was debarred. In the novel, Pt. Kali Nath, a Brahmin, takes a lot of precaution while pouring water in the pitchers of the lower caste women least he be polluted accidentally. However, all reservations are thrown to the winds the moment Bakha's beautiful sister Sohini, a sweeper girl, becomes an object of desire for him. To top it all, when Pandit Kali Nath is on the verge of being caught red-handed, he raises an uproar blaming the innocent girl so as to camouflage his own licentiousness. Gulaboo, another low caste but beautiful woman in the novel, is a long-time mistress of an upper caste man. He does not marry her because she is a washerwoman but sleeps with her because she is irresistible. He even fathers an illegitimate son with Gulaboo.

Mulk Raj Anand obviously cannot understand and appreciate a system that is helpless before such exploitation and blind to such anomalies. The whole logic of 'touchability' and 'untouchability' 'upper' caste and 'lower' caste crumbles to expose the hollowness and hypocrisy of the Hindu religion and its notions of 'right' and 'wrong.' Mythic gods and goddesses, to whom Bakha had bowed in awe and reverence just minutes before, fail to protect his innocent sister from the lecherous Pandit. Nor do the gods and goddesses do anything to give Gulaboo and her son their rightful places in the life of that dubious upper caste man.

Mulk Raj Anand shows the gradual disenchantment with religion and the reason behind this disenchantment. Bakha, in spite of the rough treatment that is meted out to him, is not averse to Hinduism. In fact, like any other Hindu he too would have loved to sing, pray and participate in the rituals. It is the religion itself and its custodians who have closed the door to him and his community. They clean the temples and the latrine of high castes but are not allowed to enter into the holy premises. It is the effort of these people that maintains the purity of the place but they are the first ones to be shown the door. Hence Bakha walks away towards Gandhi and the poet, the new messiahs who hold the promise of salvation. It is Gandhi and machines, socialism and industrialism who appear as the new gods and new mantras with a ray of hope for the future.

In fact, the bias and prejudice of the upper caste never gave Bakha a chance to know his religion fully and properly. He had only a rudimentary knowledge collected through over-hearing and observation from a distance:

> The word 'Ram' he had heard very often, also 'Sri, Sri,' and he had seen a red shrine with a monkey carved on a wall, caged from without with brass bars—that he knew was called the shrine of Hanuman. The black shrine showing a jet-black woman with a flaming-red tongue, ten-armed and with a garland of skulls around her neck—that was called the shrine of Kali. Krishna was the blue god who played the flute in the coloured pictures of the betel-leaf seller's shop in the street. But who was Hari, Narayan? (65)

Though denied proximity, he feels drawn. His curiosity becomes "more and more intense." (66) He moves as close as his courage would allow but stops because he had been taught that "an untouchable going into a temple polluted it past purification." (66) Reprimand was sure. However, his inner impulse to see god closely was too intense to ignore. The whole environment of incense, conch shell, the ringing bells and the songs mesmerized and he forgot his status in society. "Bakha was profoundly moved. . . . His hands joined unconsciously, and his head hung in the worship of the unknown god." (68) However, his quiet devotion was neither received by the celestial beings nor approved by the terrestrials. Within seconds he is discovered by the touchable Hindus who object: "Get off the steps, scavenger! Off with you! You have defiled our whole service! You have defiled our temple!" (69) He is yet to recover from this collective censure when another shock hits him like a bolt out of the blue. His innocent and beautiful sister Sohini is accused by Pt. Kali Nath of taking liberty with him. He tried to molest her but accuses the girl of polluting him to hide his crime. The crowd fails to understand as to how a young sweeper girl can make advances to an old Brahmin associated with the temple. Bakha's devotion and reverence for the divine deity bears little fruit. Both he and his sister are humiliated. Their sincerity and honesty have little value before the hegemony of the upper caste on religion and truth. The touchable Hindus decide to send Bakha packing from the temple and it is Kali Nath's opinion about Sohini that matters. No wonder Bakha felt as if "the temple stood challengingly before him. . . . The temple seemed to advance towards him like a monster, and to envelop him." (67) The same gods whom he was eager to know and see from close quarters suddenly seem distant, detached, even cruel and cold to him. It is as if they are the gods of only the more fortunate, the blessed touchable Hindus:

> His eyes caught sight of the magnificent sculptures over the doors extending right up to the pinnacle. They seemed vast and fearful and oppressive. He was cowed back. . . . He felt as if the gods were staring at him. They looked so real although they were not like anything he had ever seen on earth. They seemed hard, their eyes fixed as they ogled out of their niches, with ten arms and five heads. (72)

How could Bakha respect such a religion and approve of the social organization of 'caste system' created by its custodians? How could he or anyone with sense and sensibility approve a person like Pt. Kali Nath? He has a burning desire to hit back and teach everyone a lesson. Right from the crowd that booed him and the Pandit who took liberty with his sister. He wished to tell them and teach them a few things about 'purity' and 'impurity.' He wished to show who the real devil was and where the dirt lay—in him and his sister or with people like Kali Nath who feared neither god nor society while tormenting an innocent and defenseless girl. Moreover, what is the use of gods, goddesses when they fail to protect the innocent and vulnerable and appreciate or accept their purity of feeling? These are the questions that torment Bakha as he walks back from the temple with his disgraced sister. These are also the issues that Anand has raised as a writer and asked for more effective ideals, and ideologies in place of ineffectual gods, goddesses, hypocrite Pandits and greedy mahants.

In yet another novel *The Village (1939)* Anand shows how the rural Sikh peasants are held to ransom by the Sikh mahants. Not only is the character of the mahant suspect like that of Pt. Kali Nath in *Untouchable*, he even flinches money from them on the slightest of pretext. Lalu's family are embroiled in a law suit, have not got a fair price for their harvest, yet they have to remain obsequious and offer the *Mahant* the mandatory gifts.

Thus, it is not that Anand attacks just the Hindu religion. He objects to the discrepancy between principles and practice, and the misuse of religious authority in all communities. In *Untouchable* conversion to Christianity is one of the options before Bakha. However, Anand shows that religions may change but prejudices do not. A low caste of one community becomes an outcaste in another. If Hinduism had both a Pandit Kali Nath and Mahatma Gandhi, one a symbol of repression and the other of reformation; so too Christianity. The efforts of Colonel Hutchinson to assuage the feelings of Bakha and win over another convert for Christ are ruined by his racist and rude wife. Bakha realizes that she is no better than those Hindu touchable men and women who abuse him because of his caste. Colonel's wife, in fact, has three reasons to despise and deprive him. Not only caste but also his race and his status as a citizen of a slave country. Hence Bakha takes to his heels:

> Bakha had not known the exact reason for his frowns, but when he heard the words bhangi and chamar, he at once associated her anger with the sight of himself.
>
> 'Salaam, Saheb,' he said, extricating his hand from the old man's grasp, before the missionary realized he had done so. And he showed his heels; such was his fear of the woman. (147)

God, the tales of his kindness, talks of things such as salvation, mercy, divine justice etc. become a 'myth' for people like Bakha for whom the 'meta narratives' are nothing other than tools of maintaining the hegemony of the dominant group. This is the reason why in novels such as *Untouchable* or *The Big Heart* Anand shows his protagonists walking towards the other grand narratives of the modern era or the age of reason to escape from traditional narratives of either Hinduism, Sikhism, Islam or Christianity. In most of his novels he redefines traditional notions and turns upside down mythic 'ideals' that are unrealistic and inhuman in the context of modern men and women. Iris Murdoch observes: "We live in a scientific and anti-metaphysical age in which the dogmas, images, and precepts of religion have lost much of their power." (15)

Not only has Anand debunked mythology as a charter of conduct, he has also rebelled against myths and legends as works of literature. Originating from the word 'mythos' which means 'tale' or 'story,' myths are also colourful pieces of literature. They contain the classical rules of the archetypal hero, heroine, the villain, poetic justice and so on. The language is dignified and poetic. The stories invariable deal with either superhumans, superheroes or the royalty. Mulk Raj Anand, however, undid all such rules. His characters come from the lower classes rather than the upper or ethereal. His language is the dialect of the downtrodden laced with abuses and innuendoes. There are not any miracles. His heroines and marginal female characters are rarely submissive. His novels are pre-dominantly about men. Anand's novels, like Dickens', have children as the main character. There are not any rags to riches story. Many of his novels deal precisely with just a day in the life of the hero as in *Untouchable*. Most of them show the endless struggle of the poor and baffled people till they die as in *Coolie*. The end is often painful. Ananta dies in *The Big Heart* so too Munoo in *Coolie*.

It is not that Anand denied and disowned the myths of his culture totally. In the dedication to the *Morning Face,* he admitted that the old myths lay "dormant in my heart and mind; as these myths are inherited by every Indian." What he objected to was the absolutist nature of mythology and its bedrock, i.e., religion. He tried to show that the 'idealism' constantly hammered by mythology or religion and the 'idolatry' went towards denying even the minimum of human rights to men and women. He diligently worked towards revealing this reality in his novels. He believed that mythic, social and literary codes must be re-defined so as to give truth and justice a fair play. Hence, he denounced the 'old' rules of life and creativity and tried to promote 'new' ideas of living and loving in his fiction. His 'ideas' were not totally fictitious. Rather he tried to communicate the divergent viewpoints and ideologies current in the contemporary world that were all directed towards elevating man. Malcolm Bradbury observes: "The novelists' business at best is to make himself or herself an exemplary creative citizen in a world which is still occurring. . . . He or she works inside a convention that always has to be de-conventionalized in order to generate a new work authentic to the author and the contemporary occasion." (5)

Thus, Mulk Raj Anand is preoccupied with myths at both the level, i.e., 'form' as well as 'content.' The humanist in him goes on to subvert mythology as 'charter' of social and personal conduct. It is his conviction that there cannot be absolute truths. What was right for *Ram* or *Sita, Shiva* or *Parvati* cannot be right for all men and women. Ideals and beliefs must be revised, re-defined or re-modeled constantly. Anand was of the opinion that "there are no hard distinctions between what is real and what is unreal nor between what is true and what is false. A thing is not necessarily true or false, it can be both true and false." Hence rigidities must be avoided because human life is in flux. It is constantly changing. 'Standards' or 'morals' must also be revised so as to avoid making men and women feel guilty all the time.

Myths and legends often refer to those epochs of human existence when most of the world was divided into kingdoms.

Ordinary people were unheard of. It was either the royalty and aristocracy or gods, goddesses and nymphs who seemed to govern as well as populate the world. However modern human history shows the rise of the common man. It is the 'ordinary man' who rules the roost while gods, goddesses, kings and queens have receded into either mythology or pages of history. The advent of democracy has put political, social and financial powers in the hands of the common man. It is the life of the ordinary people that is the primary concern of all governments all over the world. It is their preferences and priorities and problems that make and unmake governments. Hence a realist author like Mulk Raj Anand rejects the 'form' of the myths as well. He does not write about the upper class. His heroes are the ordinary men and women. Even in a novel like *Private Life of an Indian Prince* (1953) he works not to romanticize or eulogize royalty. Rather he writes in this book only to show the "vices, weaknesses and extravagances" (Iyengar) of a minority unable to come to terms with reality.

Anand's ultimate analysis is that the gods and heroes, morals and ideals of the past, as depicted in myth, must give way to the gods and heroes and democratic mantras and morals of today, in life as well as literature. His creativity is a walk away from the mythology of the past to the myths and legends of today like Marx and Gandhi. Pre-historic myths and legends can, at best, decorate our imagination but should not dominate our lives. Each age must create its own mythology, must make its own charter of 'dos' and 'don'ts'.The tendency to obstinately hang on to models and morals that are outdated, incongruent, illogical and inhuman in the context of contemporary era has to be done away with.

Raja Rao's *The Serpent and the Rope*: Mesmeric Myths

Raja Rao's novel *The Serpent and the Rope* (1960) is permeated with "ancient memories" (Mackenzie xx). It is informed by not just the author's biography, his personal problems and psychology rather the whole history of the Indian sub-continent since the Vedic age has gone into the making of the novel. Fact and fiction, myth and legend mix in startling ways to document a crisis that is personal as well as universal. The narrator is a young man named Ramaswamy who carries with him the knowledge of millennium years. He lives with "the pastness of past . . . in his bones" (Eliot 294):

> I was born a Brahmin—that is, devoted to truth and all that. "Brahmin is he who knows Brahman, etc. . . . But how many of my ancestors since the excellent Yagnayavalkya, my legendary and Upanishadic ancestor, have really known the truth excepting the sage Madhava. (5)

The protagonist Ramaswamy is a young man weighed down by his own antiquity. Ancient memory takes him back to the age of sacred scriptures—the Vedas and the Upanishads. It is to be noted that the Vedas contain the religious thought and practice developed by the Aryans since their arrival in the Indian sub-continent from B.C. 2000 till 500 B.C.: "The whole of Vedic literature consists of four Vedas, or Samhitas; several expository ritual texts attached to each of these Vedas, called Brahmanas; texts giving secret and mystical explanations of the rituals, called Aranyakas; and speculative treatise, or Upanishads, concerned chiefly with a mystical interpretation of the Vedic ritual and its relation to man and the universe" (Weiler 5).

It is to the last two, that is, the Aranyakas (forest books) and the Upanishads (or Vedanta/ the culmination or end of Vedas) that Ramaswamy has mentioned directly in the passage quoted above.

These sacred texts, however, are important not just for understanding the origin and continuity of the Hindu religion but the development of Indian civilization itself. The four Vedas and the subsequent appendages are the only source of information about the time before the birth of Buddha. These sacred scriptures supply not just religious hymns, rites and mythological tales but also provide an account of the beginning of Indian culture and civilization which "does not" seem "to have fundamentally changed for many thousand of years" (Basham 4). What Raja Rao has done is to credit this period of Indian history, wherein lies the genesis of the Hindu culture, for the make-up of the collective consciousness of the Indian people and indeed of the novel's hero Ramaswamy. He has gone back to the roots, that is, to myth and to history to "extend our understanding of a present situation" (Mukherjee 137).

In fact, myths and legends have always been a great "culturing influence in India . . . potent . . . in the domestic, social, and religious life of millions of Hindus" (Mackenzie xii). Not surprisingly, therefore, myths have found their way into literature which is either a factual or fantastic portrayal of life. They are part and parcel of a common Indian's day-to-day existence. The spread of scientific temper—rationalism, modernism and secularism—in fact all the other 'isms' of the world have failed to obliterate it. At best they have only succeeded in marginalizing the hold of myth on Indian mind. Hence the tendency to go back to myth is not a relapse into obscurantism, as alleged by many, but actually an attempt to know more about ourselves. It is an effort to understand the mind, manner and behaviour of the Indian people, that is, their culture at large as they moved from prehistoric age to historic age. The purpose is to acquaint oneself with "the durable values in one's own tradition" (Lal 16), as contained in the Vedas, Veda-based 'Smritis' and 'Puranas' (the *Ramayana* and the

Mahabharata). A creativity nurtured by merely Western thought will produce literature deficient in genuineness, disconnected with the soul of the land whose people it purports to portray. "The language does not matter. If the feeling is fake, the writing will be fake. If the feeling is shallow, the writing will be shallow." (Lal 16)

None has understood this fact more than Raja Rao perhaps. His novel *The Serpent and the Rope* "splendidly conveys the attitudes of the culture from which" (Lal 16) it draws its sustenance. It goes back to prehistory and history to reveal the mysteries of Indian life. The protagonist of the narrative Ramaswamy recalls Yagnayavalkya, Madhava and Sankara—his Brahmin ancestors of pre-Vedic and Vedic times—to understand the Brahmin or the Hindu mind. The various sacred stories or myths too are mentioned by Ramaswamy in trying to unravel the Hindu consciousness and to comprehend the Hindu way of life. The whole effort is to understand "why the Indian male will not, as a rule, hold his wife . . . or why a wife will not address her husband by his first name. And big things like what is the difference between Dharam and Svadharma, the difference between avatara and incarnation, the varieties of karma, the nature of moksha." (Lal 17)

Rao, in this novel, however, does not refer to individuals—either divine or mortal. The story, though narrated by only the main character—Ramaswamy, is about couples—again both divine as well as mortal. The book is not about the individual strength and supremacy of any celestial being or about the struggle and success of any terrestrial being. It talks about and refers to 'pairs'—Shiva and Parvati, Ram and Sita, Krishna and Radha, Savitri and Satyavana, Ramaswamy and Madeleine, Savitri and Ramaswamy, George and Catherine, Father and Little Mother, Savitri and Pratap, Saroja and Subramanya etc.

In India, relationships are always 'divine.' More so in the case of opposite genders. The tie between a man and a woman is never purely physical. It transcends the limits of the human to include the superhuman. The union is seen as the re-enactment of the creation of the universe itself. Each woman in Hindu society is considered to be a symbol of the divine goddess. Each man is a representative of the divine gods. Each woman is the incarnation of 'Mother Divine.' Each man is Brahma, Vishnu and Mahesh. He is Krishna too and Satyavan as well who is restored back to life by his wife, the 'Mother Divine' of the universe. In Hindu mythology, marriage is sacred as well as sensual. Never wholly one but both simultaneously. "In western literature romance usually ends with marriage; in India the devotion of wives is of more account than yearnings of love—smitten Juliets on moonlight *nights*" (Mackenzie x-xi).

Ramaswamy arrives in India from France to attend the wedding of his sister Saroja in Hyderabad. He longs to come back to India not because she is his motherland. He looks forward to the homecoming so that he can get in touch with the great souls who have peopled the place and who do not seem to be dead in spite of having died millennium of years ago. He recalls the mythic gods and heroes of yore and feels a spiritual connection with them: "It was India I wanted to see, the India of my inner being. . . . The India of Brahma and Prajapati; of Varuna, Mithra and Aryaman; of Indra, of Krishna, Shiva and Parvathi; of Rama, Harishchandra and Yagnavalkya; this India was a continuity I felt, not in time but in space." (246)

In this novel a few mythic figures are profusely and repeatedly quoted. They are the divine couples Shiva—Parvati, Radha—Krishna and Ram—Sita. It is to be noted that Raja Rao has chosen divine couples from the abundantly populated pantheon of the Hindu religion. He has eulogized not single gods like Kartikeya, Kubera or Viswakarma. His memory keeps reverting back to the divine pairs in the context of the mortal pairs—Ramaswamy and Madeleine, Ramaswamy and Savithri, Savithri and Pratap, George and Catherine, Madeleine and George and the lesser pairs of Saroja and her groom or Litter Mother and Ramaswamy's own dead father whose life story is the subject of this novel.

The story of Lord Ram and Sita is recalled innumerable times and at the most varied of moments and hours—in London, Paris, Hyderabad. The story is the same but the occasion changes. Surprisingly, it fits in the narrative each time presenting not one jarring note. The story of Lord Ram, the crown prince of Ayodhya—the relinquisher, the vanquisher of the demon Ravana—fits in every time it is quoted whatever be the context, whichever be the place. He is there to explain what truth is, to show the Indian notion of Dharma to Anglo Saxons, to reveal the importance of religious duty or simply to make vivid the art of storytelling in India which has safely survived in the hands of women since centuries. Indian theatre critic Smita Narula has observed that the Indian woman has narrated the epics to her children or grandchildren and passed them down from one generation to another. In *The Serpent and the Rope* too, Little Mother narrates the story of Ishwara Bhatta and of Ram to Ramaswamy as if he had never heard the saga ever before. In fact, the story of Ram is narrated in many ways by many people in the novel. Some prefer making the divine figures prominent. Others highlight the devotees. Some of the narrators use Lord Ram to define 'truth' and 'dharma' (duty). Others choose to show the importance of obedience and obeisance. Purpose differs but the basic narrative does not. There is a difference in style, in motive but not in faith.

The first reference to Ram and his ancestor Harishchandra is made in the opening chapter of the novel. One of the ghats of Benaras is named 'Harishchandra Ghat.' While Ram is eulogized for his devotion to duty or dharma, Harishchandra, who was the son of Trishanku and twenty-eighth king of the solar dynasty, has "become synonymous with steadfastness and adherence to truth at any cost" (Narayan 217). The example set by him and his other descendants compelled King Dasharatha to banish his most loved son Ram to fourteen years of exile in forest.

Ram plays multiple roles and in each he epitomizes the 'ideal.' He is an ideal son, brother, friend, son-in-law, king and even an ideal enemy. Hence be it a personal situation or a social one, Ram remains a role model. In fact, the *Ramayana*, i.e., the story of Lord Ram is relevant for each one of us irrespective of what or who we are. The *Ramayana* covers the whole gamut of relationships that human beings enter into through the course of their life. Hence Ram's story is never out of context.

No wonder the epic *Ramayana* is recalled again and again in *The Serpent and the Rope* and by different people. For each the sacred saga has a special significance. It is especially relevant to them in their life at a certain moment. In other words, the Ramayana is itself a character playing multiple roles in the life of the Indian people and indeed in the life of Raja Rao's personages in *The Serpent and the Rope*.

The *Ramayana,* apart from being an eternal love-story of a divine married couple, Ram and Sita, is also pivotal to the understanding of 'dharam'—a key concept of Hinduism. Ram is considered an embodiment of 'dharma,' its incarnation. Ram's whole life is looked upon as an enactment of 'dharma.' In fact, the debate between 'dharma' and 'adharma' has been going on since centuries. The two epics the *Mahabharata* and the *Ramayana* are the finest examples of the discourse centering around dharma: "Dharma is . . . a key word of Hindu culture . . . The great epic, the Mahabharata, carries dharma as its burden . . . whereas this great epic makes its hero, Yudhisthira, the very son of the God of Dharma (Dharma-putra) and one who had no enemy (Ajatasatru), the other epic, the *Ramayana*, makes its hero, Rama, dharma itself in flesh and blood" (Embree 210).

It would however be misleading to treat 'dharma' as an idea exclusive to religion or exclusively Hindu. The term is, in fact, both sacred and secular "incorporating not only religious traditions but also social mores and the requirements of law" (Brockington 64-66). Moreover, the idea of 'dharma' is not confined to Hinduism alone. Roughly translated as 'duty,' the term finds an echo in all religions of the world, especially those this originated in India: "Buddhism was never wholly cut off from the mainstream of Indian religion. . . . Correspondence in Hinduism to the creedal statements of other religions is found, first of all, in certain underlying assumptions shared in some measure by all the Indian religious tradition. . . . Among them are an acceptance of the ideas of karma, dharma, reincarnation, and a sense of time and creation" (Embree 189-205).

In each 'yug' or epoch of the Indian civilization, dharma has been at the centre of dialectics. Leaving aside the prehistoric times, dharma has been re-emerging in each era either as a tool or as a solution of man's problems. In 'Satayug' Lord Ram was born to annihilate the forces of 'adharma' as well as to show the practice of dharma. In 'Kaliyug' Lord Krishna and the Pandavas carried the responsibility of establishing 'dharma.' In modern times, Mahatma Gandhi, according to many devout Indians, sought to restore dharma in the land and drive out the adharma. Gandhiji, in fact, frequently used the term 'Ram Rajya' as his idea of self-rule. By Ram Rajya, however, he did not mean the establishment of a Hindu state, but the creation of a nation-state which would be akin to the utopian or mythic welfare state that had been set-up by Lord Ram. Dharma, thus, has always been a "central idea of old Indian civilization, or Indo-Aryan culture, . . . much more than religion or creed; it was a conception of obligations, of the discharge of one's duties to oneself and to others" (Nehru 87).

It is not surprising, therefore, that this "central idea of old Indian civilization, or Indo-Aryan culture" will find its way in Raja Rao's novel too. Indians have been debating about 'dharma' since eternity and the easiest way of explaining the term to themselves and to others, they have found, is through the story of Lord Rama: "For vast numbers of Hindus throughout the ages, there has been no more inspiring symbol of dharma than the hero of the epic Ramayana. . . . Rama's devotion to duty, to his father, and to his people, and Sita's long suffering fidelity to Rama have been regarded as religious and ethical ideals through the centuries. Rama is seen as the embodiment of dharma, and his triumph over wicked Ravana as the overcoming of vice (adharma) in order that virtue and the moral law might prevail in personal and public life. Rama is adored also as the incarnation of the Supreme Lord who has come into the world to restore the moral order. . . . Generation after generation of poets have celebrated Rama in poems and plays in both Sanskrit and the vernacular languages. . . . Sculpture, song, and drama have told of his glory" (Embree 213-14).

The Serpent and the Rope too is one such piece of literature that unwittingly ends up discussing Lord Ram. Critics opine that the novel is about East and West encounter or about the meaning of love and marriage but in my opinion the work is, on one level, deeply engaged with 'dharma'—or rather the clash of different 'dharmas.' There are the different religions—Hinduism, Buddhism and Catholicism. Then there are the individual 'dharmas' or 'duties' which elevate or annihilate the personages of the novel. It is inevitable, therefore, that Ramaswamy would take recourse to the Ram-Sita epic to explain 'dharma' as 'Ram' is the other name of 'dharma' to all Hindus:

> What's dharma? asked Swanston. Dharam comes from the word dhru, to sustain, to uphold. It' as it were the metaphysical basis of the world—in so far as the world exists, of course—and it's the same dharma, to continue the story, that forced Sri Rama, after having burnt Lanka, killed Ravana and liberated Sita, and after returning to Ayodhya the capital, in the splendour of banners, victory—pillars, music and worship, to send Queen Sita away in exile. The fair, the pregnant Sita was sent away, for the dharma of Rama, the dharma of a king demanded it. (183-84)

The discussion about 'dharma' and the reference to the *Ramayana* to explain it, takes place in Cambridge between Ramaswamy and the friends of Savithri:

> Well, Ravana wants to possess the world—he's taken Sita, daughter of the furrow, child of Himalay and wife of Rama, away; he's kidnapped her and taken her away and made her his prisoner.
>
> "And so?" said Jack, joining the discussion.
>
> And so Rama has to fight his battle." (184)

In the passages quoted above the whole focus is on Lord Rama and how his whole life is devoted to the exposition of dharma.

'Dharma' is impersonal. It is not attached to thoughts of personal loss or gain. Ram rescued Sita not only because she was his wife but also because 'dharma' must be restored. Every creature participated and contributed towards the liberation of Sita because 'dharma' must be rehabilitated and they must discharge their 'dharma' of assisting in the noble work. Every creature is tied to another through 'dharma' which can be interpreted as 'duty' 'obligation' or 'responsibility.' One lives, thus, not just for oneself but for others. One works not just for oneself but also to safeguard the interest of others. To set the right precedence and to persevere on the right precedence, is 'dharma' and this is what the *Ramayana* is all about. To work for oneself, to think about oneself in a manner that would benefit and elevate the 'others. To annihilate the ego, the personal interests, for the larger good is 'dharma.' Pt. Nehru too believes that the term implies "a conception of obligations, of the discharge of one's duties to oneself and to others. This dharma itself was part of Rita, the fundamental moral law governing the functioning of the universe and all it contained. If there was such an order then man was supposed to fit into it, and he should function in such a way as to remain in harmony with it. If man did his duty and was ethically right in his action, the right consequences would inevitably follow" (Nehru 87).

As mentioned earlier, the novel is deeply engaged with 'dharma.' The discussion between Ramaswamy, Swanston, Jack and Savithri about 'dharma' is not a digression. It casts its shadow on the life of the hero and indeed on the whole novel. Even though Ramaswamy is not 'Lord Ram' or like Lord 'Rama,' that is, ideal, faultless or above all dreams and desires, he does, like the Divine Lord, help establish 'dharma' in the lives of those who are near to him. He assists and facilitates the performance of 'dharma.' He helps them see reason and seek salvation through duties they must or ought to perform so as to maintain normalcy and order in life. "He makes her (that is, Savithri) see that she must go back to her Pratap in India, and domesticity and fulfillment in marriage and motherhood. It's Rama's destiny to show the path to Madeleine, although it causes a wrench to him; he can give solace to Little Mother and Saroja his sister; he can help Catherine, his wife's cousin, to find happiness with Georges" (Iyengar 407).

Thus, like Lord Ram, his namesake Ramaswamy too helps many to dissolve the conflicts of their minds and seek salvation by devoting themselves to 'dharma' in the lives of Savithri, Madeleine, Catherine and George. The role that Shri Ram played in the *Ramayana*, Ramaswamy plays to a certain extent in *The Serpent and the Rope*—to explain dharma, to practice it and to help others adopt it. Ramaswamy may not match Sri Ram's idealism but in his own humble way, he helps establish 'dharam' in his small circle of friends and family so that life may go on as undisturbed as possible.

Dharma, therefore, is, crucial to the Hindu life so too the role of the 'guru' who shows the way to it. "Dharma is the foundation of the whole universe. In this world people go unto a person who is best versed in dharma for guidance. By means of dharma one can drive away evil. Upon dharma everything is founded. Therefore, dharma is called the highest good" (Embree 217). The *Ramayana* plays the 'guru' for the common Hindu people providing them with guidance in a manner they understand best—through the example of Shri Ram, Sita, Lakshman and disciple Hanuman. This is the reason why the *Ramayana* or the 'story of Ram' has been made a part of *The Serpent and the Rope*—a novel pre-eminently about the Hindu way of life in which 'dharam' is a stabilizing force and 'guru' is the one who shows the way to it.

The *Ramayana* is again narrated in the novel later on when Ramaswamy goes to attend Saroja's wedding in India. This time, however, the narrator is not he but Little Mother. But the focus, is not on Lord Ram but on the benefits of remembering Ram. Little Mother had no conflict in her mind about what her 'dharma' is or wherein lay her destiny. Hence, she does not elaborate on the endeavours of the Lord to clarify what is 'dharma' or 'adharma' either to herself to anyone else. Her main intention is to highlight the consequences of overlooking 'bhakti,' i.e. devotion to the

Lord. She highlights, through her folktale the pitfalls of ignoring 'dharma,' that is, the religious 'dharma' of remembering the Divine without whose grace no one can either live purposefully nor die peacefully. In spite all the mundane responsibilities of a normal life, man must snatch a few moments to remember and recall Ram and his fight for 'dharma': "It's Saturday today, and you've come just in time for the story of Rama, said Little Mother, and seating me beside her, she told me once again the story of Rama" (249).

The story that Little Mother narrates is quite lengthy taking up a couple of pages of the novel. She believes that she is narrating Ram's story. Actually the whole focus of her tale is on Ishwara Bhutta and his pilgrimage. Like a roaming minstrel he narrates the story of Ram to people who are willing to listen. He marries off his daughter within those twelve years. Lord Ram, moved by his worship, meets Ishwara Bhatta and bestows blessings on him. Now whoever listens to the old Brahmin, is bestowed with things auspicious. Their problems are solved. Vision is restored to an old man. Prosperity returns to his household and so does the son who had wandered away from home for years. Ishwara Bhatta, at the time of departure, had asked his own wife and son to narrate the story of Rama every Saturday so that Lord Ram may bless them. Wife Bhagirathi and son Brahma Bhatta, however, do not take the advice of Ishwara Bhatta seriously. They postpone the narration of the story of Ram because of mundane household responsibilities. Many Saturdays pass during those twelve years and the mother son duo do not narrate the story of Ram even once. Gradually all the splendor of the house of Ishwara Bhatta begins to vanish and poverty, sickness and crippling old age sets in. When the guardian returns, the wife and son are unrecognizable, so old and disheveled they are: "Ishwara Bhatta was so moved, he wept and said, 'son, how has this become? . . . Have you told the story of Rama on Saturday? . . . Then Brahma Bhatta said, 'No, Father. . . .' So Ishwara Bhatta . . . told them there and then the story of Rama" (254).

There is vital difference between the way in which both Ramaswamy and Little Mother recall the *Ramayana.* The tale of Little Mother does not elaborate the 'story of Rama.' It is as if the 'story of Rama' is known to all and, therefore, does not need repeating. She seems more interested in disclosing how Ishwara Bhatta was rewarded for his devotion to the Lord and how blessed were those who listened and narrated the 'story of Rama.' The 'story of Rama,' that is, the *Ramayana* is not directly narrated. The focus shifts on the 'devout' and 'devotion.' While Ramaswamy's purpose, in Cambridge, was not only to acquaint his foreign listeners with who Ram, Sita, Ravan were but also explain the connection between Ram and 'dharma' the impersonal 'truth,' the duty which governs the lives of all in this universe. Little Mother, a simple, god-fearing woman, however, has much simpler task on her hands. She is narrating the story of Ram to Indians, to her own son and step-son who do not need to be told who Ram was in the first place. They know Lord Ram. Only the importance of bhakti has to be emphasized. The need to follow age-old tradition has to be impressed upon so as to ensure a safe and secure today and tomorrow. Ramaswamy listens to Little Mother and peace descends upon him. In Cambridge, however, the doubts and dumbness of Swanston and Jack had irritated and angered him when he was explaining to them the story of Ram which is both 'dharma' and 'truth.'

The *Ramayana* myth, thus, is important to the novel for many reasons. It is crucial for the understanding of the narrative, of the characters and how they solve their individual dilemmas. In Hindu mythology, 'dharma' is a multi-faceted term covering not just religious rites but also simple rules of good house—keeping, family life and rules of governance. "The sacred law and the epics are viewed by the Hindus as only slightly less sacred than the Vedas and together form the body of semi-canonical scriptures called smriti (remembered) tradition: "The central concept that was elaborated and emphasized by Smriti was that of dharma. . . . Actually, the concept of dharma is all—comprehensive and may be, broadly speaking, said to comprise precepts that aim at securing the material and spiritual sustenance and growth of the individual and society. It is significant also that dharma has adjusted to changing contexts of time, place, and social environment" (Embree 214-15).

It is apparent that the *Ramayana* along with the other epic the *Mahabharata* plays a pivotal role in Hindu religious and social life. It is, therefore, inevitable that in a novel like *The Serpent and the Rope*, which is deeply engaged with Indian culture, the two epics would find mention not as a digression, but as an essential and coherent part of the story.

As mentioned earlier the term 'dharma' is central not just to Tulsidas's *Shri Ram Charita Manas* but also to the other great epic *Mahabharat* one of whose many heroes is Yudhisthira, "the son of . . . the god of justice, Dharam" (Knappert 281) himself. The *Mahabharata*, however, is a "colossal work" (Nehru 106) dealing with multiple issues and numerous personages written in 90,0000 stanzas of Sanskrit. It is "an inexhaustible mine" containing "stories within stories" (Karve 1, 4) besides the main plot of a family feud between cousins. "There are many theological and ethical passages, as well as many narrative episodes. Some of the latter tell legends of the gods, but others are more or less secular, including the famous stories of Ram and Sita, Shakuntala, and Savitri. The longest narrative episode is the story of Nala and Damayanti, told to Yudhisthira" (Basham 411). Realizing that "no one person can encompass it entirely," Indian writers of all the native languages, including Indian English authors, have tried to use "part of this cultural wealth according to" their "own ability" (Karve x). They have selected one or the other myths and mythic characters of Vyas's poem as source material for their own narratives. Raja Rao is no exception.

The first name that strikes the reader in *The Serpent and the Rope* is 'Ganga'—a goddess, a river and a character who is at the genesis of the whole drama the *Mahabharata*. As mentioned above, this epic is about the dispute between two groups of cousins—Kauravas and Pandavas. Ganga happens to be the great grandmother of these heroes. Apart from this she has—her own separate identity among the pantheon of Hindu gods and goddesses. Mythologically Ganga is "the daughter of the mountain—god Himavan, . . . And sister of Parvati, spouse of Shiva. In the earlier times the gods kept her all to themselves, for they considered her too precious and too beautiful to share her with terrestrials. It was Bhagiratha, son of Dilipa, son of the pious Ansuman, King of Ayodhya, who, with his prolonged asceticism, induced Brahma to grant him a boon. Bhagiratha prayed that the sacred river Ganga might be allowed to descend to earth, so that the 60,000 burnt brothers of king Ansuman might be brought back to life. Brahma warned him that it was only possible if Shiva consented to let Ganga flow through his hair. After a long period of asceticism, Bhagiratha finally persuaded Shiva to agree. Roaring and foaming she came down and would have drowned India, but Shiva's hair was like a dense forest where she became the gentle river" (Knappert 109). She has been flowing ever since offering salvation not just to the 60,000 burnt sons but also to all of humanity in life as well as in death. Perhaps it is because of this mythic story about Ganga, Bhagiratha and the sons of Sagara, or, Ansuman that it has become a custom to pour the funeral ashes into the river. It is believed that the soul would be purified and liberated of sins and fallacies so as to join ranks with supersouls—the sages, rishis, munis, gods and goddesses.

This celestial lady, the Ganga, has a role in the poem of Vyas too. She is the mother of Bhishma, and the first wife of Shantanu. Shantanu, in turn, is the great grandson of King Bharata. King Bharata on the other hand, as told by Kalidasa, is the son of Shakuntala and Dushayanta. The following is the family tree of the Kurus:

Menaka Vishwamitra (Sage)

↓

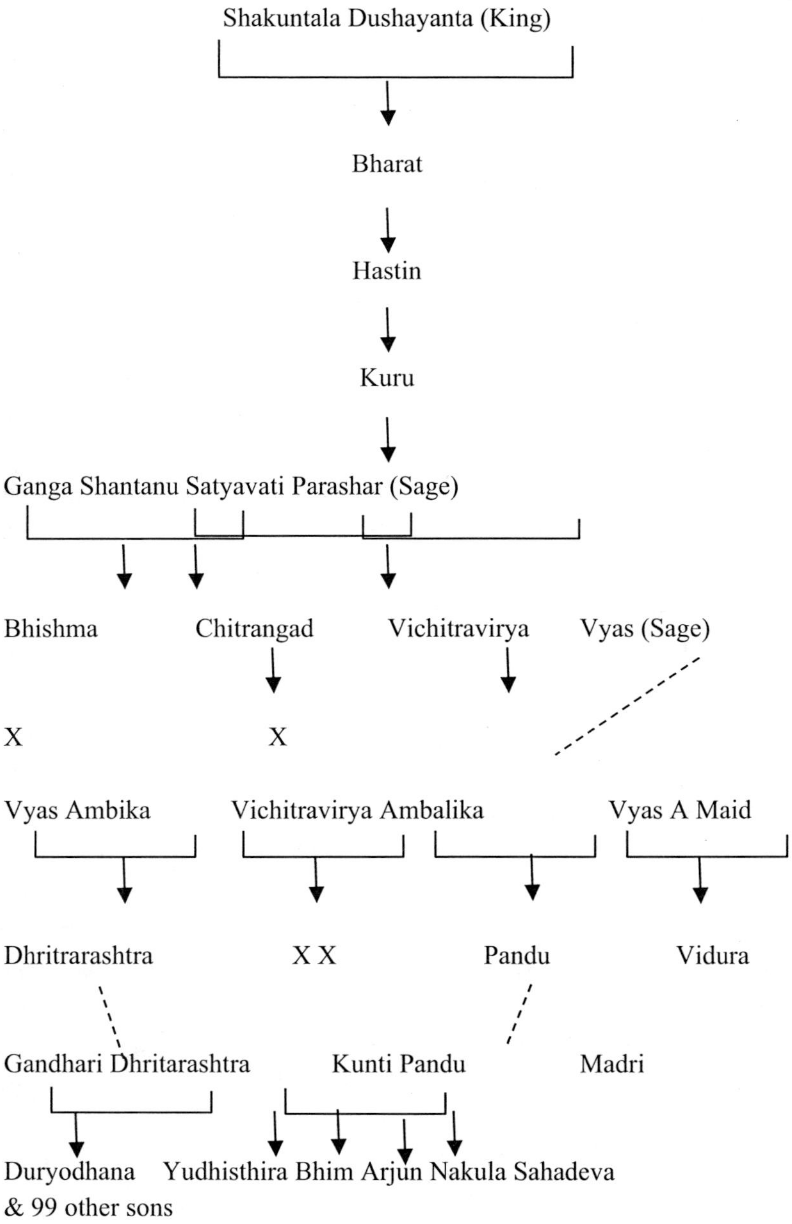

It so happened that Ganga, presumably flowing from the toe of Vishnu, had to marry a mortal so that the Vasus might be rescued from the curse of Brahma to live in the human world. The Vasus requested her to become their mortal mother. Ganga descended on earth and sat on the lap of King Pratipa and proposed marriage. The king refused on the ground that she chose to sit on thigh that is meant for the son or daughter-in-law. Hence, she should wait for a son to born who would then marry her. Ganga agreed to the idea of Pratipa. In due course of time Shantanu was born as son of Pratipa. Irawati Karve in her *Yuganta* recounts the story: "For some reason Ganga had been forced to live for a time on earth" (9-10).

Shantanu, the father of Devavrata or Bhishma, latter remarried thanks to the extraordinary sacrifices made by his Gangaputra. He fell prey to the charms of Satyavati, a fisherman's adopted daughter. Her father Dasharaja demanded that the right to ascendancy to the throne must be shifted from Ganga's son to the children of his daughter. Realizing how earnestly his father yearned for Satyavati, Bhishma promptly agreed to forgo his right to kingship and brought Satyavati home as his step-mother.

In time Satyavati gave birth to two sons Chitrangada and Vichitravirya. The eldest died in a battle. Vichitravirya became king. He was married to two sisters but died childless. The Kuru clan was under the threat of extinction but ultimately Satyavati's eldest son, Vyasa, born before her marriage to Shantanu, was told by her to perpetuate the Kuru line. Bhishma refused to break his vow of celibacy. Dhristrashtra, Pandu and Vidura are therefore the grandsons of Parashara with whom Satyavati had first got involved and not the blood of the Kuru clan. Bhishma, the son of the river Ganga, thus was the only the real Kuru among the Kauravs as well as the Pandavas. He played god-father to generations of Kuru children and managed the kingdom till they came of age. The children of Dhrishtrashtra and Pandu, however, failed to live amicably. They later fought the famous war in Kurukshetra and Bhishma, blessed with the boon of death at will, lived to see the carnage of almost the whole Kuru clan whose regency he had painstakingly managed. Ganga had given him life. It was again Ganga who took him back. Arjun pierced an arrow in mother earth so that Ganga may quench Bhishma's thirst at death-bed and grant him final reprieve from the trap of death at will. Thus, the saga 'Mahabharata,' in a way, starts with Ganga and ends with Ganga.

It is Ganga who is profusely mentioned in the novel. She is the river flowing in Bharata since the day Bhagirath brought her down on earth from her abode in Shiva's hair. The hero Ramaswamy is deeply impressed by the river and she too becomes a character just like Madeleine, Savithri or Little Mother. Critics opine that Savitri alone epitomizes the feminine principle in the novel. The fact, however, is on the contrary. The river Ganga is as much a strong representative of the feminine principle as Savithri, Little Mother, Saroja or Madeleine in *The Serpent and the Rope*. In fact rivers "have always had a special place in Indian life. Rivers have held the Indian mind captive with their economic, ecological, mythic and beatific significance. They have been hailed and revered as benefactresses and feared as ruthless destroyers out to punish humanity" (Jaya Prasad 2003: 81). G.N. Devy opines in his article 'Timeless Metaphor': "Accordingly, our relation with rivers is intensely emotional. Song of hunting beauty and tales of mystery, involvement and separation articulate this relationship." Consequently, in *The Serpent and the Rope* river Ganga symbolizes for Ramaswamy many things. She is reprieve, she is salvation, she is peace, and she is journey to Moksha or truth. That is why Benaras is so dear and precious with the river Ganga with all her multiple significance flowing there: "The Ganga is always there" (11). Even the concubines take a dip in her waters and become luminous. No wonder, observes Ramaswamy, "the concubines of Benaras are the most beautiful of any in the world" (12). Raja Rao writes: "That is why Damodhara Gupta so exaltedly started his book on bawds with Benaras. 'O Holy Ganga, Mother Ganga, thou art purity itself, coming down from Shiva's hair" (12). Ganga, for the hero, is a link between the past and present. Generations of his family have come to her banks to seek salvation for themselves and their dead relatives.

In Indian mythology rivers have always been regarded as feminine. They have been hailed as goddesses. Rivers, like mother earth, are supposed be the givers of everything a human being aspires for. Ramaswamy observes in the novel:

> One remembered that it was here that the Aryans, when they first entered the country, camped under the ancestors of these trees, and the Ganges flowing by brought them the richness of green wheat—stalks, the yellow of sesame and the gold of sugarcane. It was somewhere here, too, that Gargi and Yagnayavalkya must have walked, and out of their discussions by wood—fire and by river steps was our philosophy born. (33-34)

In other words, rivers in general and Ganga in particular have nurtured civilizations in their lap. The hero Ramaswamy mediates over the role that the holy river has been playing in the life of the Indian people. He repeats the songs of eulogy and reverence penned by the ancestors in the honour of Goddess Ganga: "Devi Sureshvari Bhagavathi Gange. . . . Saviour of the three worlds of restless waves, Clear is the water circling upon the head of Shiva, May my mind ever repose at Thy lotus—feet" (32).

In the first few pages of the novel, Ramaswamy recounts the whole story of Goddess Ganga. Mythically she has originated from the toe of Vishnu and resides collected in the bun of Shiva. Only after the onerous efforts of Bhagirath was she allowed to descend on earth to "purify mankind" (32).

However, geographically she has originated from the Himalayas. She rises in the Gangotri glacier at a height of about 6,000 metres. Crossing the Siwalik Range near Hardwar, she enters the Great Plain of India. The Ganga has many tributaries that swell its waters. The most important among them are the Yamuna, Gomati, Ghaghra, Gandak and the Kosi. The Yamuna, with her tributaries—the Chambal, Betwa and the Ken—empties her water into the Ganga near Allahabad. The tributaries of Yamuna have their source in the Vindhya Mountains of the south. Near the Raj Mahal Hills in Bihar, the Ganga turns south-east and flows into West

Bengal and Bangladesh. Before she joins the sea, she is united by the silt—laden waters of the Brahmaputra, which, before joining the Ganga, flows through the plains of Assam. Before entering the sea, she divides herself into many in the east and the Yamuna in the plains, forms a vast depression that is extremely fertile and has supported great civilizations through the course of history. Ganga and her sister rivers have not only provided water but also fertile soil essential to support and sustain population and economy. This perhaps is the reason why Ganga has been hailed as a 'goddess' by the Hindus. Water and food are the essentials of life. Just as a mother looks after her young ones and makes arrangements to feed them, the Ganga, flowing down from the Himalayas, has provided the essentials to sustain life. Hence, she is loved and regarded as a mother.

In fact, contrary to popular perception, Hindu mythology is deeply influenced by economic and social factors. Whatever is essential for human life and happiness has been given immense importance. Rivers, plants, trees, birds, animals, soil, sun or even primary human relationships have undergone a process of apotheosis. They have been made divine in mythology precisely because of the important role they play in the sustenance and perpetuation of life, culture and the civilization at large. In fact, what is brushed aside in the scientific age as obsolete, obscure, illogical, primitive and false or 'myth,' is, more often than not, backed by solid social, economic, environmental and psychological reasons. The only problem is that instead of explaining the reasons, our ancestors tried to indoctrinate us, in ornate language, about worshipping this creature or following that practice. Why we should do this? This question has been largely left unanswered. By chance if any explanations have been given, these too are told in such a roundabout manner that they only add to the confusion surrounding mythology. However critics, anthropologists, sociologists—all are slowly realizing that mythology of different cultures is based on economic, environmental, political and social logic. Any person, any living being or non-living object is revered not unnecessarily but because of its direct or indirect, overt or covert contribution to existence: "Hindu worship was not confined to the propitiation of gods and demigods, for the whole of nature was in some sense divine" (Basham 321).

Ramaswamy, therefore, is shown enamoured of the river Ganga. He is only repeating the obligations that Indians owe to the river for centuries. He is praising her and acknowledging her role in his life, his family's life, in the life of the whole Hindu community and in the nation state of India. He realizes that at the expense of her own purity, Ganga washes the sins of humanity: "It was Ganga . . . for she it was, from age to age . . . who had borne the sorrows of our sorrowful land. Like one of our own mothers, Ganga, Mother Ganga, has sat by the ghats, her bundle beside her. What impurity, Lord, have we made her bear" (33).

Ramaswamy, a motherless child, sees in the river a reflection of his own dead mother. He never mentions this fact but the way he is reminded of the river again and again in the narrative shows that Ganga is almost a mother figure for him. He does not remember his biological mother but time and again at crucial junctures of his emotional life, he recalls the divine river goddess. His father, his mother Gauri, his first son Pierre Krishna all have mingled with the waters of Ganga and thus do not seem to have abandoned him. They have only gone to reach the 'truth' via Ganga. Truth is always white like snow. Hence to reach truth one must reach the Himalayas from where Ganga begins her journey. Ganga is the link between mankind and god, between humanity and truth, between the earth and heaven:

> My Aryan ancestors went up the Ganges to seek the solitude of the snows and the identity of Truth. . . . Truth is the Himalayas, and Ganges humanity. That is why we throw the ashes of the dead to her. She delivers them to the sea, and the sun heats the waters so that, becoming clouds, they return to the Himalayas. (35)

The young hero, who lost his mother in childhood, his father and his son as an adult, is a deeply sad man. He never overcomes his loneliness but discovers the mother figure in Ganga. The image of his father's third wife merges into Ganga to reinforce in the hero's life her place as a Mother figure: "The Ganges alone seemed to carry a meaning, and I could not understand what she said. . She seemed like Little Mother, so grave and full of inward sounds" (26).

While on pilgrimage with his stepmother to perform the funeral rites of his father, Ramaswamy visits not just Benaras but also the Himalayas from where Ganga surges forth. He gets an opportunity not just to ponder over the spiritual and religious role of Ganga but also on the material contribution made by her. He does not go into mathematical details of her long journey from the Himalayas to the sea in Bengal but does recount and describe her long journey as succinctly as possible:

> There beyond the folds of the snow was Gangotri, where the holy mother took her birth; and the barbarian began where she started. Tibet lay beyond, where Sister Brahmaputra cuts herself gorges in the Himalaya to feed the barbarian; then mingling with the Ganga and become holy she enters the sea conjointly. Duality is anti-Indian; the non-dual affirms the truth. (41)

Ramaswamy seems to derive from the visit to these places a certain degree of mental peace for himself. The sight of the holy places by her bank, the dip into her divine waters is catharsis for him. It rejuvenates him, resurrects his mind and soul. In fact it is believed that "physical contact with the body of the goddess Ganga has the magical effect of transforming automatically the nature of the devotee. As if by an alchemical process of purification and transmutation, the base metal of his earthly nature becomes sublimated; he becomes an embodiment of the divine essence of the highest eternal realm" (Zimmer 111). While visiting Benaras, Hardwar, Rishikesh, Badrinath and Gangotri, Ramaswamy and his widowed stepmother derive emotional support and succour. The river herself and the beauty of these places nestled in the Himalayas refreshes them, soothes their tormented and disturbed mind, convinces them that they have not lost their near and dear ones forever. They are in the Himalayas and also in the fluid lap of Mother Ganga. This is the reason why the time of departure for both Ramaswamy and Little Mother is heart-wrenching:

> Little Mother and I left the mountains and the Ganges with immeasurable pain, as though we had been visiting some venerable relations and had to leave them, with a broad kumkum on our faces and their hands on our heads, the perfume of their feet in our Mother Ganga had her feet all yellowed with turmeric, and she carried the flowers of our evenings in her hair. (42)

The point is why has Raja Rao taken such painstaking efforts to eulogize the river? Ganga is not unknown to Indians nor her holiness new to them. Ganga and the sister rivers have all along been looked upon as "female divinities, food and life bestowing mothers, and as such are prominent among popular divinities" (Zimmer 109).

Perhaps Raja Rao wants to stress the point that a melting pot like India is kept united by a number of things and mother Ganga, like the twin epics the *Ramayana* and the *Mahabharat,* is one of them. She units the big Hindu community, internally a divided house on caste, class, sub-caste, linguistic, gender, region, sect lines, under the single umbrella of her name. The sentiments of the hero are not unique they are shared by many. His praise for the mighty river finds an echo in many souls. It keeps Hindus connected to one another as they make common cause in worshipping her or fearing her. Let us recall the reaction of Little Mother, a south Indian, to the whole of north India. She would not have liked to step into the upper part of the country if Ganga had not been flowing there: "Benares seemed hateful to her: the whole of the North, but for the Ganges, was one desolation of dirt" (27).

It is the shared tradition of myths, epics, gods, goddesses, rivers and mountains that keeps Indians united: "No Hindu ritual at birth, death, marriage, house-building and house—warming can to this day take place in rural as well as the most sophisticated sections of India without the Ganga water and without reference to Kasi" (Narasimhaiah 78). In other words, despite all the external dissensions, the emotional and spiritual life of Indians is one and this perhaps keeps the country united. This is what foreigners have to understand about India. Geographically, socially, economically, linguistically the country is diverse, but emotionally it is one. The *Ramayana*, the *Mahabharata*, the Ganga & the Himalayas, constitute the soul of India and this is why Raja Rao has included them in his narrative.

As mentioned earlier the *Mahabharat* is an abundantly populated epic crowded with heroes and superheroes, princesses and goddesses. River Ganga is one of the them. Yet another important character, the most popular and revered of all, is Lord Krishna whom Rao has used in his narrative to discuss, define and direct the relationship between his hero Ramaswamy and his Lady-love Savithri.

Mythologically Lord Krishna is the incarnation of Lord Vishnu, the second deity of the Divine Trinity. "Vishnu is generally thought of as wholly benevolent. The god works continuously for the welfare of the world, and with this end in view he has from time to time incarnated himself either wholly or partially. . . . The Avataras ("Descents") or incarnations of Vishnu are, according to the most popular classification, ten. An incarnation might be total or partial. . . . In this sense every good or great man was thought as a partial incarnation of Vishnu. The chief ten incarnations, however, are of a more special type, for in them the full essence of the god is believed to have taken flesh to save the world from imminent danger of total destruction. They are as follows: The fish (Matsya), the tortoise (Kurma), The Boar (Varaha), The Man-Lion (Narasimha), The Dwarf (Vamana), Parasurama (Ram with the Axe), Ram, Prince of Ayodhya and the hero of the *Ramayana*"; last but not the least "Krishna . . . Undoubtedly the most important incarnation of Vishnu" (Basham 203-4).

No mythic figure of the Hindu religion has had as much

impact on Indian culture as Krishna. Music, dance, painting, sculpture, literature—Krishna can be found everywhere. His colourful personality, especially his 'raas leela' with the gopis has fired the imagination of many since ages and added colour to the fine arts of the Indian sub-continent. "There is an immense literature dealing with Krishna, who in bhakti tradition is worshiped and celebrated, not as the great austere teacher of Bhagavad Gita, but as a god who is playful child, a great lover, and a worker of miracles. These stories have also been the inspiration of important traditions of painting as well as festivals and music" (Embree 51). Krishna has been a perennial source of inspiration for everyone and everything. While the other gods and goddess are uni-directional in their temperament, either full of angst or benevolence or both; Krishna is the only mythic figure who presents himself as both human and superhuman combining the mundane as well as the marvelous, the serious as well as the comic.

In Krishna's colourful and multi-faceted persona, intelligent artisans and writers, dancers and sculptures see immense potentiality for artistic inspiration and creation. Each phase of his life has given stimulus to umpteen ideas of creative expression. Roughly, Krishna's life can be divided into four phases. First is his childhood spent in Mathura in the house of his foster parents Yashoda and Nanda; his adolescence spent in the company of the village women or gopis; then his conquests as an adult in Mathura and Dwaraka; and finally his role as friend, philosopher and guide of the beleaguered Pandavas. Depending upon creative requirement, writers and artists have used one of these four phases of Krishna's life in their works of art. While Krishna as the counsellor of the Pandavas is the favourite of spiritual people who like to pour over his *Bhagavad Gita*, others like Suradasa prefer to highlight the childhood pranks of the flute player Krishna, still others wax eloquently over the love escapades of the deity, like Jayadeva in *Gita Govinda*.

While in the literature of the native languages, almost all the phases of Krishna's life have been adequately and abundantly used, interpreted and interpolated, the same cannot be said about Indian English literature. There is too much of emphasis here on Krishna, the voluptuous pastoral god, "the flute player and dancer, the shepherd loves of the Gopis or herdsmaids" (129), the partner of Radha or the unattained love of Meera. The innocent, mischievous childhood pranks and tantrums so lovingly and beautifully portrayed by Surdas has been almost completely ignored. Krishna as the ultimate philosopher too has been largely overlooked. What instead can be found in Indian English literature repeatedly and frequently is Krishna as the romantic hero of the milkmaids, of Radha and Meera. In fact the Krishna—Radha pair or Krishna and Meera have entered the annals of literature as quintessential parallels for unrequited love or clandestine relationships of men and women outside marriage. In *The Serpent and the Rope* too the mythic god and his lady-loves, serve the same purpose.

Overtly Ramaswamy's marriage with Madeleine was perfect. She was a good wife sensitive to his needs and moods and trying all the time to adjust as much as possible. Any man other than Ramaswamy would have been happy with a wife like Madeleine. The Indian, however, hankered and hungered for more. The weakness for things 'Indian' never left him. The stay abroad and marriage to a westerner only increased it and created space for the 'other' woman who happens to be Savithri in this case.

Savithri was a young Indian girl belonging to a Rajput royal family whom Ramaswamy met in India while going around the pilgrim centres of northern India with his step-mother. She was not a very beautiful Indian woman. Neither was she traditional: "There was nothing in her round, almost plump face and her thick spectacles to show but the most ordinary upper—middle class Indian . . . I felt I did not like her, she was too modern for me. She had already started smoking" (31).

Yet it was Savithri who made the world seem "familiar and whole" (57) to Ramaswamy. "Her presence never said anything, but her absence spoke . . . one longed for her to be back" (31). Perhaps Savithri was, for Rama, metaphor of India. He looked upon his motherland "as tradition, as the Truth" (246). For him India was "my breath, my only sweetness, gentle and wise" (246). In his opinion Savithri exhibited similar qualities. To be with her and near her was to have a piece of India beside oneself. Savithri's image tallied with the idea of the country that the hero carried within himself: "The India of Brahma and Prajapati; of Varuna, Mithra and Aryaman; of Indra, of Krishna, Shiva and Parvathi; of Rama, Harishchandra and Yagnayavalkya; this India was a continuity I felt" (246). Savithri, despite all her westernization, participated in that continuity. Early in the novel, when Ramaswamy had just met the Indian girl, he had observed: "We had one thing in common: we both knew Sanskrit, and could entertain each other with Uttara Rama Charita or Raghuvamsa" (31). For the hero, India was the land of the gods, of truth and of women who would understand that "Every gesture, idiosyncrasy or mole—mark . . . traced back to some cousin, aunt or grandfather" stood for "a complex oneness, from which one could never get out save by death, and even after that one would get into it again in the next life, and so on till the wheel of existence was ended" (277). Savithri more than shared these feelings of Rama. She, in fact, sharped them and helped him realize where his calling lay. Ramaswamy observes in the novel: "There is only one woman, not for one life, but for all lives" (230). Savithri was for Rama that "only one woman" (230).

As mentioned earlier Ramaswamy looked for a woman who would understand the significance of "every gesture, idiosyncrasy or mole-mark" as well as participate in the "complex oneness" created by customs and traditions in India. Madeleine, however, in spite of all her best efforts failed to become a part of that "oneness." When Ramaswamy brought gifts from India, Madeleine was disappointed to know that they were not from her husband but from his sister and mother. According to her viewpoint, there was a dichotomy between Rama and his family. For Savithri, however, Rama and his family were one big continuous whole. She accepted him and with him accepted his whole world comprising of long dead ancestors. The toe-rings, the kumkum were given to her by

Ramaswamy because she alone, and not Madeleine, understood their significance: "Slowly I anointed her with kumkum from my home, offered her the coconut and the betel nuts—there were eight, round and auspicious ones. . . . The toe-rings were the precise size for her" (212).

Savithri's acceptance of the gifts brought by Ramaswamy from India symbolizes her acceptance of everything related to Ramaswamy. Not just the individual self of Rama but his whole family, ancestry and legacy. She acknowledges him with all the plurality of his existence. Rama too could hand over the family heirloom only to a woman like Savithri who grasped fully the significance of the present as well as the past, the single as well as the whole. Love for both Ramaswamy and Savithri was not something individual. It had to be plural and universal wherein love for Rama, the man, became a symbol of love for the whole family, the whole of mankind, the universe and finally the almighty. This is the reason why Savithri repeatedly addresses Ramaswamy as 'Krishna' or as 'Shiva.' She constantly compares or rather calls Ramaswamy either "my Krishna" or "Shiva" thereby placing herself in the shoes of these deities' divine consorts—Radha and Parvati. Ramaswamy too looks up to Savithri as Mother Earth, Queen, Princess and as Radha, Meera, Parvati and even Sita. They consider each other not merely as a man, or a woman but as 'Purusha' and 'Prakriti—the dual forces of nature which generate and sustain the whole universe. Hence their love affair takes on a philosophical colour beyond the merely physical. There creeps in an element of transcendentalism in their relationship.

Both Savithri and Ramaswamy repeatedly look beyond the human world and seek guidance, solace and solution from the mythic world. They draw parallels between themselves and the celestial beings in an effort to comfort each other and solve their dilemma of having extra-marital affair while being socially committed to Madeleine and Pratap. They make attachment to each other not the raison de etre of their lives. Rather they guide and goad each other towards the 'dharam' or 'duty' that they owe to their kith and kin and society at large. They make themselves each other's 'deity' and 'guru'—to be worshipped, not to be possessed physically but shared with all. Their mutual admiration becomes a catalyst transforming their whole vision towards themselves and those around them.

Rama was basically a man with "ancient" needs in spite of all scholarly pretensions. He was not above enjoying carnal pleasures with women ranging from his own wife to his friends' wives and prostitutes. Savithri, too, was not exactly a very virtuous girl—falling in love with a married man and heralding the break-up of a home. Yet these initial realities and the upheaval of divorce between Rama and Madeleine pave way to a larger good—that of the reformation of Ramaswamy. He finally moves towards becoming a true spiritualist rather than a pseudo spiritualist who was caught in the web of carnal pleasures in spite of all Vedic and Vedantic scholarship. The encounter with Savithri paved the way of his 'moksha' from 'kama.' In trying to guide Savithri, in order to prevent embarrassing situations such as the break-up of Savithri's engagement or his marriage to Savithri, Ramaswamy learns something vital and teaches the same to her: "Rejoice, Savithri! Rejoice in the rejoicement of others. That is the Truth" (364). He sends Savithri back to Pratap, accepts Madeleine's decision of separation, decides to return to his roots and the obligations that he owes to his family at home. Saroja writes to him: "Brother, come back soon" (368). For these reasons and for the sake of "Truth" that is "meta-physical" (350) he returns to India as soon as possible. Mental peace, emotional anchor, freedom from physical comfort and desire—Ramaswamy seeks at the feet of a Guru. He seeks not God but urgently and desperately a Guru who would hold him by the finger and guide him to spiritual salvation: "No, not a God but a Guru is what I need. 'Oh Lord, my Guru, my Lord,' I cried, in the middle of this dreadful winter night. It was last night. . . .' Lord, Lord, my Guru, come to me, tell me; give me. Thy touch, vouchsafe, I cried, the vision of truth. Lord, my Lord" (402-3).

This realization in Ramaswamy——the need to seek spiritual

guidance; to get in touch with someone who would free him from the burden of guilt as well as sacrifice; finally calms his tortured soul and he emphatically asserts: "I had reached Benaras—Benaras. I had risen from the Ganges, and saw the luminous world, my home. I saw the silvery boat, and the boatman had a face I knew. . . . He called me, and said, 'It is so long, so long, my son. I have awaited you. Come, we go.' I went, and man I tell you, my brother, my friend, I will not return. I have gone whence there is no returning" (403).

However Rama and indeed Savithri too could not have possibly reached this stage of spiritual growth had not the Radha—Krishna myth acted as a catalyst. Their inability to give a permanent shape to their relationship because of Pratap and Madeleine push them into the refuge of Radha and Krishna. These two mythological figures have always been looked upon as a symbol of love, of eternal and universal love though not belonging to the category of love-stories such as Romeo and Juliet, Laila and Majnu or Heer and Ranja. Radha-Krishna myth is similar to them as well as very different and deep operating both on terrestrial as well as celestial sphere. It is not confined to a particular man or a woman. It does not refer to merely one Krishna and his Radha. It is the story of many young men and women who face the predicament of living with 'one' while loving the 'other' yet never failing in the primary responsibilities or 'dharma' that a person owes to family or society.

Radha and Krishna is a love-story that constructs and not destructs. It maintains order rather than generate or spread disorder. It does not end with death or bloodshed as is the case with other famous love-stories of human history. Rather there is a healthy and natural change in keeping with the demands of time. Radha and Krishna are not rigid. They are rigid in their attachment to each other but not in terms of physical proximity. In fact after a brief period of togetherness, they never meet again. Krishna goes on his own way while Radha remains behind. Krishna has to rescue the world from evil. Radha does not tag along. She has her own world to look after which includes a husband. Krishna goes and grows away from her yet their spiritual commitment never breaks. They remain an eternal symbol of love at its purest, sublime and benign. Radha shares Krishna with the milkmaids, with the numerous princesses who married him, with the Pandavas whom he helped, with Draupadi and Subhadra who were his sisters, with the Yadava clan which had to be put in order, with sages and saints who needed respite from demons, with devotees like Meera and with disciples like Surdasa who recreated the Lord's life through his poetry for posterity. Radha loved Krishna only to return him to the world. She never came back to stake claim on him. Nor did Krishna look back at her. He had other issues to look into. He couldn't be so selfish as to remain engrossed in the beauties and pleasures of the *raas lila* provided by Radha and the milkmaids. Radha, on her part, saw to it that her love did not become a possession, obsession or infatuation. The understanding between Radha and Krishna was tacit. They were to be together for only a brief period till Krishna's adolescence and during this phase of his sojourn on the earth, Krishna showered love and attention not only on Radha but also the humble village folks, the cows, the rivers (Yamuna in particular), the mountains (Govardhan) the snakes and the flowers—who all had their claim on the Lord. Radha facilitated their association with Krishna. Gokul and Vrindavan were the venue. Radha was an excuse through whom the Lord had to bless each and every aspect of nature. He had to give joy to many. He needed Radha to build an atmosphere of joy, to show the multiple meanings of human love, what true friendship is all about, care for animals, the way of community living, of God's impartiality and kindness towards all. Radha played her role to the hilt. She had to help Krishna explain the meaning of all the softer emotion of human life. She had to help him show the beauties of nature. Then came a time when she had to let go so that Krishna could highlight the dual nature of the world. The ill and the evil that had to be cured and eradicated so that poetic justice prevailed and the rule of 'dharam' was restored. Hence while Radha remained behind in Barasane (her village), Krishna moved ahead to Mathura, Dwarka and off and on to Hastinapur—the 'karma-bhumi' of his adult life. Their bond was thus, mental going back ages and was to continue in the times to come. Till date the idols of Radha and Krishna adorn temples across the Hindu society scattered the world over.

Radha and Krishna are of course colossal figures whom Ramaswamy and Savithri could not dare to compare themselves with. Rather what they did was to draw consolation and inspiration from the way in which the mythic love story progressed. Ramaswamy became Savithri's 'Krishna' whom she could love but not marry. Savithri became Ramaswamy's 'Radha'—a disciple as well as a Guru, a symbol of the Mother Divine, the creative energy of the world. Rama becomes for Savithri an incarnation of man as well as God. God cannot be possessed. He has to be shared. God cannot be married to. One revers God and eulogizes him, seeks guidance from Him, looks up to him for clarity of vision and to find a purpose of life. Ramaswamy does all these for Savithri. He is, therefore, for Savithri not just Ramaswamy but also her Krishna and Shiva. Her love for him is the love of Radha for the flute playing lord:

> The tales of the women's love for Krishna concentrates on one girl in particular, Radha, about whose yearnings for Krishna many poems and songs have been composed, complete with music, in the appropriate 'raga' mood. . . . The lover is always Krishna, the god, represented by a royal crown, a blue skin and sometimes with four arms. There is no doubt . . . the Beloved is God, not a man. Thus we must conclude that the loving woman is not a sensual, wanton adulteress but a devout worshipper, indeed the human soul herself. Without this knowledge neither the myths of India nor its art can be understood. The soul is constantly yearning to unite herself with God, the spiritual reality of the other, better world. (Knappert 144-45)

Savithri bows before Ramaswamy like a devotee in ecstasy. Ramaswamy becomes a symbol of the God to whom she devotes herself spiritually, mentally and emotionally.

The dilemma of Savithri and Ramaswamy was that no matter how much they adored each other, however indispensable were they for one another; they could not legalize their relationship. Matrimony was simply out of question Ramaswamy was wedded to Madeleine—a good wife in her own way. Savithri, on the other hand, was an aristocrat engaged to another aristocrat chosen by her father. A break of this arranged match would have brought defame to herself and discredit to her whole family among the royal Rajputs of the Indian society. However the yearnings of the heart could not be ignored. Hence the duo philosophized their attachment to a spiritual level where permanent proximity became immaterial. They made Radha and Krishna their idol derived and comfort from the example of these mythological lovers and their numerous and various famous devotees like the gopis of Vrindavan or Meera of the Mughal Period. It is to be noted that Ramaswamy compares Savithri not just to Radha but also Meera—yet another female worshipper of Krishna who abandoned home, husband and all royal trappings in the pursuit of her obsessive love for the divine flute player.

It seems Ramaswamy and Savithri likened themselves to the mythic figures not only because their relationship could not be legalized but also to protect it from being interpreted in purely physical terms. For them their mutual admiration was something very sacred and serious beyond the merely physical or sensual. Even though Ramaswamy was a man with "demands . . . ancient primal, inevitable" (219) he did not wish to view his affair with Savithri on purely sexual lines. Similar was the case with Savithri. She too was not exactly a woman of extraordinary restrain to deny herself the pleasures of the flesh. She was on the verge of being swept off her feet by a debonair Muslim in London. However both Savithri and Rama were ashamed of viewing each other as objects of desire. All the more so when both their legal partners—Madeleine and Pratap—trusted them so blindly. Pratap, in fact, had commissioned Ramaswamy to rescue his fiancée from the charms of the Muslim suitor and stop her from becoming a run-away bride. How could Rama, then, have Savithri for himself? Or how could Savithri turn a blind eye to Rama's French wife who was painstakingly and desperately trying to build a cosy nest for herself and Rama with failed attempts at motherhood? There was too much of hope, faith and effort by their respective lawful partners that Rama and Savithri could not allow passion to overpower them. Had they done so they would have gained nothing other than discredit in their respective circle of friends and family.

However in spite of all the restrain, the extra-marital angle of their relationship was a fact. It had to be justified somehow to end their own sense of guilt and doubt lurking in a corner of their heart. They also had to somehow sanctify their relationship because they knew it was going to be a life-long affair at least mentally. They were, henceforth, going to be unfaithful to their respective partners if not physically at least mentally. How was this reality to be ignored or justified? How were they to balance their love for each other with their social and domestic commitment to Madeleine and Pratap? It was in this context that the Radha and Krishna myth became relevant for Rama and Savithri. The myth of Radha and Krishna showed that one could love without being sinful. Both Rama and Savithri finally went their different ways with a heavy heart but a clear conscience.

It is to be remembered that Radha, Meera and the Gopis were married women yet marriage was never a hurdle in the way of their love for Krishna because Krishna was not looked upon as an ordinary man. Since the time of his birth, Krishna had repeatedly revealed his divinity. Hence, he was not looked upon as an ordinary mortal. He was Divine. He was God and love for him was considered a kind of 'bhakti' or worship. Hence rarely did the husband of the gopis resent their wives' liking for Krishna. In fact, married women tend to look upon, ever since Krishna's time, their husbands as 'Krishna' i.e. God as well as lover. Even unmarried girls in India, sentimentally, consider themselves and their lovers as 'Radha' and 'Krishna' respectively. The divine duo, therefore, are symbols of marital as well as pre-marital love in Hindu society "wherein human love" becomes "a metaphor for divine love", thereby avoiding baser interpretations such as physical attraction or lust:

> When the moon shines over the Jamuna and lights are lit in the households, Krishna dances on the red earth. What Gopi, my Lord, would not go to this festival of love? Women lose their shame and men lose their anger, for in Brindavan Krishna the Lord dances. (209)

Radha and Krishna myth has been quoted by Raja Rao directly in the narrative. The use of myth in this context is overt. A covert use of myth is naming a character after a mythic figure thereby making an important suggestion of some connection between the present and the past. "Finally we have the example of authors who use myth not as part of a digressional technique (as in *Kanthapura*), not as a central structural device (as in *The Maneater of Malgudi*) but employ mythical parallels only incidentally to illuminate certain situations or characters" (Mukherjee 161). In the novel under discussion, an example of this is the character of Savithri.

It would be foolish to assume that this name has been chosen by the writer accidentally or unintentionally. A perusal of the novel reveals striking resemblance between the ancient episodes of the 'Mahabharat' and the situation created by Rao in the novel. However the mythic name 'Savitri,' during the pre-Vedic Age, was also used to refer to one of the three forms of the sun god. It would be interesting to find out whether Rao has alluded to both the mythic contexts or only one of them.

"The Indian sun god Surya, like the Egyptian Ra, had three forms. The rising sun was Vivasvat; the setting sun was Savitri . . . who had yellow hair, was of pre-Vedic origin. He was the 'Stimulator.' When he commanded Night to approach, men ceased their labours, birds sought their nests and cattle their sheds" (Mackenzie 32). Surya is an Aryanized sun god. He drives a golden chariot drawn by seven mares, or a mare with seven heads; he has golden hair and golden arms and hands. Since he is alluded to as "the eye of Varuna and Mitra," and a son of Aditi, it is evident that if Surya did not originally belong to the group of Adityas, he was at least, strongly influenced by them.

> In his Savitri character, which he possessed at morning as well as at evening, he stimulates all life and the mind of man. One of the most sacred and oldest mantras (texts) in the Vedas is still addressed by Brahmans to the rising sun. It runs:
>
> Let us meditate on the excellent glory of the divine Vivifier. May he enlighten (or stimulate) our understandings. (*Ibid.* 33)

The excerpt quoted above discloses a rare and forgotten connotation of the word 'Savitri' that was believed in pre-Vedic times. It refers to a stage of the sun god both in the evening and morning when he provides impetus to mental as well as physical growth. In other words, it can also be said that the sun creates conditions for civilizational as well as cultural progress. The sun sets in the evening paving way for rest, recreation, recollection and speculation. Man gets an opportunity to rest his tired bones and indulge in mental activity, meditate over the hours passed by or plan for the future. At the break of dawn, however, the sun rises on the horizon signaling that the time of rejuvenation is over. Man must resume work so that civilizational progress continues unhindered. In the refulgence of the day he must renovate as well as innovate so that mankind makes solid and sophisticated achievements. The sun God, thus, as 'Savitri' in the evening and in the morning ensures mental as well as physical exercise taxing and relaxing the mind and the body alternatively. This is true not just for mankind but for every other creature; that is the whole flora and fauna. As 'Savitri' the sun god provide 'pause' as well as 'progress.' This mythic reference associated with the word 'Savithri' is little known today in comparison to the widely believed and revered myth of 'Savitri and Satyavana' contained in the epic 'Mahabharat.' The story is too well known to be repeated in detail yet it is necessary to recall the original version of the story.

The Savitri-Satyavana story is all about a wife's heroic fight against the God of death to save her husband's life. Even though the 'life' of her husband abandons its earthly abode, that is, the body; she continues to chase it and its carrier, Yama. Conversation ensues between the two with Savitri outwitting the God with her intelligence, her fortitude and resolute devotion to her husband. Her clever arguments compel the God to grant one boon after another till Savitri manages to extract her husband's life from his clutches:

> Said Yama: "The more thou dost speak, the more I respect thee, O princess. O thou who art so deeply devoted unto thy husband, thou canst now ask of me some incomparable boon."
>
> Savithri said: "O mighty One, thou bestower of boons, thou hast already promised what cannot be fulfilled unless my husband is restored unto me; thou hast promised me a century of sons. Therefore, I ask thee, O Yama, to give me back Satyavan, my beloved, my Lord. Hear me and grant this boon: Let Satyavan be restored to life so that thy decree may be fulfilled.
>
> Said Yama "So be it. With cheerful heart I now unbind thy husband. He is free . . . Disease cannot afflict him again and he will prosper. Together you will both have long life; you will live four hundred years; you will have a century of sons and they will be kings, and their sons will be kings also." (*Ibid.* 54-57)

This myth about a pious but adamant wife, purportedly an incarnation of celestial Goddess Gayatri, (the wife of Brahma, the Supreme Creator) who wages a battle royal to save her husband from the clutches of death, has inspired many since centuries. It has fired the imagination of poets, writers and dramatists of both the vernacular languages and Indian English. The story has been interpreted allegorically, metaphorically and philosophically. It has been seen as the triumph of the feminine principle, the victory of creativity over negativity. The story of Savitri, Satyavan, Yama and Ashwapati—has been interpreted as the effort of nature to protect herself from annihilation. The masculine and feminine principles or are required to run and rule the world. They cannot exist or survive alone. Both must co-exist to perpetuate as well as to maintain the balance. Hence the appeal of Savitri to return Satyavan's life. Such are the interpretations offered by Indian English writers who have used this myth in their creative work. Raja Rao too is no different. Savtri is both 'light' as well as 'learning' that man requires: "The Savtri of the Vedas, of the Mahabharata story, and more recently of Sri Aurobindo's epic of the name—symbolizes the birth of a new knowledge with which man conquers death or ignorance and gains his release from the flux of life."

In *The Serpent and the Rope*, the protagonist Rama had already a quite good rapport with all the women in his life—from Madeleine to Lakshmi and the various professional girls he hired in hotel rooms. This shows that in spite of all the pretensions of philosophy and scholarship, Rama was actually an ordinary man who routinely succumbs to carnal pleasure even outside marriage. 'Dharma,' 'morality,' fidelity, etc. were never an issue either for him or the various women who kept entering his life. In other words, in spite of all the learning that Rama possessed, spiritual content was missing from his life. He was leading a fairly debauched life in the name of normality. It was Savithri who saved him from this and prevented him from degenerating into one of those Indian Yogis who preach ascetic Indian philosophy to all and sundry only to lead an extravagant, opulent and licentious life behind the curtain in their ashrams. Savithri came into Rama's life like a beam of light to dispel the forces of the dark that were encroaching upon his existence. "The name 'Savthri' is obviously symbolic indicating both the sun and that paragon of wifely devotion, the Savthri of ancient Hindu legend, who rescued husband Satyavan from death. Savthri's role in the novel is the same—to bring enlightenment to Ramaswamy and save him from dying into a purely worldly life Savithri further represents the eternal feminine Principle." (Naik 169)

All along Rama preached 'dharma' without actually practicing it. He was infidel, abandoned a slaved motherland (did not participate in the freedom struggle) for greener pastures abroad, was never at home to take charge of family responsibilities as the eldest. He was sympathetic towards his sisters but never took any concrete steps to help them realize their aims and ambitions. It can be said that Rama was a fairly self-centered individualist man. He was too engrossed in his own academic and carnal pursuits to really bother about his duties and obligations that he owed to his French wife, his family in India or his beleaguered country struggling to achieve political freedom. He was caught in the labyrinth of 'maya' and 'kama.' He was not even like Pratap whom he himself described as "steady, and . . . devoted" (28).

Savthri's association, however, cured Rama from all ills and illusions. She was the 'unattainable' love of his life who turned the 'bhogi' into a 'yogi.' Her association taught him the true meaning of 'dharma.' While teaching her, he taught himself. While interacting with her and replying to her intellectual queries, Rama became 'learned.' As Iyengar has noted about Savithri and Rama, "each has a catalytic effect upon the other, each grows upon the other's consciousness" (401). She became "a companion of pilgrimage" (98) who helped Rama to discover "the gods that reside in us" (90). The novel's scholarly hero soon realizes that "every man is like a Christ on the Cross" (370) and that true 'dharam' mean rejoicing "in the rejoicement of others" (364). The love for Savithri and the subsequent estrangement from her for the sake of religious, moral and social propriety leaves Rama wiser. He surrenders his 'Savithri' only to gain greater wisdom and maturity. "He realizes that his love for Savithri, far from being of the kind that would find fulfillment in physical union, is actually an instrument of achieving the higher Love, the ultimate union of the soul with God" (Naik 168). If women like Lakshmi or the various prostitutes Rama hired, pushed him into the dark recesses, Savithri saved and salvaged him from moral degradation and showed where his true vocation lay. Thus, both as solar deity of the Vedic age who provided impetus; and as an incarnation of Goddess Gayatri who rescued Satyavan from Yama, Rama's Indian soul-mate justifies her name 'Savithri' in the novel:

> The ancient Savithri myth is central to *The Serpent and the Rope* in the sense that the Savithri of the novel has, as shown earlier, an equally stimulating and life-giving role to play in the life of the hero here. She is, in effect, the feminine principle incarnate; and self-realization through the agency of the feminine principle is, as already seen, one of the major themes in the novel. The following dialogue between Rama and Savithri, when he is convalescing from his lung operation, is significant:
>
> "Will you exchange places with me"? I asked.
> "Yes, if you like this wretched cloak."
> "If you become me, then there is no problem."
> "How so"?
> "Then you, become me, will be the real Savithri."
> "And who's the Satyavan"?
> "The self, the Truth."

This interpretation of the Savithri legend is in line with the symbolism with which Aurobindo has invested the age-old story in his great epic *Savithri*. Here, Satyavan is truth, married to Savithri who represents love and the power of devotion, the meaning of the legend being: man can transcend death by uniting truth and the power of devotion.

The symbolism of the ritual marriage between Rama and Savithri is plain: the individual self (Rama) has been united to purity and power of devotion (Savithri), or the masculine principle has been wedded to the feminine principle. The outcome of this union is self-realization and illumination. On the other hand, the fact that the marriage of Rama and Madeleine ultimately proves barren, both their children dying in infancy, may be considered symbolic of Madeleine's failure (from Rama's point of view) to be the true feminine principle. (101-3)

The global nature of Raja Rao's characterization made it necessary the inclusion of many things. If he included Indian stories to explain, probe and emphasize the Indian psyche; he needed the European myths, legends and pieces of history to delve deep into the Western mind:

> Being a product of many cultures Rama's mind is a seething whirlpool of cultural currents and cross-currents. Unlike the simple storyteller in 'Kanthapura,' who knew only Indian myths and legends, Rama is familiar with myths and legends of different civilizations and he can discern parallels between them and forge a link between the past and the present. (Raizada 5)

Thus, one finds in *The Serpent and the Rope* the Hindu pantheon rubbing shoulders with the Greek. Rama, Savithri, Madeleine talk in the same breath about Krishna, Radha, Isuelt, Tristram, Achilles, bearing testimony not only to their learning but also to their understanding that the complexities of human life are the same everywhere. Continents, civilizations, cultures, centuries, and characters can change but the basic human emotions and the problems born out of these are similar. Hence the past is never out-of-date and the present not completely new and the future not exactly unforeseen. What is needed is the ability to see everything in proper perspective. Some see. Others don't. The characters of Rao, however, decide to see things in proper perspective. Hence, they recall gods, goddesses, heroes and heroines, leaders and philosophers to realize, sooner or later, "not only . . . the pastness of past, but its . . . presence."

Madeleine, the French wife of Ramaswamy, is much like her husband. She too, to base her feeling somewhere, looks back to the past of her continent, specifically the Greeks—the saddest, the bravest and the most complicated pantheon of divinities and heroes:

> The child in the cradle. And the cradle against the Mediterranean, the Mediterranean the cradle of our civilization. I slept, Rama, night after night in the nursing home, not thinking of Pierre or of you but of Demeter and Poseidon and the voyage of Ulysses. In fact at first I thought a second name for Krishna would be Ulysses. How I rounded the names on my tongue: Krishna Ulysses Ramaswamy. Absurd, absurd, said something to me, but I repeated them so often together, thinking that with familiarity it might become natural. No,

> the name seemed so absurd. Then I thought of Achilles, as I told you; Achilles was the name of one of the servants in the clinic, but I thought it too heroic for the son of a Brahmin. Well, there is no hurry and Krishna was Krishna. Krishna, Krishna, I said to myself, as one repeats a mantra, and I was filled with delight. (37)

Madeleine continues in the same vein and says: "Like Penelope I sat on the seashore, weaving my web. When will you come, O Ulysses?" (39)

The two excerpts quoted above show that Madeleine had a predilection for Greek tragic heroes and deities with strong tragic streak. While Savithri recalled Hindu mythic figures like Krishna, Radha, Shiva, Parvati, Savitri and Satyavan, who, in spite of initial struggle do get to lead more or less contented lives; Madeleine thinks of Ulysses, Achilles, Penelope, Demeter or Poseidon—mythic figures saddled with lingering pain and failure. Their life is more or less lopsided while the Hindu gods and goddess lead eventful lives full of variegated colours.

Why this selection of the gay and the contented for Savithri and the sad and somber for Madeleine? Did Rao and his protagonist Rama consider Savithri more of a 'complete' woman and a 'round' character? Was Madeleine as a 'woman' not up to the mark—a 'lesser' woman or a 'flat' character? Did her repeated failure at motherhood cloud Rao's and Rama's assessment of her? Did her background, a childhood without parents and an adulthood without children, turn her melancholic forever? It seems so. Perhaps Madeleine had an inkling of what fate had in store for her and that is why she says: "I who love the Greeks" (23). She loves the Greek who are fatalistic, ferocious and promiscuous—three qualities enough to ruin anyone's happiness.

Ulysses (actually Odysseus) was a Greek hero who was unable to return to his home Ithaca after the end of the Trojan war. He wanders in alien lands amongst alien people, monsters and demons for thirty years. When he returned to Ithaca, he had to rescue his wife Penelope besieged by suitors. The result was that he had to go for another ten years of exile. Penelope waited twenty years for her husband to return who, though always pining to return to her and home, had wedded twice (to Circe and Calypso) and fathered sons. Their reunion too was brief as Odysseus was again exiled. In other words, Penelope woes were never over. Her suffering was unending like Sita of the *Ramayana*. However unlike Sita, it was not she but Odysseus who had to go away. Unlike Sita, she did not have to relinquish Ithaca. It was Odysseus who had to leave his land for long periods while she remained stationed in Ithaca with her son. However, while Sita did not have to share her husband with any woman, Penelope repeatedly lost her man to other women one of whose sons killed his own father Odysseus.

Madeleine's selection of this myth was ominous. Little did she know the realities of her husband and realize the parallel between herself and Penelope, Odysseus and Rama developing slowly but steadily. It was probably a wave of emotion for her lost child, her distant husband and nostalgia for the past that made her think of the Greeks. She loved them and she loved Rama too. Hence, she could think of her child, herself and her husband only in the terms of these pagans. However this imaginative link did not stop in her mind but slowly descended on her life.

Rama was not faithful to her. Prostitutes visited him off and on. Indian women like Lakshmi seduced him or he seduced them while Savithri, the Rajput princess, consumed him completely. Like Ulysses, Rama loved Madeleine but strangely there always remained a space between them to be encroached upon by other women. No wonder Madeleine calls herself Penelope. Ironically Madeleine's Odysseus becomes Savithri's Ram, Krishna and even Satyavan. It is to be noted that Ram, Shiva and Satyavan were ideal husbands, faithful to their respective wives. Rao's Savithri calls her lover—'Ram,' 'Krishna' or 'Shiva' alternatively because Rama is as enamoured of her as Lord Ram, Shiva and Satyavan were of Sita, Parvati and Savitri respectively. If life with Madeleine reached a dead end, Savithri meant a new beginning to Rama (as he himself believed). She was the feminine principle incarnate for him and he eulogized her a great deal. She was the 'force' of creativity or creativity herself. He considers her '*Parvati*' too who married Shiva and gave birth to Kartikeya so that the world be saved by her son from capture and annihilation at the hands of the demons. If Madeleine was the end, Savithri was the beginning of a new life for Rama—his resurgence as a true 'spiritualist.' This is the reason why Madeleine thinks of tragic heroes and gods such as Ulysses, Achilles, Poseidon. Rama and Savithri, on the other hand, recall Sita, Savitri, Parvati, Ram, Krishna, Shiva, Satyavan the Hindu gods and goddesses of resurgence who are perennial source of strength, survival—ever living and ever giving.

Thus, with the change in perspective, myths change in the context of some characters. Madeleine's Ulysses and Poseidon, that is Rama, is Savithri's Krishna, Ram, Shiva and Satyavan. "Raja Rao has used the myths and legends to highlight the situation of characters or the relationship between them and to substantiate or concertize the abstract thoughts of the hero."

Another alien myth, referring to a pair of lovers, has been taken from the Arthurian Romances of Britain. This time it is not Madeleine, the French, with her love for the Greeks, who takes recourse to Arthurian tales but both Rama and Savithri who separately and together turn to this bundle of legends to define their relationship:

> "When Tristan died, Iseult came. Iseult always comes too late."
> "If Iseult had died"?
> "Iseult was death itself. When death dies . . ."
> "Tristan is born. And there never, never is an Iseult."
> "What happens to Iseult, then?"
> "She is Tristan."
> "Iristan, do not die"!
> Satyavan will not die, Savithri." (360)

This dialogue takes place when Savithri visits Rama in the hospital. Few days before Rama too had been reading Thomas le Trovere, that Anglo-Norman poet, to whom England and France were as Tristan and Iseult:

> You could imagine Tristan le Preux moving on the boat, with Iseult, the daughter of the king of Ireland, she, the beautiful, who was to be married to king Mark. And the nephew was bringing her to him, for it was a promise that the young had made to the old and come fire, come water, it had to be respected and obeyed. But the winds rose on the sea, and the sun was hot on the oceans; and one night while they were playing chess they asked Brangien, the faithful, for wine and for more wine to drink. Brangien, the faithful, being full of sleep, it was the potion of love meant for King Mark that she gave unto one first and the rest to another; and such passions rose in them that not even the waves in the sea would know of such rising and such demand. Just as the castle of Tintagel rounded itself and shone, on the rocks there, in the country of King Mark in Cornwall, Iseult gave herself unto Tristan, who through fire and forest, through torture and exile, was to be her love. And when he went away and tried to warm his heart through another Iseult of the white Hands, no warmth came for there was no love in him. So the ships brought the news of his illness and hopelessness to Iseult of Cornwall, and she took her boat and sped towards him. But when she came Tristan was just dead, and she lay beside him dead. A bramble linked them even in their grave; it rose from the grave of Tristan.
>
> Sometimes I thought how beautiful it would be to have a tomb over oneself. (355)

It is in the hospital when Rama is sick and when Savithri is already married to Pratap that both of them think of Iseult and Tristan. As is evident from the excerpt quoted above, the lovers die. In the novel Rama and Savithri survive but only after arriving at a death like decision. The meeting in the hospital turns out to be a turning point in their lives when both of them finally come to an understanding (or realization) that they must give each other up. They must root themselves elsewhere. In the context of Savithri, it is to be Pratap. In the context of Rama, the change is going to be more drastic. He will have to leave Madeleine, leave France, leave a life full of women such as Lakshmi, return to India and start life afresh as a true spiritualist under the guidance of a 'guru.' He does not, lying in the hospital, foresee all this about himself but he definitely guides and goads Savithri to her new destination, her true mooring as wife and mother. He had seen the unhappiness of Madeleine over her lost children, that is, her unfulfilled motherhood. Perhaps he did not want Savithri to suffer a similar fate. He wanted her to become a 'complete' woman—to become a wife and above all a mother—the greatest duty of womankind as the 'Feminine Principle' of the world. Hence, he convinces her to be true to her husband and to the 'dharam' of marriage: "Pratap is a very fine person, Savithri. As a husband one needs nothing better" (362).

Savithri does not give up so easily, demands Brindavan and Krishna. She argues but ultimately and tearfully surrenders before Rama's reasoning and accepts her fate, her marriage as 'dharam' to be obeyed and respected:

> "What shall become of her that does not belong to herself."
>
> "Then must she belong to someone."
>
> "But if she belong to one wholely, or rather almost wholely, and to another she be tied, as a calf is tied to the tether, or as the plane is tied to the radar."
>
> "The plane must accept the direction of the radar, that there be no accident.
>
> "So the plane must obey the radar"?
>
> "Yes, that is dharma. The law is dharma . To disobey dharma is to give pain."
>
> ". . . So what shall I become?" She heard her voice choke in herself."
>
> "A wife, Savithri, a wife. A true wife." (363-64)

Why is that both Rama and Savithri refer to the Arthurian myth of Tristan and Iseult in their own love story? It is because both Rama and Savithri, Radha and Krishna and Iseult and Tristan have lot in common. Like Iseult, Savithri was promised to be the wife (she already was when both Rama and she recall this romance) of one man while she loved another. Radha, too, was wedded to another while she loved Krishna. Like Iseult she was a married woman but her attachment to Krishna remained as strong as ever. Rama too was married to Madeleine just as Tristan had wedded Iseult of the

White Hands. However both Rama and Tristan continue to love and long for Savithri and Iseult of Cornwall respectively. Just as Iseult and Tristan continued to meet surreptitiously so too Radha and Lord Krishna as well as, the novel's characters Rama and Savithri. It is worth noting that the stories belong to different historical periods and different cultures but the problem or the predicament of the lovers is the same—love outside marriage in a world that fails to sympathize or empathize before it is too late. It is ironic that as long as people like Tristan and Iseult, Romeo and Juliet, Laila and Majnu or even Meera were alive, they were an object of ridicule and scorn but the moment they died the same world placed them on a high pedestal and immortalized them through legend, folktale and mythology.

The myth of Tristan and Iseult are the only tragic figures whom Savithri and Rama use in the context of their relationship. Otherwise they always refer to such Hindu deities who are an epitome of strength and success, the eternal 'Masculine and Feminine Principles' having the power to annihilate as well as create the world. Madeleine, on the contrary, thinks of Ulysses, Achilles, Poseidon and Demeter—whose lives are heavily loaded with struggle, pains and tears. Perhaps Rao wanted to create a pensive and melancholic character in the form of Madeleine, a character who would go on to renounce the world, become a hermit. Hence such sombre myths for her in which the heroes / gods/ goddess struggle endlessly having little peace and contentment in their lives. Savithri, on the other hand, has to get on with life, marry and procreate. Hence tales of struggle and success, passion and restrain, spiritualism and marital bliss for her—Shiva-Parvati, Ram-Sita, Radha-Krishna, Yagnayavalkya and Maiteryi.

Madeleine seeks refuge in Buddha who becomes a pauper from being a prince, abandoning a beautiful wife as well as an infant son. From the highest denomination of worldly achievements, he comes to the lowest in search of the ultimate truth. Madeleine joins his order leading an austere and ascetic life. Savithri doesn't. She has to join the humdrum (or normal) world that Madeleine leaves. The task left unfinished by Madeleine, at which Madeleine failed, Savithri has to complete and succeed. Hence positive mythic stories for her wherein human endeavour triumphs even in the face of divine obstruction as in the case of Savitri who fought to save Satyavan from Yama, the God of death, and left him humbled.

It must be recalled that just hours before her first son's birth, Madeleine has a vision:

> One night, the night before his birth, a great sweep of minstral cleared the air. . . . You were away in the hotel, but I told you later of the vision I had that night. Demeter, with fruits and stalks in her hand, rose out of the invisible sea, as though she was made more of silken thread than of substance. . . . Beauty filled the magnanimity of creation and I was happy, Rama, happy as I have never been. (38)

Her son Pierre Krishna was born in Bandol. When Rama left for India to perform the funeral rites of his father, Madeleine, too, allowed herself to slip into the memories of her dead son, heir of Rama and grandchild of her dead Indian father-in-law. She quietly stole a visit to Bandol, the place of his birth, to recall and re-live those moments and hours just before and after he was born. She later wrote a letter to Rama disclosing the secret visit as well as describing the memories that haunt her. When she first had the vision of Demeter just before Pierre's birth, little had she realized that the "Greek gods are jealous. They are jealous of happiness" (39). With the "love of the Greeks" (23) embedded in her heart, she embraced her son only to lose him seven months later. It is on her second visit to Bandol that the ominous significance of that mythic vision becomes clear to her:

> The Greek gods are jealous. They are jealous of happiness. My votive offerings brought no answer. No Demeter came in with polos and veils, nor did the sea throw up a broken raft on which was to be found the golden child. Like Penelope I sat on the seashore, weaving my web. When will you come, O Ulysses? (39)

Demeter was an Olympian Greek female deity. She was the goddess of vegetation and fertility. She was Zeus' sister. Demeter had a daughter Persephone. Persephone was abducted by Hades, the God of the underworld, the abode of the dead. In retaliation and in grief, Demeter, the mother, made the earth barren. At last it was decided that her daughter would return to her every six months. Demeter, the goddess of vegetation and fertility, revoked her curse and the earth was restored to health and happiness.

The myth about Demeter is the story of a mother, her grief and struggle to recover her lost child. It is, therefore, not surprising that Raja Rao chose this mythic parallel for Madeleine. He made her see a vision of Demeter. It is left to Madeleine and the readers to draw conjunctures. Madeleine, however, does not understand the hints hidden in the myth. She does not realize its ominousness. She does not foresee the death of her son. She is, on the contrary, rather happy and feels blessed to have seen the vision at the time of her child's birth. Only later, when Pierre is dead and she pays a second visit to Bandol, does she realize what the vision forebodes. She comes back and sends up a fervent prayer with the vain hope that like Demeter's daughter her child too would be returned to her if not in reality at least in a vision. Alas! it is not to be: "No Demeter came in vision. . . . Nor did the sea throw up a broken raft on which was to be found the golden child" (39).

In her letter Madeleine writes to Rama that he would "never understand what it is for a mother, and a French mother, to bear a child. It is the birth of the god in a chalice, the Holy Grail; you know, Christian or not, one feels the birth, and even one who is not a Christian would almost look around and see the stable and the Rois-Mages bringing offerings to the Lord" (36). Thus, Madeleine, the mother, feels deeply for her lost son and makes his birth sacred—the re-enactment of the birth of Christ himself. For the first time, she, a French, refers to the English Arthurian romance of the Holy Grail. The Holy Grail was the plate or the cup used by Jesus at the Last Supper, in which one of his followers is said to have received drops of his blood at the Crucifixion. It somehow got lost and had to be recovered by the knights assembled by King Arthur:

> The Grail legend derived from the 'Mystery Cult' just as surely as the 'Mystery Cult' derived from the 'Nature Cult.' The later literary form of romance, which in the case of the Grail narratives involved the quest of a knight for the lost cup containing Christ's sacrificial blood, was firmly rooted in fertility religion; only it had developed by way of a detour through mystery. What was constant was the idea of the body and blood of the saviour offering new life, whether the communal life of fertility or individual life of enlightenment. (Coupe 28)

Madeleine looked upon her son as Jesus just as for all Hindu mothers their tiny-tots are Krishna. This sentiment of hers is understandable but why has she talked of the Holy Grail in the context of her son? The Grail contained the blood of Jesus. Such a situation is not palatable for any ordinary mother. No mother would like to see the blood of her child in a cup. With Jesus the case was different. Neither He nor His Mother Mary were ordinary people. Jesus was the son of God, the saviour, who had come for the salvation of the people so as to remove suffering. That is why every act, every word and every drop of his pious and pure blood was precious. It was meant to protect the world from annihilation. His sacrificial blood stood for fertility and fruitfulness of the natural world as well as the human world. The loss of it meant 'waste land' and the recovery of it implied redemption of the waste land, that is, deliverance of creativity from misery, misfortune, mistake and malady. Recovery of the Holy Grail implied restoration of health and happiness to all.

For Madeleine her child was as precious as the Grail. His death turned her life into a waste land with no hope of redemption. Even her second attempt at motherhood bore no fruit. Her second child was stillborn. Her last-ditch effort to save her marriage, to seek happiness in domesticity failed. Her marriage reached a dead end. She never got her 'Holy Grail' that would give her happiness and completeness. Unlike the Arthurian romance wherein the knights—Sir Gawain, Sir Launcelot, Sir Percival, Sir Bor and Sir Galahad—managed to find the Holy Grail, Madeleine could not find the 'Holy Grail' of her life. She ultimately left the chase of worldly or domestic happiness and became a hermit. She divorced Rama.

Whereas the story of Demeter and the Holy Grail give expression to her deep anguish as a mother, as a failed mother let down by even the gods, the myth of Poseidon expresses her pain as a wife. It is again in the context of her son that she thinks of Poseidon. She recalls these Greek mythological figures because she loves the Greek pagan stories. She is trying to select a name for her son. Should it be Krishna, Ulysses, Poseidon or Achilles? Little does she realize the similarity between her life and these mythological entities: "I slept, Rama, night after night in the nursing home, not thinking of Pierre or of you but of Demeter and Poseidon and the voyage of Ulysses. In fact at first I thought a second name for Krishna would be Ulysses." (37)

Poseidon was the son of Cronus (the son of Uranus and Gaea) and Rhea. Cronus was in the habit of swallowing his children. Rhea managed to save her sixth child Zeus. Zeus grew up in secret and later contrived to bring back to life his brothers and sisters—Hestia, Demeter, Hera, Hades and Poseidon. Cronus was then dethroned by Zeus and bound in Tartarus. Poseidon, like his younger but more powerful brother Zeus, was a habitual womanizer—having one affair after another. The legitimate wives were very unhappy and resentful of their husbands' extra marital affairs. Poseidon's wife was Amphtrite while Zeus' wife was Hera. Besides this weakness of character, which he shared with brother Zeus, Poseidon was also a greedy and quarrelsome deity becoming unpopular as a result of it. He waged many wars to expand his realm but failed. He had to remain content as the god of horses and the sea.

Madeleine's predicament as a wife was similar to that of Hera and Amphtrite. Rama, in spite of being a learned man, was prone to womanizing. He was unfaithful to Madeleine repeatedly. It is alleged that even she had an affair but it is clear from the narrative that the so-called affair was purely a platonic relationship based on like—mindedness. Madeleine's gradual involvement with ascetic Buddhism made it impossible for even her husband, leave alone any other man, to have anything to do with her. Her stand was that if she could not be happy with her husband Rama, she was not interested in being happy with any other man. She did not give herself a second chance. She turned towards a spartan life in search of mental peace and consolation. Even Buddhism could not re-kindle the fire between her and Rama. It drove her farther away from him. Madeleine was betrayed by the gods who snatched her sons and by her husband who got involved with Savithri. She let the matter rest at that.

Ram and Savithri loved each other and in the process, Madeleine got ruined. She lost everything. She gave up everything—home, hearth and husband, even her original religion—Christianity. So serious was the spiritual crisis created by the death of her sons and the estrangement from Rama that she no longer could remain Christian. She adopted Buddhism and wanted to be cremated. Ram, on the other hand, was like Zeus and Poseidon—getting involved with many women and justifying it all with the argument that he was a 'man' after all with "demands . . . ancient, primal, inevitable" (219). He never felt guilty because as he said he "hated this moral India" (349) which stressed abstinence. Even the much glorified and sublime relationship with Savithri is not purely intellectual. The meeting of the two in the hospital bears testimony to this fact.

Although oblivious of all this, Madeleine keeps thinking about Demeter and Poseidon. Like Demeter she lost her children to the gods. Like Poseidon, her husband is a womanizer, and like the Greek god did not gain much either. Madeleine gave up Rama and Rama had to give up Savithri. He returned to India empty handed. He stayed in France long enough to witness Madeleine turn an ascetic. Eventually he too had to embrace a similar fate. Only Savithri, though under pressure, returned to home and husband. Madeleine, unlike Hera and Amphitrite, never got to know the whole truth about Savithri and Rama but her unconscious mind repeatedly warned. The names of Ulysses, Achilles, Demeter and Poseidon echoed in Madeleine's mind without she realizing their relevance to her life.

It is worth noting that the mythic figures used in *The Serpent and the Rope* have been culled from the mythologies of different cultures. Yet they have much in common and perhaps this was the reason why Rao created this cocktail of myths, legends and histories in the novel. The final analysis being that cultures change, characters change, time changes but the basic human emotions and predicaments remain the same. Hence problems, solutions and situations of one culture have a resonance in the other. No myth or story, therefore, goes out of date or is out of place. Radha-Krishna myth is re-enacted by Savithri and Rama. Tristan and Iseult come alive in Romeo and Juliet, Laila and Majnu, Heer and Ranjha. The myths are never or rarely useless even though life-styles change, time changes. It is because man, at the psychological level, has remained human all along.

Whether it is the pre-historic age of the Vedas or 500 A.D. of King Arthur or 1946—the year in which Raja Rao situates the novel, relationships outside marriage remained a sore in the eye of the world. Hence one story after another continues to be weaved around it—Radha and Krishna, Tristan and Iseult, Savithri and Rama. The list could go on so too the description of their heroic struggle to keep their attachments intact in a world that has always been hostile to such relationships since time immemorial.

Thus, the myths in *The Serpent and the Rope* are not ornamental. They have been included in the narrative to make important connections and clarifications. The novel opens when India was at the threshold of independence. Though published in 1960, it portrays events taking place from 1946 to 1954. Old socio-political system was giving way to a new era under the premiership of Pt. Jawaharlal Nehru who pinned great hopes on socialism, modernism and industrialism. This socio-political dynamism, gathering force since the arrival of Mahatma Gandhi in India from South Africa in 1915, was influencing literature too. Writers like R.K. Narayan with his middle-class stories and Mulk Raj Anand with his working-class heroes became fairly well established. Gods, goddesses, kings, queens were quite out of fashion and out of reckoning in literature, society and polity.

Rao, however, refused to render redundant gods, goddesses, kings, queens, superhuman heroes, heroines, mystics and yogis. It is not that he was their blind votary bend down by a sense of servility. Neither was he overwhelmed by nostalgic romanticism. Rather he knew, even in those heady days of modernism (*ring in the new!*), liberalism, Marxism (religion is the opium of the mass!), socialism (classless society!) and industrialism (science and technology!), that the end of old beliefs is not as imminent as visualized by iconoclasts and mavericks. Rather these are one of the few immanents of the human world rooted in human emotional needs and in human perception of what is right and what is wrong.

The novel also questions the vision of politicians, bureaucrats and industrialists vis-à-vis the country's future. In the novel Rama observes that 'modern' India "would never be made by our politicians and professors of political science" (352). True India was not "where the new crude Congressmen and the old vulgar aristocracy mingled for the building of a magnified India. . . . It would in fact be nobody's India, till someone sat and remembered what India was" (375). Little Mother and Savithri too repeatedly compare 'north' India with 'south,' 'modern' India with 'ancient' and express dismay over the former. They do not hanker for Brahminical purity or aristocratic splendour. Their disappointment stems from unsystematic urbanization and blind westernization in the name of progress. Savithri is aghast that India should look towards

China and Europe to move ahead when all that the country needed was to look within: "Ministers, Secretaries come and go, and I think, what is this India we are building? Oh! Rama it makes me sad, sad! some want it to become like our neighbour China, and others like their foster-mother white England. And nobody wants India to be India" (340).

The work is a desperate attempt to convince one and all that progress does not lie in merely brick, concrete and iron. True happiness does not lie in money, material comfort and free relationships. The country as well as the people also need nourishment of the spirit and the soul, the purity of which must be protected and preserved by the values enshrined in myths, legends and folktales. It is not merely 'law' but the fear of divine retribution and poetic justice, the stories of which are replete in myth and history, that keep alive the conscience of the people. Mythology and historical precedence control and console people. They prevent them from becoming utterly selfish and self-centered. They fulfill the moral and emotional needs of people. This is the reason why G.S. Kirk says that "myths and rituals . . . constitute a cultural storehouse of adjustive responses for individuals" (262).

Rao shows that all the 'isms' of the modern world can, solve the life-style and livelihood problems of man but not the emotional tangles born of love, longing, promise and betrayal. Hence the recourse to myths and legends that strike a chord at the deep levels of the human psyche.

Rao seems to believe that myths can neither be completely rejected nor abjectly accepted. Myths are, in fact, good as well as bad. Only oppressive rituals and superstitions need to be removed or overlooked so that the 'beauty' of myths and the 'truth' inherent in them become clear to us. Raja Rao makes use of the 'myth' in *The Serpent and the Rope* to help his characters cope with 'reality' and to make coherent the 'present' to them.

Githa Hariharan's *The Thousand Faces of Night*: A Modern Woman's Quest and Tryst with Myth

Githa Hariharan's *Thousand Faces of Night* (1992) is a novel about both 'real' and 'mythic' women. She shows how the 'real' and 'mythic' women stand in contrast as well as in convergence with each other; their trails and travails equally happy or horrifying. Hariharan makes use of 'myth' to explore the joys and burden of womanhood, wifehood, motherhood as also the social censures of infertility.

The novel revolves around protagonist Devi, grandmother Pati, mother Sita and the in-laws' maid Mayamma. The narrative is divided into three parts portraying different stages of Devi's life—her childhood, her conjugal life and the final resolution in part three. The novel records the attitude and experience of these women as they come to terms with life in a patriarchal society. The focus is primarily on women while the men are either subsidiary or shadowy characters. It would be a mistake, however, to assume that this novel is yet another anti-male tirade. On the contrary, the novel reveals how "a woman may be both the oppressor and the oppressed" and that "quite often she becomes an ally for instituting patriarchal authority over the other female members" (Desai and Thakkar 75). Moreover the novel brings to the fore the reality that if women experience care and security in the family "it is also a place where women suffer a number of tensions" (*Ibid.* 70).

Githa Hariharan's story reveals the psyche of women caught between 'ideal' models of mythology and 'practical' realities of contemporary life. She explodes the 'myth' that contemporary or modern times are, in anyway, liberal for women. The pressure to conform to cultural normative model remains even in the context of educated and urbane women so much so that "the modern educated Indian woman is neither happy nor contended nor socially useful. She is a misfit in life. She is highly suppressed and needs opportunities for self-expression" (*Ibid.* 40). Education or employment do not free her from traditional expectations. On the contrary her assimilation into or approval from her own caste, community or family becomes dependent on how much she underplays her intellectual abilities, academic achievements or professional qualifications in the name of 'modesty' and 'decorum.' Demureness is much encouraged while assertiveness is despised in young women. At the same time, education today also implies that women not only play traditional roles with greater aplomb; earn well; but also know how to flaunt their feminity with efficiency and sophistication as shown in commercial advertisements and popular cinema.

A 'myth' that needs to be busted in the context of modern Indian women is that they are under pressure to conform to Sita and Savitri model only. In fact, there is another current, equally strong, that is trying to compel women to 'open up' sexually. In this context too 'myth' is expediently used. The myth of Radha-Krishna and Meera or of the 'Pancha Kanyas' is used by both men and women to encourage as well as justify extra-marital and pre-marital affairs despite the inherent risks. Thus, if 'myth' is becoming a strategy of 'confinement,' it is also becoming a tool of 'motivated' liberation in the hands of cunning perverts who take advantage of gullible girls, women and even men. In *The Thousand Faces of Night,* however, the female protagonists do not face such a problem. In their lives it is the myth of Sita and Savitri that dominates. Escape through the mythic method of Radha does take place but it is more a matter of choice than coercion.

Pati, Sita, Devi and Mayamma are all trapped in mythic moulds. Yet, except Devi, neither do they realize this nor raise a murmur of protest. On the contrary, they push each other back into the trap of 'myth' so as to seek solace and solution of problems that need rational redressal. Instead of liberating each other from cultural structures whose oppressiveness is quite known to them, the women keep finding newer entrants for imprisonment. Maternal love and the element of 'romance' in cultural structures and cultural narratives are expediently used by elderly women on gullible girls to make ineffective the lure of liberal ideologies of modern era. The motive is to turn each girl into a model 'woman,' 'wife,' or 'mother' with whom the men would be completely at ease. A Sanskrit couplet describes a wife thus: "Karyeshu Mantri, Karaneshu Dasi, Rupeesha Lakshmi, Kshamayaa Dharitrii, Bhojyeshu Mata, Shayanetu Rambha, Shat Karma Yukta, Kula Dharma Patni." Thus, in the Indian tradition a woman must act like a secretary and servant to her husband while he is working, she must be beautiful and lucky like Lakshmi, earth-like in forbearance, like a mother while cooking and serving food to her husband, like the nymph Rambha in bed, participant of the 'Saptapadi Rit' and co-sharer of religious and family responsibilities.

Needless to say, normal women like Devi in 'The Thousand Faces of Night' find such multiple and varied expectations or expertise a tall order, fit only for either the ethereal or superhuman. Devi opines about her grandmother and the 'myths': "Her stories fashioned moulds. Ideal moulds, impossibly ambitious, that challenged the puny listener to stretch her frame and fit into the into the vast spaces, live up to her illustrious ancestors" (27). It is not that women like Devi oppose marriage. It is an important and useful institution that gives happiness, fulfillment and even 'purpose' to not just women but men as well. The modern concept of 'marriage', which is strictly monogamous, ensures physical, emotional and financial security in society. Devi realizes in America itself, when she is far from Sita's influence, that in all societies (not just Indian) marriage is considered a "logical outcome" (5) or a natural and normal occurrence in a person's life. Her black American boyfriend Dan, after going around with her for some time, wanted to marry her. It is another matter that Devi turns down his proposal and opts to obey her mother.

It is this decision that proves to be the most momentous in Devi's life exposing her to host of such issues that have strong bearing on women's lives. Her sad experiences raise numerous questions. Are women born only to play the role of 'wife' and 'mother'? If they fail to be both what would be their position in society? Are women without children and women without husbands burden for family and liability for society? Why this pressure to be 'perfect'? Why do women force each other to do the men's bidding?

The novel brings to the fore, as mentioned earlier, the agonizing reality that before battling the men; women must struggle against their "own internalized oppressions" (Katrak 241). They must allow each other to talk freely and express openly their dreams, desires and wishes. They must assist each other in the realization of the 'self' instead of muzzling in the name of gender hierarchy, propriety or family responsibility. Women as mothers, sisters or mothers-in law must give girls the opportunity to 'grow' rather than nipping them in the bud.

The grooming of girls is in the hands of women. It is women who transfer patriarchal pride and prejudice to their children thereby maintaining the status-quo of unbalanced power equations between men and women in society. The women must re-think about gender sensitization so that girls get opportunity for individual advancement too rather than playing merely the biological and social roles of wife and mother "subordinating the self and giving priority to the needs of other kin members" (Desai and Thakkar 75). It is to be noted that these kin members are not just the men of the family but women too like the mother, grandmother, mother-in-law, sister-in-law, sister or maternal/ paternal aunts who have the advantage of either seniority, experience, connection or money. Sometimes 'well-placed,' 'clever' and 'established' female relatives manage and manipulate the lives of younger, dependent and inexperienced women in a manner that would either stifle growth, ruin brighter prospects or simply suit them more than the recipients.

Often marriages are 'arranged' or 'not arranged' not with the best of intentions but with vested interests. Innocent boys and girls are used as pawns on a chess board with the intention to extract maximum mileage through marriage alliances. Desperate parents often fall prey to such manipulative mediators masquerading as well-wishers. This is not to say that all marriages are solemnized with such nefarious motives and that all families are battle grounds and all female relatives each other's enemy. However the leg-pulling and back-biting that goes on in Indian families over the issue of marriage cannot be ignored. 'Marriage' remains one of the main tools of 'pinning' a girl down, of 'sealing' her fate or of showing a girl 'her' place. Sometimes patriarchal notions and values are just an excuse for women to settle scores with one another. Men are often 'toys' and 'trophies' in the hands of women engaged in one-upmanship with one another. When women are possessive about their husbands, it is quite understandable and also justified. However matter does not end here. Some women are seen eager to 'pocket' not just their own husbands but the husbands and sons of other women too. There has been, thus, an unprecedented rise in the rate of extra-marital and pre-marital relationships and in divorce cases. The credibility of the institution of 'marriage' is at stake today more than ever before.

It is this moral degradation and disintegration of families that makes 'myth' relevant as well as necessary. Moralists and traditionalists clamour for old world values to bring some sanity, order and decorum in society at large and personal relationships in particular. Mythic women like Sita, Sati, Parvati and Savitri and mythic men like Ram and Shiva are revered. Monogamy, chastity and fidelity are thereby loudly eulogized.

However the problem with both traditionalists and mavericks is that they do not know where to stop. In the zeal to further their interests and ideologies they go to the extreme. They overact or overdo ruining the very purpose for which they are purportly fighting. If the excesses of the mavericks have given rise to promiscuous relationships and consequential health and psychological disorders, then the traditionalists have to answer for dowry-deaths, female infanticide, child-marriages and the over-all dissatisfactory status of women in Indian society in the matter of education, employment and health.

The title *The Thousand Faces of Night* refers to an Arabian folktale in which an emperor was in the habit of marrying a girl every day of the year. He also got each bride beheaded the morning after the wedding night. Horrified by this practice of the emperor there came a time when no one in his kingdom was willing to give his daughter. However a courtier's daughter pressurized her father to make a proposal of her marriage to the emperor. The eccentric king gleefully acceded and the marriage was solemnized with due pomp. However this girl had no suicidal intentions. She had her own plans to dodge the sword. When the emperor came to meet her on the nuptial night, she started a conversation with him. In no time the emperor found himself listening to a story being narrated by his latest bride. The 'story' was long enough to last all through the night but not short enough to end at dawn when the girl was scheduled to be killed. The emperor found the story so interesting that he would have none of it without hearing the 'end.' He broke the horrifying precedence so that he could hear the 'conclusion' on the second night. On the second night, however, the clever girl did not only conclude the first story but also began narrating another equally enchanting if not more. Her death sentence was again deferred till the third morning. In this manner the new bride kept narrating one story after another so as to keep the king awake all through the night but not short enough to end in the morning. In all she told a thousand different stories and consequently she survived a thousand days. At last the mesmerized emperor decided that he would not only spare this intelligent and talented girl from the sword finally but never remarry. The courtier's daughter was to live and rule as his one and only queen.

Hariharan alludes to this folktale so as to stress the need for women to 'talk,' to share their stories as also the stories of their ancestors who might have lived millions of years ago before days could be counted or numbered. She emphasizes the need to 'share' experiences, agonies, joys and knowledge so that women learn and know from each other's lives. Women must talk about themselves as also about goddesses and princesses to find out how the 'real' as well as the 'mythical' live or lived, survive or survived. What options and opportunities are or were available to women? What mistakes are to be avoided and what knowledges and wisdoms are to be transferred from one generation to another. They must let each other speak. They must talk and interact so as to learn, rectify and encourage themselves and others before it is too late.

In *The Thousand Faces of Night*, Hariharan shares the story of many women and the men related to them. Devi, Sita and Mayamma share their innermost thoughts about their married life. One also meets Pati, Devi's paternal grandmother. Through Pati, mythical women and their 'stories' are brought before the readers. One meets Parvatimma, the absentee mother-in-law, whose story is revealed by Mayamma. Then there is Uma as also Annapurna. There is Mahadevan, Mahesh and Dan too with their own stories embedded in the bigger stories of the women related to them. Devi talks about herself, her mother, about her marriage, about her grandmother and the mythical stories that she heard from her. Sita too talks about herself, about her plans and ambitions and the painstaking efforts that went into them. Mayamma discloses the gory details of her infertility, her cruel and crooked mother-in-law and the horrifying rituals that she had to put up with so as to bear a child. All except Sita also talk and discuss the goddesses, the princesses and the nymphs whose assistance they must seek to ease the problems of a woman's life.

Pati, Devi's grandmother, is the woman who takes Devi and the reader back in time. So as to know 'us,' we must know our ancestors. So as to know the 'future' one must know the 'past.' So as to prepare for life ahead, for its unpredictabilities, one must know all that has already happened. Life is indeed unpredictable.

It is for the sake of this that Pati makes use of the 'myth.' Devi, her golden grandchild, the apple of her eyes, must be made aware of a woman's life in its totality, its bright as well as dark colours:

> My grandmother's stories were no ordinary bedtime stories. She chose each for a particular occasion, a story in reply to each of my childish questions. She had an answer for every question. But her answers were not simple: they had to be decoded. A comparison had to be made, an illustration discovered, and a moral drawn out. (27)

The first myth that Devi recalls is about Nala and Damayanti.

In this myth narrated to her by Pati, Devi heard how gods and princes queued before Damayanti. The suitors came to her doorstep. It was for her to pick and choose amongst them. There was no pressure on her even from her parents to select this or that particular candidate. The preference was solely to be Damayanti's. Moreover no one stopped Nala to join the *swayamvara*. She was free to select Nala from the assembled suitors. There were no horoscopes to be matched. Just her 'decision' mattered. In those mythical times if a girl made clear whom she wanted to marry, she was ordinarily not stopped provided the person in question was equally willing. The system of *swayamvara* was primarily to give girls the freedom of choice and lovers a chance to legitimize their attachment. Grooms were selected or rejected by princesses and not vice-versa. Even gods could not force a woman to marry against her wish. If anything of the sort ever happened, there were upheavals serious enough to make the culprits repent for eternity. Someone or the other always rose to the rescue of such hapless women so as to ensure poetic justice.

This ancient Hindu method of marriage, however, has undergone great change. It has been turned upside down. It is the boys who select or reject the girls. The fate of the girl is made or marred on the basis of birth-charts—'kundali.' These charts, however, are expediently used. It is actually the 'dowry' that matters. The 'heavier' the dowry paid, the brighter seems a girl's horoscope to the prospective groom's family. The horoscope, in fact, becomes irrelevant in such scenarios. On the other hand, even a genuinely good horoscope is rejected if the dowry is not up to expectations. Her own likes and dislikes matter little. It is the 'horoscope,' the pandits who analyze them, the parents and the men and women who come to 'see' her are the people who rule supreme in this matter. Even the 'boy' for whom the whole charade is carried out is sometimes a mute spectator doomed to put up with whichever girl his kith and kin dump on his head. The girl or boy is lectured to 'adjust' no matter how unhappy they might be with one another.

Devi in *The Thousand Faces of Night* went through a similar ordeal. She met four to six eligible bachelors. Some of them were too traditional to have a 'look' at her. So they sent their parents to do the job. Others were too 'modern,' that is, almost amorous. They met Devi not to make her 'wife' but probably to have an evening out with an intelligent woman good enough to sit and chat with but too bright and wise to be wedded. There were no princes, kings or gods vying for her hand. She had already left behind Dan in America who could have been a 'Nala' of her life. The grooms were short listed after the matching of horoscopes and then meetings were arranged. Some wanted not just an intelligent girl but adequately beautiful too to show off. Others wanted an up-to-date girl who would be adequately dull and dumb as well or at least adept at keeping 'secrets.' One of the boys asked Devi to be frank about her life. He encouraged her to be honest. Devi disclosed about Dan. The boy even danced with Devi and had heart-to-heart talk with her that evening like a perfect prospective husband. The next morning Sita informed Devi that she was not to the boy's liking. What had the boy come for? To have a good time with Devi? Why did he take so much of liberty when he knew he would not marry her?:

> The next morning I woke up late, with a mild tremor of anticipation. But Amma met my looks without a smile. . . . She announced, as if I had asked her, that I was not quite what the young man had in mind. I was not disappointed, but surprised. (20)

Of this motley crowed of boys, Mahesh appeared the most sensible. Their horoscopes matched. They met and accepted each other. Mahesh was not given to pondering over an issue too much. Devi seemed to him adequately educated as well as adjustable girl. He met her a few times before they were married off in a traditional ceremony. He did not believe in displaying emotions too much. He was, moreover, not interested in her past. He was least interested in what she did in America. Thus, Devi's marriage took place without "the feast of a bride's choice, the regal dignity and solemnity of a swayamvara" (18). Devi was no Damayanti nor Mahesh a king dressed in "robes and jewels" (18), Devi observed: "If I was going to play out a travesty of the myths that had filled my childhood, I would tear aside all pretence, I thought, I would be as matter-of—fact as Mahesh" (23).

Perhaps the Indian female population would have had an easier life if generations of them were not fed with stories as fabulous as the myth of Damayanti and Nala, Radha and Krishna, Dushyanta and Shakuntala: "In my grandmother's stories, there was room only for heroes and heroines. Princesses grew up secure in the knowledge of what awaited them: Love, a prince who was never short of noble, and a happy ending" (20). On the other hand, there were also horrifying tales about married life which would push any woman to depression and dejection. There seemed to be no middle path. Either the extreme romanticism of Damayanti, Shakuntala and Rati or the extraordinary struggle of Savitri and Sita, Kunti and Draupadi. "Ideal moulds, impossibly ambitious" (27).

In fact not just 'myth' but also movies, romantic novels, advertisements or the sculptures found on the walls of ancient temples coalesce in conditioning women to talk, behave, look and dress in a certain 'acceptable' and 'desirable' way. Shashi Deshpande in *The Stone Women* observes: "Were real women ever like that or are they simply the projection of the male mind? The male imagination, as it depicts women, tends to be stereotypical and the male gaze all conspire to contain women within an image, an image that women find static and narcissistic and even cold" (178-79).

The question arises as to why even the women cooperate in the conspiracy of the men to 'contain' women in certain images? Grandmothers, mothers and mothers-in-law become "an ally for instituting patriarchal authority" and also 'fantasy' "over the other female members" (Desai and Thakkar 75). By narrating their own tales of woes, they rationalize and legitimize the pains of all the other women. They narrate 'myths' and 'legends' to show that even goddesses and princesses believed that "female submission" and silence' is "the basis of a harmonious man-woman relationship" (Jain 162). Why this eagerness and anxiety to mould every girl in a manner that would suit the men? Why this implicit emphasis that contentment and salvation of a woman lay only in "subordination of the self and giving priority to the needs of other kin members"? (Desai and Thakkar 78). In Shashi Deshpande's short story 'My Beloved Charioteer' the grandmother narrates her own experience as a wife to her granddaughter:

> I lived with him for 25 years, I knew he didn't like unstringed beans and stones in his rice . . I know he didn't like tears. . . . He didn't like to see women with loosened hair. . . . And once a year he bought me two saris, always colours that I hated. But he never asked me and I never told him. . . . And once, when I asked whether I could sleep in another room . . . he said nothing. But the next day, his mother . . . told me bluntly about a wife's duties. I must always be available. So, I slept there, afraid to get up for a glass of water, scared even to cough. (Jain 163)

With such 'true' tales along with the 'mythic' ones, generations after generations of women tutor each other about the tricks of 'managing' men and making a marriage click. In *The Thousand Faces of Night* too, Pati's narration of 'myths' to Devi is "a case of the older generation trying to shape the younger generation in the same mould of social and familial docility."

After narrating the myth of Nala and Damayanti, Pati began to talk about Gandhari. Damayanti's story allowed Pati to show "happiness and tragedy in conjugal life" (P. Mukherjee 42), of a wife's resolute love for her man and triumph over struggles. Damayanti was basically a lucky woman who managed to marry her beloved and hold on to him in spite of umpteen upheavals. The two got separated only to reunite and live happily ever after. Nala was Damayanti's selection and she made a success of it. What about women who are not so fortunate? What about those brides who end up having incompatible grooms? What about those innocent young girls who marry with dreams in their eyes only to realize later they have been deceived? How are they to cope with the tragedy as well as seek revenge for the injustice done to them? It is in the context of such possibilities and eventualities that Pati finds the 'myth' or story of Gandhari relevant:

> When Gandhari came to her husband's house, dressed in her bridal finery, her heart beat like a drum . . . her . . . eager eyes lost their shyness as she sought those of her new husband. . . . He stood by the window, his noble head looking up at the sky. But when he turned around, she saw the white eyes, the pupils glazed and useless.
>
> In her pride, her anger, Gandhari said nothing. But she tore off a piece of her thick red skirt and tied it tightly over her own eyes. She groped towards her unseeing husband, her lips straight and thin with fury. (28-29)

Devi recalls that even as a child she could sense that even in their own family they had a 'Gandhari.' In fact all Indian families have one or the other women like her who do not protest vociferously to avoid upheavals but silently 'protest' against what they perceive as 'injustice.'

Devi's own mother Sita was a girl gifted with musical talent. She had a rare expertise on the strings of the veena. She could have blossomed into a major musical name if given the opportunity. Look wise, however, she was a 'plain' girl. She was dusky, unlike the fair-complexioned maidens whom Indian families eagerly seek as brides for their sons. Consequently, Sita got married much after her cousins "at the age of twenty, late by family's standards" (101). If it had not been for the veena perhaps Sita would not have been Devi's mother and Pati's daughter-in-law: "By the time she played an ashtapadi about the sweet poignancy of love, Nindat Chandana, her examiners had forgotten about her dark skin and the severe face that met theirs without a smile; they were overwhelmed by her talent and their good fortune" (102).

However when she was already married and settled with her in-laws, she had to abandon that for what she was selected. If Gandhari had to blindfold her eyes; her counterpart in the novel had, literally, to cut her fingers. Sita's father-in-law thundered about household responsibilities as a wife and daughter-in-law. Sita retaliated with equal sharpness. She did not look for excuses or plead for concessions. She simply took the extreme step like Gandhari; humiliating all with a masterstroke making them regret, repent and remember forever;

> Sita hung her head over the veena. . . . Then she reached for the strings of her precious veena and pulled them out of the wooden base. They came apart with a discordant twang of protest.
>
> She looked up at my husband, her eyes dry and narrowed, and said in a clear, stinging whisper, "Yes. I am a wife, a daughter-in-law." (30)

Pati, Devi's grandmother, further recollected: "We never saw her touch the Veena again. She became a dutiful daughter-in-law the neighbours praised, and our household never heard the heart-rending music again" (30). Pati knew that Gandhari was not the only one of her type. She survived and lived in the spirit of women like Sita. 'Gandhari' is not a 'myth' but a 'reality' of Indian society. It is the silent sacrifice of women like her that have built the foundations of the Indian nation. The household hearth has been kept ablaze precisely because women like her have burnt their dreams, desires, aims and ambitions in it and have instead nurtured generations after generations of kith and kin, giving priority to 'family' over the 'self.' Somehow, even as child, Devi knew this reality. It lurked around her. It was familiar to her:

> I said nothing, and was not precocious enough to ask how

> Gandhari's story and Amma's came together. Or perhaps I knew. I must have known, even then, that Gandhari's pride, the fury that was to become her life-force, the central motive of years of blind suffering, was no piece of fiction. Gandhari's anger, wrapped tightly round her head in a life-long blindfold, burnt in a heart close, very close to mine. (29)

Gandhari was the princess of Gandhar. She was blessed with exquisitely luminous eyes. Bheeshma, in his eagerness to fetch the best possible brides for his handicapped nephews, wedded the luminous eyed princess to the visionless Dhritarashtra as if to compensate for the latter's blindness. To top it all, the fact of Dhritarashtra's visual disability was not disclosed to Gandhari. She came to know of it when nothing could be done to change her fate. It was deceit. It was an insult to a woman who was famous for the beauty of her eyes. Gandhari, hurt, shocked and finally angry, was not to take Bheeshma's decision lamely. She retaliated in her own way:

> For a young girl, embarking on adulthood and marriage, to vow never to see the world again! what it must have meant to her to make this sacrifice, to blot out the world to conform to an idea of matrimony even fiercer and more intense than that handed down over generations. What was it that drove her to this extreme act of self-denial? Not just tradition, for even the tradition of the dutiful wife, the Sati, Savitri myth and legend, did not demand so much. Not love, for she had never set eyes on Dhritarashtra before; not admiration, for the days of his greatness still lay ahead. No, it was some mysterious inner force that led to this young girl to will herself into blindness, to give up the glory of the sunlight. (Tharoor 64)

The blindfold on her face did more than match Dhritarashtra's blindness. It reminded everyone of the injustice that had been done to her. The marriage to him plunged her into life-long darkness. It brought forth children who were equally blind. Blind in animosity, in hatred. Blind to morality, good sense and propriety. Not physically blind but mentally blind. Ironically the boon of a hundred sons that Gandhari was blessed with in her maidenhood benefited the Kuru clan little. Bheeshma had selected her precisely because of this boon. However, it rebounded on the clan and none survived. Bheeshma's effort was in vain. The marriage was a waste. The Kuru clan was punished severally. The boon turned to be their nemesis. It was rather late when Dhritarashtra apologized to his wife. The great war was over with only the five sons of Kunti alive:

> You were deceived. Without being told of my blindness you were married to me. We did you a thousand wrongs Gandhari. . . . We Kuru men have done great injustices to women. And we have paid in full for them too. In Amba's wrath Bhishma was burned. I am still burning in yours. Kunti also was married to a deficient man. . . . I wronged you. Pandu wronged Kunti. . . . I am pleading with you. (Karve 37-40)

Pati felt there was some link between the mythical woman Gandhari and her own daughter-in-law Sita. Gandhari has, in fact, never been an exception. There have been more of her ilk in all ages of Indian civilization. Women compliant but paradoxically defiant too. Registering their protest in a silence that has been louder than words. She remembered, along with the story of Gandhari, the cold and decisive compliance of her daughter-in-law that put to end all complains as also the possibility of a reappraisal.

Sita, with a woman's pride and anger swelling in her breast, broke the veena wires and resolved to be a 'perfect' wife and daughter-in-law. The way she did it shamed her father-in-law and shocked her genuinely sympathetic and supportive mother-in-law. Pati was unable to protect Sita from the patriarch's wrath. As a mother-in-law she did not resent Sita's veena playing but she was unable to pre-empt the volatile confrontation between Sita and the head of the house. The dice was cast. Anger was met by not scared surrender. Rather it was greeted with a silent but destructive fury which burnt all bridges of reconciliation. The veena bore the brunt of it. It was never heard again. Sita obeyed her father-in-law to the hilt. So much so that Pati never forgot the silent rage and resentment implicit in the obedience. Sita burned her talent and her individuality in the kitchen fires to become a model housewife and mother. She lost her cool only when Devi betrayed her:

> Sita was in fury. So this was what she reaped after years of sacrifice, years of iron-like self-control. And what had Devi done in return? She had torn her respectability, her very name, to shreds. And for what prize? A year or two wallowing in the arms of an illusionary lover, in a den of riff-raff; then total, abject degradation, the slime and filth of an uprooted woman's decay. (108)

Around the same time Devi got to know about Gauri. Gauri was the maid of Pati. She toiled hard to collect gold coins enough to make her marriage possible. It did take place with as much fanfare as Gauri's family could afford. The wedding was graced by none other than the excited Devi herself escorted by a maid on either side. The memory of this pleasant participation, the beholding of a joyous event, was marred some years later. Gauri's marriage too ran into rough weather with she taking extraordinary liberty with propriety to seek happiness. Pati was shocked as much by the break of Gauri's marriage as by her strange ways to rebuild her life:

> Gauri came to see Pati some years later, to ask if she could have her old job back. Her husband was an animal, she said. They treated her like dirt, she said. But Pati had already heard several stories from the servants. She had heard that Gauri had fallen in love with her younger brother-in-law. They plotted behind the elders' back and ran away one night.
>
> Pati would not give her work to do in the house again, but she sent her away with a ten rupee note. That night, she sat by my bed, unusually quiet, with a kind of hurt bewilderment. (32)

Why was Pati hurt? Did she consider the decision of Gauri unwise? Did Gauri's unashamed assertion of her independent 'will' and 'sexuality' offend Pati's sensibilities? Did she believe that situations like these should be handled differently? It seems so. Later that night when Devi demanded another myth from the ancient epic *Mahabharata*, Pati refused. "No not today, Devi. But I will tell you about the beautiful girl who married a snake." (36) She married him, and was a devoted wife, looking after all his needs.

> One night, the serpent slithered out of the chest in her chamber and crawled into her bed. When she clasped her arms about him, she felt the scales soften underneath her hands till they touched tender human flesh. She embraced the good fortune she had brought about with her loving hands, and they spent a night of warm caresses. Towards dawn, the young woman slipped out of her husband's embrace and got out of the bed. On the floor she saw yards of cold snake—skin ripped apart in the middle. She quickly dragged the skin outside and burnt it to ashes. Then she went back to her bed, where the sweet-smelling youth slept on, unaware of his rebirth. (34)

It is clear that Pati strongly disapproved of Gauri's conduct. She narrated a myth in which the husband was a 'snake' who changed into a human being probably softened by the wife's good conduct and patience. Taken metaphorically, the myth's message is that even if a man is virtually as poisonous and dangerous as king cobra, patience and devotion by wife can reform him. Love has a strange power that tames even wild animals. When they can change why can't human beings? This is Pati's logic and this is what she wants her granddaughter Devi to understand and remember. Never break a marriage or run away from husband, home and hearth. Silently, patiently persist till things change for the better. No human being, man or woman, is faultless. There is bound to be some flaw somewhere. At the same time there is no problem, no hurdle, no defect, no error that cannot be rectified, solved or removed. Hence Pati believes that no decision must be taken in haste. Before making a final decision, effort must be made to see if things can be improved for the better.

Yet another important reality that Pati has, unconsciously or consciously, highlighted through this 'myth' concerns 'men' and their 'mothers.' Pati unintentionally raises finger at the grooming of boys and puts in the dock their mothers. In the myth, the 'son' is a 'serpent' whom his mother nurses till he becomes a "fifteen feet of sinuous coils" (33). She insists that this venomous serpent be married off too.

In Indian society too all men are not saints. A girl has to be extremely fortunate to have protective and progressive father, considerate brother and a humane husband. Facts and figures, however, show that such pious male members are numbered or else why would there be so many dowry deaths, female infanticide, cases of gender harassment, illiteracy, unemployment and poor health of females? Such disheartening status of women is undoubtedly the consequence of patriarchy.

It has been observed that a man may be an 'ideal' at home only to turn a 'devil' outside with women not related him. On the contrary a man may be chivalrous publicly but a wife or woman beater privately. All these men are 'sons' of such mothers who have groomed them to be 'snakes' in the guise of humans. The question arises as to how do 'mothers' groom their 'sons' that they become a liability for women folk in particular and society in general? Why is that mothers are not as cautions and careful about the conduct of their sons as they are about their female progeny? Why aren't right values imbibed by the male child too? Who is to be blamed if a boy goes astray? Does the responsibility of a mother end merely with feeding her children with nutritious food? Is the physical well-being, the health of the male child the only responsibility of his parents? What about his mentality? His attitude? Does the pride of being a boy's mother make women blind to the necessity of inculcating 'right' values in their wards? If a man is insensitive to his wife or disrespectful towards other women does it not reveal the mental culture of his family, of the woman who gave birth to him? Who is to be held responsible for such a behaviour apart from the man himself? Why are such devils not brought to book? Why do mothers nurse and pamper such notorious progeny like the mother of that 'snake son' in the myth? Last but not the least, why are wives expected or tutored to 'adjust' or 'tolerate' such beast like husbands? Why aren't boys groomed in a manner that their wives, daughters, daughters-in-law, sisters, colleagues or women in general would have a better life?

The reader also comes across the story of Mayamma's aunt, an old village woman Lakshmiamma, who sat wasted in the village while the son was least bothered about either her life or death. The old woman ultimately resorted to defaming her son by complaining about his negligence before neighbours. Only then was he shamed into taking cognizance of her existence:

> The sole heir to this family . . . her son, lived forty miles away in a town. He sent her money orders once a month, twenty rupees, and a line to say he was busy, he would visit next year. Then the money orders stopped coming. Lakshmiamma complained in the temple every evening. She wailed in impatient neighbours' homes. (125)

Mayamma's own son, whom she had given birth after years of entreaty to the gods, was no less than a devil. He did not need a wife to show his fangs. He was eager to show his true colours as soon as possible. Mayamma found herself at the receiving end of the very son for whom she had prayed, fasted and pleaded before all and sundry—from gods and pandits to planets and trees: "The son, fed on lavish helpings of tenderness and yearning even before he was born, turned sour early. At fourteen he threatened to beat his mother and sold her last pair of gold bangles. . . . The wastrel son kept Mayamma busy" (81).

Thus, in this novel Githa Hariharan compares myth with reality. She tries to bust illusions about the mother-myth in the context of both sons and daughters. The mother myth is busted with reference to the mothers themselves. As mentioned earlier in this chapter, motherhood enjoys a reverential status in Indian society. She is a figure that is considered the epitome of love, care, kindness, devotion, fortitude, all unconditional. The male progeny is much sought after and fussed over while the girls realize gradually that mothers and mothers-in-law are, often, not goddesses with impartial hearts and eyes. The love of the mother is tilted and tinted by gender bias in favour of brothers and sons. Mothers themselves, on the other hand, often live to regret and repent when they see their grown-up sons raise their hands on them in old age. It is not just wives but even mothers who need to be extremely fortunate in having sons who would be respectful and caring. The reverential status accorded to mothers often turns out to be a myth when parents are overlooked socially, neglected physically and exploited financially by sons for whom they had left no stone unturned. Maternal love makes women fatally blind to the mistakes of their male children. Consequently, their male progeny grows into arrogant, obstinate, negligent individuals with little sense or sensibility. The rise in the number of old age care homes exposes how children, including daughters, in India are shamelessly and selfishly shaking off filial responsibilities. The exalted parent-child relationship in India is, thus, turning into a 'myth,' a facade. Neither are mothers or fathers divine nor their sons or daughters like the mythical Shravan Kumar.

In some households, mothers are insignificant figures losing grip on their male children rather early. The father, male relatives, and associates stoke male chauvinism in male children so much so that they begin to distance themselves from mother or mother figures before time. It is the mother and other female relatives who instill religious and moral values in children. But in many families, they rarely get an opportunity to play their traditional role. The sons grow up believing that manliness lies in being brazen, brawn and insolent. The male ego is stroked so much that they turn a deaf ear to all voices of sanity and restrain. In their eyes, even the mother becomes a woman to be respected but not listened.

Thus, the role and status of the mother assumes great significance. In the hurry to impart masculine training, the mother should not be marginalized. At the same time mothers themselves have to be balanced in handling their male child. Neither can they afford to be too lenient nor can they be too strict. Being mothers of 'sons' is, in fact, more onerous. Daughters can be sent away via marriage. It is the vice and virtue of the son a mother has to put up with lifelong. They have to not only educate their sons properly so that their professional settlement is smooth but also impart right values to the boys least a lifelong of effort of parents is ruined by their sons courting and creating trouble.

It is in the context of the 'serpent-son' myth that Pati unwittingly brings into focus the mother-son relationship. Devi, the grandchild, on the other hand, has other ideas on the matter. She begins to draw parallels between Gauri and the wife of the serpent man. In Pati's version, the husband was the serpent. In Gauri's story, believes Devi, there were two serpents—one physical, the other mental. In Devi's analysis of Gauri's story both the husband and lover were 'serpents.' The husband was as dangerous as a venomous reptile, a king cobra. Gauri's brother-in-law was physically a snake. He was ugly, suffering from a skin disease that turned his body into a canvass of coloured patches, pink prints that don't gel with Indian complexion. However he, from Gauri's perspective, was no less a prince. A saviour in shining armour who came to her rescue. Devi ruminates over such interpretations contrary to what Pati had wanted her to understand:

> I remember I spent days trying to unravel this message from my grandmother. Should Gauri, my happy, down-to-earth Gauri, have married a snake? And who was the snake in her story—her bestial husband or her freakish lover? (34)

Gauri was not the only real woman whose story Devi got to know at her granny's house. Another 'real' woman, whose reality made a great impact on Pati's psyche and indeed on Devi's, was Uma. Uma was a distant cousin of the little girl. Uma had spent her childhood with an "indifferent father and a hostile stepmother" (35). When she came of age, she was married into an affluent family. The marriage was solemnized in Pati's house with fanfare and hope that the motherless girl would now get a home and hearth of her own. However happiness and hope proved to be ephemeral. Uma returned to Pati's house within a year as a sexual victim of her drunkard and lecherous father-in-law.

Uma had been married off with the best of intentions. She was considered a lucky girl to have been accepted by a well-off family. It was thought she would, at last, get the happiness that had eluded her in her father's house because of the step-mother. However it was not to be. Uma returned more broken in spirit and body than ever before. She remained with Pati henceforth. Her marriage broke forever.

The experience of Uma hurt Pati badly. Gauri's story had saddened her but Uma's shocked her. Her faith in natural goodness, her optimism towards life was severely jolted and challenged. She had faith in the inherent and innate goodness of people. Now she began to have doubts and fears. Apprehension and a sense of resignation began to encroach her mind. She was badly and rudely hurt. She was a person who believed that 'goodness' is ultimately reciprocated by 'goodness.' A man or woman who is pious may struggle but not fail. Justice may be delayed but not denied. However the experiences of Gauri and Uma made Pati doubt her beliefs. She felt the necessity to acknowledge these ugly realities as a fact of life. At the same time she also realized, with urgency, that one must be mentally or emotionally, strong, that is, defiant in the face of struggle and sadness. A woman must, at all cost, salvage her pride from the worst of mess. She must never allow circumstances to subdue herself. She must muster courage to hold her head high. This was what she wanted her grand-daughter to understand. Hence, she quickly dried her tears and turned to Devi. She rationalized that it is not just mortal women but even goddesses and princesses who suffer and struggle but they salvage their pride with conviction and courage:

> 'Ah, Devi,' she said, 'why weep over Uma? A high-born prince, or even a goddess, has been the victim of disaster. But a woman like Amba, a truly courageous woman, finds the means to transform her hatred, the fate that overtakes her, into a triumph.' (36)

A woman who prided in talking about Nala and Damayanti, Gandhari and Dhritarashtra, soon found herself talking about serpent husbands and women avengers like Amba, the nemesis of Bheeshma. Devi observes:

> Did my grandmother know what she was saying? On the threshold of senility for years—she collected in her old age more and more wounded refugees in her house, stray objects of charity—her stories reached a frenzied pitch of fantasy. Close to death, she made me a gift of the ultimate fantasy: a woman avenger. (39)

What Devi took as Pati's senility was actually the old woman's urgency to impress upon all women, including Devi, to combine in themselves the 'kind' as well as the 'cruel.' Women must be soft as well as strong so as to tackle the unpredictable turns of life not just for themselves but for the sake of others too. After all it was Goddess Durga whose refuge even the gods sought when tormented by the buffalo demon:

> The demon Andhaka is on rampage. . . . The gods are worried. Very worried. This demon is proving to be too tricky, too mobile, too adept at changing himself. The occasion calls for a superior power of the sort they only possess in portions. He has to be destroyed by a sublime power that challenges the demon's dark arrogance while its own appearance carries no hint of the real ingenuity, cunning and indomitable courage within.
>
> In short, a female worrier. (Pande 13)

Amba was the eldest of the three Kashi princesses kidnapped by Bheeshma for his step-brother Vichitravirya. It is surprising that in the epic 'The Mahabharat' only the cousins Kauravas and Pandavas fetched their brides themselves All the other Kuru men born before them never attended any *swayamwara*. It was Bheeshma, the eternal bachelor, who went about snatching princesses from *swayamwaras* for his step-brothers Chitrangada and Vichitravirya and step-nephews Dhritarashtra and Pandu. Amba was one such princess plucked from her *swayamwara* by Bheeshma to be married to Vichitravirya along with her two younger sisters.

The Kuru family was "a lineage that was fragile, often broken, compromised, and patched up, enfolding within its dark secrets of sexual excess and denial, and the trauma of sexual inability" (Varma 6). Bheeshma and Amba were two victims of this lineage from amongst many. In Bheeshma's case his own father's sexual lust and Dasharaja's greed for power pushed him towards life-long loneliness. The young man had to sacrifice his natural and normal right to marry and procreate because of his father Shantanu's objectionable desires. He had to forgo kingship because of Satyavati's father Dasharaja's jealousy. Bheeshma catered to the needs and demands of these two old men but with grave repercussions. The extraordinary demands of abdication and life-long celibacy from Bheeshma, the legitimate claimant to the throne, produced results that humanity regrets and rejects to this day.

Bheeshma remained the only original Kuru in spite of his father's second marriage to Satyavati. The throne of the Kuru kingdom ultimately went not to Satyavati's descendants as planned by Dasharaja but to the progeny of the five celestial gods with whom Kunti mated at her husband's instruction. A liaison based on lust brokered through an innocent person's extraordinary sacrifice brought forth heirs not just equally and fatally lusty but also short-lived. Chitrangada, Bheeshma's first step-brother, died in war childless. The second step-brother Vichitravirya married but died "eventually of sexual excess" (*Ibid.*). He had two healthy wives but their wombs remained empty. Vyas did mate with them but again produced unlucky and impotent heirs. While Pandu died cuckold, Dhritarashtra did have a hundred sons, thanks largely to the boon that Gandhari was blessed with, but none survived the great war of Kurukshetra. Bheeshma who had arranged the marriages of the four Kuru men lived to see the futility of his efforts. He remained, till his death, the only true Kuru in spite of so many marriages in that adulterous and dubious family.

The main fault of the Kuru men such as Shantanu, Vichitravirya and Pandu was that they forgot that marriage was a sacred institution and not just sensual: "The various Vedic mantras recited by the bride, the groom and other parties concerned at the vivaha ceremony reveal some of the vital social implications underlying the Hindu views and aim of vivaha. . . . The couples . . . are exhorted to strive their best to fulfill their marriage vow of not failing each other in the pursuit of dharma, artha and kama" (Prabhu 198). Shantanu, Vichitravirya and Pandu, however, got carried by sensual desires to the utter neglect of the first two duties of married couples—dharma and artha. Artha, the kingdom, already possessed. It was dharma that the Kuru clan repeatedly and habitually over-looked and paid for it dearly. Shantanu already had a worthy son from celestial woman Ganga. There was no compelling reason to wed a second time, other than lust. He was already past his prime. Old enough to take 'Sanyasa,' i.e., retire from worldly life and reside in the forests. However he went hunting and returned 'hunted' by Satyavati, a woman in the prime of her beauty, young enough to be his daughter or daughter-in-law. It seems neither Shantanu nor Satyavati had any conscience. If Shantanu was blind before 'beauty,' then Satyavati was dazzled by 'royalty'—the prospect of becoming 'queen.' Shantanu overlooked the fact that he had a virile son. With the flimsy excuse of wanting more heirs he wed Satyavati. The real compulsion was nothing more than lust. Vichitravirya, too, used matrimony to indulge in orgy. He treated his two wives not as 'mothers' of his future progeny but probably as 'harlots' to play with. No wonder he died abruptly because of perversion. Pandu inherited the malady of his step-father Vichitravirya. He was impotent. In order to somehow continue his name he told wives Kunti and Madri to cuckold him. Thus Shantanu, Vichitravirya and Pandu entered the annals of religious and literary history as great-grandfathers, grandfathers and fathers of the children of other men with whom their wives—Satyavati, Ambika, Ambalika, Kunti and Madri—willingly or unwillingly got involved.

It would have been better if Bheeshma had not contributed to this sexual pandemonium. He had vowed to be a bachelor. Hence, he should have refrained totally from matrimonial matters. On the contrary, he went on assisting and facilitating the debauchery of old, effete and impotent men—from Shantanu to Pandu. He also remained a silent spectator of Draupadi's trauma at the hands of Dushasana. In the name of 'dharma' he remained quiet and watched the spectacle.

Bheeshma, in the name of discharging family responsibility, kidnapped one princess after another from different kingdoms and shoved them towards his step-brothers and step-nephews. He sacrificed normal and healthy princesses at the altar of mentally as well as physically abnormal men such as Vichitravirya, Dhritarashtra and Pandu. Bheeshma's conduct gives rise to numerous doubts and questions.

Did Bheeshma raid palaces and *swayamwaras* to show that though he had vowed celibacy, he was strong enough to win any woman he liked? Did he derive some kind of vicarious pleasure in plucking princesses? Why did he not allow the three Kuru men to find wives themselves? Did he visit '*swayamwaras*' to keep reminding his family and people at large of his terrible vow? Did he want to subtly demoralize the other Kuru men that their 'wives' were his 'gifts' to them? Did he want to, somehow, hint that he deserved to marry such beautiful and blessed women and not them? Did he think that the so called Kurus—his step—brothers and step-nephews—got to marry such exceptional brides only because he had intervened?

Questions galore about the psyche of Bheeshma who had vowed to remain unmarried but never stayed away from the matter of marriage. He was not to have anything to do with women but strangely enough went around hunting for them. What kind of abstinence was this? Bheeshma, in fact, was never sufficiently detached or removed from women even though he was to remain above and beyond both the fair sex and the institution of marriage. If as a care-taker of the kingdom, the responsibility rested on his shoulders, why did he not adopt more decent methods of arranging the marriages of his step-brothers and step-nephews? Why did he soil his hands? He could have acted as a negotiator or as a mediator, honest and impartial. Rather he chose to act either like a martyr in the context of Shantanu and Satyavati or like a raider in the context of Amba, Ambika and Ambilika.

The women suffered enormously because of Bheeshma's interference as well as non-interference. He did not intervene where he should have, especially in the context of Draupadi and Dushasana. He intervened where he should not have, like the many marriages that he got solemnized from Satyavati's to Kunti's. Marriage is, all said and done, a very personal and serious alliance which requires, above everything else, consensus between two individuals and not coercion. Bheeshma, however, over-looked this fact. Apart from Satyavati, all the other Kuru brides were helpless before the will and power of Bheeshma's biceps.

The women had, except Satyavati, done Bheeshma no harm. He was a *brahmachari.* Yet he pursued them and pushed them in the lap of either old, abnormal or impotent men, who in turn, shoved their women towards other men, terrestrial as well as celestial. No wonder it was a woman who became instrumental in ending Bheeshma's earthly sojourn. Bheeshma was responsible for mismatched and abnormal marriages by taking the vow of celibacy. If only he had put his foot down before Shantanu and Dasaraja, several princesses would have been saved and the great bloody battle would have never taken place.

Women bore the brunt of Bheeshma's *pratigya* and the expedient ways by which he contrived the marriages of others. The *pratigya* itself was unnatural. No wonder it led to one abnormal decision after another till the Kuru clan itself was exterminated. It seems as if the collective curse of the women gobbled up the clan in which the woes of women seemed endless. The attempt to disrobe Draupadi was the last straw.

Amba was the woman who played a crucial role in Bheeshma's end. Amba and the king of Salwa were in love with each other. The king of Kasi organized a *swayamvara* for his three daughters. Salwa too was present on the occasion so as to formalize his relationship with Amba. However, Bheeshma's intervention ruined the plans of the lovers. It is not that Salwa did not try to rescue Amba from Bheeshma. Gangaputra, however, was way ahead of Salwa as a warrior. The three princesses were successfully taken away to Hastinapur. Amba disclosed her heart's desire to the Kuru family. Consequently, she was let free to marry the man of her choice while her younger sisters were wedded to Vichitravirya. Amba, full of happy hopes, proceeded to meet Salwa:

> She walked with a bride's grace up to Salwa's throne. "I am her, O king," she said for all the court to hear, "to keep the promise I almost made earlier. You are my chosen husband. See the wife who stands before you, pure and untouched as her garland of fresh flowers.
>
> Salwa roared with crude, mirthless laughter. His face twisting with rage, he said, "Do you think I feast on leftovers? I am a king. I do not touch what another man has won in battle. Go to Bheeshma. He won you when his arrow struck my eager hands on your luckless garland. He is your husband. What have you to do with me?
>
> Even when she had been kidnapped from her father's palace, Amba had not felt as orphaned as she did now. (37)

A shocked Amba returned to Hastinapur. Vichitravirya would not accept her because she had been in love with Salwa. She, then, requested Bheeshma to accept her as wife:

> She crept back, shrunken in her bridal robes, to Bheeshma's palace. She waited at the door of his bedchamber, her face wreathed in the shadows of the oncoming night.
>
> When Bheeshma had put away his armour of courtly robes, she ran in and shut the door behind her. "Take me for your wife, Bheeshma," she wept. She tore her frail veils aside. . . .
>
> Bheeshma trembled with desire, but he had spent his youth building thick walls of masculine deafness around himself. The echo that sent a tremor along his spine was, however moving, muffled. He sent Amba away, his face safely averted. (37-38)

The dejected and rejected princess remained in Hastinapur for a few years waiting for either Vichitravirya or Salwa to have a change of heart but it was all in vain. Even her second entreaty to them failed to elicit any positive response. It was obvious she was destined to remain single lifelong. She held Bheeshma responsible for this. He kidnapped her when she was on the verge of settling down with a man of her choice. It was because of Bheeshma that now she had become taboo for even her lover. He won't accept her. On the other hand, the man for whom she was kidnapped too would not have anything to do with her because she had made public her love for Raja of Salwa. Bheeshma himself refused to offer matrimonial sanctuary to her even though it was he who had kidnapped her and created the whole mess. A young, beautiful, normal princess was pushed to lifelong spinsterhood against her will. Her bitterness and rage had no end. She held Bheeshma responsible and wanted to, somehow, teach the warrior a lesson:

> The young princess had lived several lifetimes in a week or two. She cast aside her finery, the trappings of a life denied to her, and set out for the forest, a new hardness in her heart. She no longer thought of silks, thrones, flowers, children, she had thrown away her woman's lot when Bheeshma scorned her offering. Now she was a woman only in name.
>
> Lost in her insatiable desire for revenge, Amba spent long years in the forest, with her hatred as a faithful companion.
>
> When she had, with superhuman energy, piled penance on penance; . . . Amba stood ready to meet Shiva, a garland of thick-skinned, flesh coloured nagalinga pushpa in her hands.
>
> Shiva saw the desire leap into her eyes; he knew what she strained towards. He took the garland from her, gently . . . and promised Amba her revenge. Whoever wears this garland will surely kill Bheeshma, he said. (38-39)

Blessed with the garland of *Shiva*, the injured woman approached many kings to wreck revenge on Bheeshma on her behalf but all declined. What she was looking for was just a man and a Kshatriya to challenge the Kuru. However the fear of Bheeshma was widespread. No royal warrior dared to invite the wrath of Ganga's son in spite of Amba's entreaties and Shiva's floral armour.

After the refusal of the royals, Amba hung the garland on the palace gates of *King Drupada*. She then took the refuge of the forests. The ascetics there advised her to seek the help of *Parasurama*, the eternal enemy of the Kshatriyas. Amba's poignant story moved him and he challenged the mighty Bheeshma but how could *Goddess Ganga's* son be defeated? The fight ended inconclusively. Amba again returned to the forests. She "practised rigorous austerities. . . . Siva appeared before her and granted her a boon, that in her next birth she will slay Bhishma" (Rajagopalachari 16). Amba wanted nothing more and saw no reason to live any longer. "She made a pyre and plunged into the fire—pouring out the flame in her heart into the scarcely hotter blaze of the pyre" (*Ibid.*).

Born as Drupada's daughter, Amba saw the fresh garland hanging on the palace gates. Her destiny motivated her to wear it around her neck. Drupada got petrified by his child's audacity. He packed her off to the forests least the Kurus got wind of her intentions. Years of meditations transformed her into Shikhandi—the man born to be Bheeshma's nemesis. It was this revengeful young fellow who became the charioteer of Arjun on the tenth day of the great war. Both the warrior and the charioteer cornered Bheeshma. When Shikhandi came into picture, the elder Kuru realized that his last days have come. Hence, he did not retaliate and fell on the bed of arrows created for him by Arjun. This was how the wounded and wronged woman Amba took her revenge from Bheeshma—the man who had shattered her dreams and pushed her towards a life without home, hearth, husband and children.

The 'Amba myth,' quoted, by Pati in *The Thousand Faces of Night* raises certain, hitherto, incommunicable realities about her and all the other women in Indian society concerning their rights and status. Bheeshma's rash act did harm Amba gravely. Thereafter she became an untouchable for all royal men. She was a normal woman who wanted to marry and settle down. She was in love with Salwa. However, Bheeshma's adventures on the behalf of step-brother Vichitravirya ruined her life. Unwillingly she had to remain single. She was compelled to become an ascetic.

The Kuru kingdom and indeed all the other kingdoms were being governed, ostensibly, in the name of *dharma*. Why was justice then denied to her? Why did not Bheeshma feel guilty of ruining a woman's life? Did he consider himself above *dharma?* Why were fingers not raised at him? Why did he take women for granted? Why did Amba's cries fall on deaf ears? Did women have no right and status before the powerful men? Were women mere 'commodities' to be possessed or abducted, purchased, rejected or pawned at will? Why did not Amba's own family support her crusade for justice? Why was she left to roam around like a vagabond? Was her family also scared of Bheeshma to stand in support of their daughter? Last but not the least, why were Ambika and Ambilika or even Satyavati silent towards Amba's suffering? Why didn't they do anything for the hurt and humiliated woman? Did the women have no power, no role other than dancing to the tunes of the men?

Ostensibly, the Kshatriyas refused to challenge Bheeshma because he was too powerful. However it seems they considered a woman's injured pride too small an issue for men to fight amongst themselves. Was Amba's hurt feeling too unimportant to take cognizance? Did Amba's anger and protests against injustice made her loathsome? Did the men dislike Amba for highlighting the fate that had been heaped on her for no fault of hers?

> Men have let them down all through their lives, yet it will always be to men that they'll turn for protection, and for guidance.
>
> Such stubbornness. Such sorrow. Such shame. (Pande 159)

The Kuru men and their associates, however, suffered immensely for their negligence. Amba, Gandhari, Kunti, Draupadi, and all the other women had the satisfaction of seeing their different tormentors breathe their last in the war of Kurukshetra. Either they themselves, like Amba, or their sympathizers, like Bhima in the context of Draupadi, punished the guilty. The saving grace of these women was not that they were vindicated. Rather their triumph lay in their will to survive and persevere in spite of relentless struggle and commotion. A clan that had made women suffer so much did not finally survive. All except the Pandavas, perished in the great battle.

The Pandavas lived and ruled not because they were merely brave. They tasted success because they did not allow masculinity and male chauvinism to overpower them. Kunti, the mother, and later Draupadi, their wife, stayed all along with the five brothers not as shadowy figures like the wives of the Kurus but as important and indispensable part of the Pandava faction. In fact the war between Kauravas and Pandavas was actually the clash of patriarchy with matriarchy. The Kauravas had the support of the majority of the men up in arms against the sons of Kunti and their supporters. Pandu was long since dead. Consequently his sons were also known as Kunti Putra. The battle of Kurukshetra was actually the fight of a widow and her sons whose share of ancestral property was gobbled up by the other men of the large family. The victory of Pandavas was the victory of matriarchy over patriarchy and male chauvinism. Duryodhana rarely listened to women. Yudhistra, on the other hand, always had his mother's wise counsel to bank upon. Later Draupadi assumed that mantle. The Kauravas, on the other hand, basked in masculine pride and cunning personified by Shakuni but paid for it heavily.

It should be noticed, however, that the Kauravas, in spite of being painted culprits, transgressed warfare rules less. "The Kurukshetra war of the Mahabharata is generally believed to be a war between justice and injustice. The Kaurava side of Duryodhana is unjust and the Pandava side of Yudhisthira is just . . . but the question remains how to determine justice and injustice, who should be the judge" (Web 50-52). A stark reality is that, at least, during the Kurukshetra confrontation "violation of all rules of war were perpetrated by the Pandavas, not the Kauravas! . . . here are many instances of Pandava's satanic cruelty" (51).

The role of Lord Krishna too is not infallible. It is alleged that he acted less like a god and more like a politician. He instigated the fratricidal war for the sake of *dharma* or justice only ostensibly. The real motive was to settle scores with the Brahmins who would not accept the ascendancy of Krishna, a non-Aryan and a non-Brahmin, in the matters of *dharma* and *karma.* However

Krishna's supporters counter that the blue god intervened for the sake of establishing political unity in Bharatvarsa. The smaller kingdoms, in a constant state of battle with each other, were to be destroyed so as to pave way for a big nation ruled by the single authority of the Pandavas. Krishna's detractors again point out that the "killing of Kansa by Krishna was not inspired by any noble objective" (53). In fact it was the result of property dispute between nephew and maternal uncle. "Krishna was not a prince like Rama. His father was an official in the royal court. He was the nephew of Kansa, the king of Mathura" (53). Krishna was an expert manipulator who outwitted not only his maternal uncle Kansa but all his other detractors including the Kauravas.

In some way or the other even the Pandavas are guilty of running amok. It is not just the Kauravas but also the Pandavas who have behaved expediently as far as *dharma* or ethics are concerned. Why, then, did the Pandavas win? Why were they ultimately better off than their cousins? Why Krishna, in spite of indulging in conspiracy and deceit, enter the annals of religious history as a god? Why is he considered an incarnation of Vishnu who is one of the divine trinity of Hindu religion? The reasons are not difficult to discover and they are all related to women.

In their dealings with the feminine gender both Krishna and the five brothers were better than the Kauravas. Neither the flute god nor his devotees ignored or brushed aside the pain, problem or opinion of the women. This is not to say that their conduct was above reproach. Yet it is also true that in an era when "even the small children" understood "that women are inferior and subordinate, dependent on men," (59) the Pandavas and their mentor Krishna were surprisingly very accommodative towards the fair sex. Kunti, Draupadi, Radha, Rukmini enjoyed prominence and power whereas the Kaurava women were invisible entities having little 'presence' or 'say.' The Pandava faction took due cognizance of their women and tried to atone for mistakes that they committed towards the fair sex. They fought as much for their share of power as for women's happiness and dignity. Krishna rose to Draupadi's rescue in the Kaurava court. The Pandava brothers did not allow their mother's lifelong struggle to go waste. Bhim killed Dushasana most savagely to avenge Draupadi's humiliation in the Kaurava's court. Yudhisthira did stake his brothers and his wife in the game of dice with cousin Duryodhana. However, he redeemed himself in his queen's eye by saving his brothers from the water Yaksha. He answered all the queries of the Yaksha aptly thereby reviving his brothers and regaining the respect that he had lost in Draupadi's eyes because of the dice episode. The Pandavas, thus, had more than just male prowess to upstage the Kauravas. They had the backing of women's blessings. They won because they fought not just for themselves but also for the grace of the feminine gender.

The Pandavas respected the fair sex more than the Kauravas and had a conscience to admit as well as atone for mistakes. They offered sanctuary to Amba reborn as Shikhandi. They gave Shikhandi the opportunity to settle scores with Bheeshma. Arjun was capable enough to seal the fate of his great grandfather. Yet the Pandavas and Lord Krishna allowed Shikhandi to take the credit of removing Bheeshma from the battlefield. Amba's soul could finally heave a sigh of relief after the Pandavas gave her a platform to confront Bheeshma and punish him as best as she could. They had witnessed the struggle and trauma of Kunti and Draupadi. They understood well the pain, problem and helplessness of womenfolk. They were receptive to the beauty as well as vulnerability of the feminine folks. Hence, they did as much as they could to come to the rescue of women in need of 'help' or 'acceptance.'

Shikhandi, in fact, had two reasons to take umbrage. He was not just Amba re-born. He was also Draupadi's elder brother. When his younger sister was being disrobed in the Kaurava court, Bheeshma had remained a passive spectator doing nothing to stop the outrage. Strangely, all through his life Bheeshma kept siding with Kauravas when he could have easily brought them to book. What is the use of an elder who does not put the weight of his or her seniority against even the most objectionable of acts? It is surprising that right under the nose of such a righteous personality as Bheeshma, the hundred sons of Dhritarashtra grew so venomous that they were not willing to spare even the family daughter-in-law Draupadi. Duryodhana was inimical towards the Pandavas since childhood. Why did not the seniors like Bheeshma nip the animosity in the bud itself? Why had Kunti to struggle so much to save her sons? Were the senior Kuru men also jealous of Kunti and her children? Krishna realized well the need to punish people like Bheeshma. Hence, he exhorted Arjun not to hesitate before the elderly Kuru and allowed Shikhandi to become the charioteer on the fateful day of the battle.

Devi's grandmother, thus, narrated the myth of Amba to highlight the survival instinct of the womenfolk, their zeal to somehow salvage themselves from crisis and chaos. She wanted Devi to understand that if women were weak physically, then God compensated for it by gifting them an indomitable spirit. The courage and will to subdue circumstances always lie in a woman's heart. She only has to listen to her inner voice and never waiver from her stand. Amba, Kunti, Draupadi all stood firm for what they believed in. They contributed a great deal in ending a clan in which women had suffered endlessly. Women, as symbols of *dharma*, were much abused by the Kuru clan. It was *dharma* that ultimately triumphed. Yudhisthira the "human manifestation of Dharma" (Zimmer 62), the son of Yama, the law-giver, was crowned king after the Kurukshetra war.

Real life cousin Uma and mythic woman Amba made a chilling impact on Devi's mind. She got terrified by the ugly realities of a woman's life—the stories of denial and perversion. Hitherto, she had encountered either Nala, Dhritarashtra or the snake husband in the myths of Pati. In real life she saw her father Mahadevan, men who were human as well as humane. However the story of Uma and Amba introduced Devi to the presence of such lechers as Uma's husband and father-in-law or a man like Bheeshma whose self-righteousness bordered on insensitivity and cruelty. Devi was scared to her bones:

> I was terrified by Uma's marriage, but I was also terrified by the vengeful Amba.
>
> Amba's story, or maybe it was Uma's, made a deep impression on me, like an irresistible horror film, and I day—dreamed more and more about female avengers. (40)

Amba's myth was the last that granny narrated to Devi. Her motive was not to alarm Devi. Rather Pati's intention was to educate her about the good as well as grim realities and possibilities of life. Men and marriages can be good as well as bad. A woman must be able to make the most of them. From Nala to Bheeshma; from Devi's father to Uma's father-in-law. Unlimited possibilities and immense challenges, unpredictable and unforeseen. Divine as well as damnable. Pati's repertoire of myths and life's true stories presented both the 'sacrosanct' and the 'sacrilegious' to Devi:

> My grandmother's stories were no ordinary bedtime stories. She chose each for a particular occasion. . . . She had an answer for every question. But her answers were not simple: they had to be decoded. A comparison had to be made, an illustration discovered, and a moral drawn out. (27)

Devi, the little girl, understood the explicit and implicit morals of the myths less and got scared more. They added little to her maturity and more to her anxiety. Her own father was very different from the men described in the myths. She found it difficult to reconcile to the idea of predators like Uma's father-in-law or indifferent and imperious men like Bheeshma. Devi shuddered to accept that men could go to such extents to torment women and women could go to these extremes to seek revenge. She had been a witness to an apparently decent relationship between her parents but Pati revealed to her another world in which the two opposite genders could be each other's worst enemy with the scale tilted more in favour of the men than women.

Bewildered as only a child can be, Devi could not visualize normal relationship between men and women. Pati's stories led her to look upon the two genders as two warriors or rivals in a state of constant combat. The men were always 'victimisers' and the women 'victims' turned avengers who combined in themselves the 'power' and 'purpose' of both Kali and Atlanta.

Deeply affected by the trauma of women about whom she had heard from Pati, Devi began to fantasize herself as a female phantom or Robin Hood who would rescue women from the clutches of evil men: "I lived a secret life of my own: I became a woman warrior, a heroine. I was Devi. I rode a tiger, and cut off evil, magical demons' head" (41).

Devi, the teenaged girl, retreated into a fantasy world wherein she translated her cherished desire to vanquish all the tormentors of the womenfolk. She could not travel back to the mythical era where extraordinary women warriors or goddesses fended off demons with ten hands. Nor could she possibly run away to a forest, meditate and win boons of power so as to teach culprits a lesson. She, instead, used her imaginative faculty to transform herself into a Durga-like figure. It is worth noting in this context that in mythic literature or history, female demons are invariably eliminated by male gods and male monsters are killed by female deities. The female demon Putana, who had come to nurse Krishna to death with her poisonous milk, was sucked to death by the baby god. The male demons Shumbha and Nishumbha, on the other hand, were put to death by Durga. These instances are only two of the many in mythology in which the divine and powerful of the two genders taught a lesson to the notorious of the opposite.

In *Durga Saptashati* Parvati, wife of Lord Shiva, undergoes ten incarnations to kill demons who are all males. In fact, it is the gods themselves who set Parvati on this mission. Outwitted completely by the demon duo, the gods realize that only a 'female' power can beat the devils at their own game and in their own den. In *The Thousand Faces of Night* it is not the gods but Devi who transforms herself imaginatively into her namesake of the myths. However, unlike Goddess Durga who was baptized by the gods, Devi is toned and trained by a female deity—the 'mountain' goddess:

> She was a mountainous woman, beautiful, but with the strong limbs of an ox. She led me to her mountain retreat. . . . She said: 'Will you take me for your mentor'? I bowed low to touch her feet. She raised me up and said, 'Good, we will begin tomorrow.
>
> . . . My pile of weapons grew as the years went by, and my body grew rapidly also, in spite of our meagre hermit's diet. She gave me a magic vest covered with little mirrors and told me, 'Now, my faithful disciple, you are ready for your battles with men. Put on the vest only if your other weapons fail you.' (41-2)

Fully trained and armed to the hilt, Devi bid adieu to her patron and marched ahead to meet her enemies, that is, those men who make life difficult for women and girls and are absolutely impertinent about it:

> I met my first enemy the very same day after I slipped down a long, golden rope that fell down to the earth. . . .
>
> A fat, greedy man, who kept innocent village girls imprisoned in his harem. . . . One lash with my faithful chain of iron and spear—like spikes, and his head rolled to the ground in front of me, spluttering with bloody agony. (42)

Devi's fame traveled fast. Men, helpless before her power and unwavering sense of justice, changed tactics. They tried the old dictum "if you can't beat them, join them" with her but to no avail. They tried to bribe her, tantalize her with offers of post and position but the superwoman was above such greed. She possessed not only extraordinary level of physical strength but also wisdom to match. Like Mahishasur Mardini, she punished the men for their temerity of making to her proposals as well as propositions:

> I became famous, a woman more sought after than the loveliest of half-naked, full-breasted nymphs. Men who dared come up to my ear whispered about each other.
>
> 'Join us,' some said, 'we will be your loyal warriors, we will anoint you Queen.'
>
> But my heart, crystal pure as the spring that flowed by the giantess' hut, spurned these fawning offers. (43)

The impious men in the context of Devi and the demons in the context of Goddess Durga committed the folly of seeing them as 'women.' Shumbha and Nishumbha had defeated the gods and captured paradise. This emboldened them to consider themselves eligible for the Divine Mother herself. How could Goddess Durga ignore such audacity? She knew well their offensive and overbearing pride. She knew too that they would foolishly make a proposal for her hand without realizing that a bait has been laid for them. She punished them soundly for their haughtiness, for their arrogance and for their foolishness.

Devi's pursuers met a similar fate. Their 'little' minds lacked the capacity to comprehend that what stood before them was no ordinary woman with ordinary feminine weaknesses. Rather she was divinity incarnate gifted with rare spark and sparkle that only an extraordinary man, equally valiant and virtuous could match. Devi soon met such an eligible youth. He was to her what Lord Shiv was to Goddess Parvati: "He was young, but wise with his years of seclusion in the mountains, and on seeing my craggy, wind-beaten face, he fell on his knees and called me his goddess" (43).

Thus, even while relapsing into an imaginative world wherein Devi was an incarnation of Hindu goddess Durga and Greek goddess Atlanta, she was not immune to a normal woman's desire of home, husband and children. Even goddess Parvati married Lord Shiva and Devi married the "mountain youth." This proves that neither extraordinary nor ordinary women are against the male gender as such. They know the difference between the wheat and the chaff. Even goddesses aspire for home, husband and hearth. They do not deny or ignore their nature ordained roles of mother and home-maker. What they strongly resent, however, is the victimization of women and of even hapless men by men and women of crooked and cruel nature. While the female goddesses punish the 'bad' they respect and care for the 'good.' Devi's inclusion of matrimony, husband and children in her fantasy shows that even though she had got scared by Pati's myths and Uma's experiences, she had not given-up hope all together as far as men and marriage was concerned. She still believed, even in the subconscious state, that virtuous and worthy men did exist in the world after all and that a 'good' marriage and a 'happy' family life too was possible.

Devi, thus, in her 'Durga' avatar, does not seem to make sweeping observations about men. She is not allergic to the institution of marriage and the responsibilities of motherhood either. Far from considering these as burdensome, she finds a sense of contentment and completeness in them. Her rage against the 'bad' does not make her blind to the 'good.' She does not desist from tying the nuptial knot with a compatible man worthy of the honour. To be brave and powerful is one thing. Wisdom and judiciousness quite another. Luckily the warrior woman shows herself to be in of possess both. Devi combines in herself both the conventional and the unconventional. She is unconventional in the sense that she is exceptionally strong, mentally as well as physically. She uses her energies to bring to book the dubious. She takes to task the tormentors of women. On the other hand, she is conventional in that she does not deny herself either matrimony or motherhood in spite of being a goddess. She seems to believe firmly in the *shastras* that ordain that all women must get purified by marriage rites:

> There is a story in the Mahabharata of a lady who remained single because she could not find her equal to marry; she then devoted her life to the practice of hard penance till old age with a view to obtaining moksha. But the sage Narada rebuked her for remaining unmarried; he told her that it was impossible for her to gain the ultimate bliss as long as she was not sanctified (asmaskrita) by marriage rites. (Prabhu 150)

Thus, the warrior woman shows that raising one's voice and hand against atrocities does not imply that a woman deny herself the peace and contentment of domesticity. Even goddesses want a home, hearth, husband and children. Given a chance, even the most ferocious of female fighters do not fail in creating a happy home caring for husband and children and getting cared for in return.

The superwoman would have remained lost in domestic bliss had not her own daughter's plight reminded her about her 'weapons' and her 'objective' in life: "When my youngest daughter . . . came back to us, limping, broken, a rag doll mauled by a careless hand" (43). The father rose to avenge the injury inflicted on his daughter but Devi restrained him. The culprit had dared to offend none other than daughter of Durga's avtaar. Hence it would be she who would go to punish the culprit:

> My husband looks up his hunting spear and his iron rod, but I held him back. I had to pay back the mentor of my youth; appease her with my cupped hands, full of my blood.
>
> I met my enemy, an iron—like villain who flexed his muscles and bared even, sharp teeth as he laughed in wild defiance.
>
> We fought for days on the arid plain. . . . I fought like a lioness that had just escaped long years of captivity. (44)

The youngest daughter's trauma showed chinks in the grooming techniques of Devi. As a mother she had failed to groom her daughter in a manner that no one would be able to take advantage of her least of them the men. Unlike the mountain goddess, who had taken Devi under her wings and turned her into a formidable woman, Devi, as a mother, had made her daughter neither strong nor wise to fend off philanderers and paedophiles. The armours that she had stitched for her children were not as impenetrable as she had imagined. Hence, it was she who decided to go and set things right. Her 'motherhood' had been challenged. Her invincibility was at stake. The time had come for her to remind the malevolent men once again about her 'existence' and 'power.' Her anger was implacable as she descended to teach the villain a lesson. Goodness must also possess fangs to survive and subdue evil. This probably was the truth that Devi did not tell her daughter. Goodness must be indefatigable in its clash with malignity. This was the lesson that Devi recalled. She went ahead to remind the devil who she was, what she could do and most importantly that she still existed. Neither her daughter nor any other woman needs cry helplessly. She was there to wipe their tears and give them the satisfaction of seeing their tormentors punished:

> I shot my fine arrows of invisible speed; I flung my trusty discus; I heaved the blood-splattered club at his thick, curly head. . . . As the life choked out of me in big gasping sobs, I aimed for his neck, and cut off his head in one quick, arrow-like movement. (44-45)

The battle that Devi waged with the enemy of her daughter is reminiscent of the battle royal that took place between Bhagavati Durga and Mahishasur in *Durga Saptshati*. In the religious epic, Goddess Durga was requested by an assembly of gods, led by Indra, to vanquish the demon duo Shumbha and Nishumbha, who had forcibly captured Indralok, the abode of the celestials. The gods, together with the Divine Trinity of Brahma, Vishnu and Mahesh, donated their weapons to the Goddess, who was actually Parvati, for the purpose. Adorned with jewellery and armed to the hilt, the Goddess lured the demon brothers into the battlefield. Driven crazy with the desire to capture and wed this exquisitely beautiful woman, Shumbha and Nishumbha first sent an emissary to the Divine Mother. The quietly amused Goddess sent the emissary back to the demon king's court with mock politeness and veiled challenge. Offended by the Goddess' intrepidity, the devil royals gave marching orders to their army of bizarre soldiers so as to tame the defiant woman. The Divine Mother and her loyal lion wiped them in no time. Finally on the eighth and ninth day, the demon kings themselves descended on the battlefield. First the younger brother was eliminated. Thereafter the elder brother Shumbha. In the course of the duel with the Goddess, Shumbha changed his physical form. He transformed himself into man and animal alternatively. The most famous of these transformations was into a buffalo. However the goddess, with much superior power put the mad animal to sword thereby ending finally the tyrannical reign of Shumbha and Nishumbha in *devalok* as well as *manavlok*.

In the context of Devi, her battered and bruised daughter becomes almost a metaphor for Indralok /devalok. Shumbha and Nishumbha are the devil who give pain to her daughter. She herself is the Mother Divine, the wife of Shiva, who teaches the guilty a final lesson that puts an end to the existence of evil. The kingdom is restored to health and happiness.

It is to be noted that the Durga tales were not narrated by Pati. The myths that she selected were primarily from the epic 'Mahabharata.' Yet in her hallucination Devi alludes to the nine-day battle between Durga and Mahishasur. There is an uncanny resemblance between the female warrior conjured by Devi and the myth of Shiva, Parvati and Mahishasur. This suggests that Pati may have narrated many more myths to Devi other than those included in the narrative or Devi might have got to know about Goddess Durga through her father. It is to be noted that in the novel, Sita, that is Devi's mother, is shown rebuking Anna for pushing the girl towards an illusionary world by gifting her with "picture books . . . fairy stories of gods and goddesses" (45). Thus the grandmother was not the only one to introduce Devi to the fascinating myths and legends. It seems the motive of Anna was not only to nourish Devi's mental faculties but also to acquaint her with cultural narratives that is the bedrock of Indian society's notion of 'do's' and 'don'ts.' He did not believe in depriving the child from recreational activities. At the time same he seemed eager to tell her about her religion and culture in an easy and interesting manner. He seemed to disapprove of Sita's too much of emphasis on "the mundane, literal world" that left little scope for "noble life of the gods" (45).

The lives of the goddesses were never easy. Parvati managed to marry Shiva after years of gruelling meditation in the mountains. Sita's kidnapping, the purity test of fire and the banishment to the forests again shows that her life was in some ways tougher than even Lord Ram's. Savitri remained single for years before she could find a mate. Even after marriage she spent a torturous year fearing for her husband's life and had to confront and convince Yama himself, the god of death, to regain her conjugal bliss. The lives of the *panchakanyas*, that is, the famous five iconic heroines of Hindu mythology—Ahilaya, Tara, Mandodari, Kunti and Draupadi—are nothing but stories of horrifying trails. Similarly, Saraswati, the third of the female trinity of mother goddesses, had to put up with her own father Brahma's incestuousness. Brahma created Saraswati and he forced her to marry him. Saraswati led a restless and unhappy life frequently running away from Brahma and disobeying him. In other words, rarely did the goddesses have a 'happy' or 'normal' life even if they were wedded to equally divine or powerful gods and sages. The trails and travails of these divine women too were almost unending. The only difference between these 'mythical' ladies and 'real' women is that while the struggles of the formal is recorded in religious history, the mortal women's pain and problem remain unheard. While these mythic women have undergone apotheosis so as to honour their efforts, the ordinary or mortal women live and die unsung.

The question arises as to why even goddesses can't be happy? Are they 'goddesses' precisely because they put up with unsurmountable challenges to their 'being'? Were the goddesses too at the receiving end of male gods' whim? Moreover why are ordinary women expected to worship and emulate such unhappy goddesses whose struggles are unending and value systems are too exacting?: "To mediate upon the various forms that the Goddess takes, is to enter a precarious and ambiguous cycle of moral and intellectual nomadism; a world without a fixed address, full of stars and star—turds, shiftings and migrations, in short, a land of visions, hallucinations, fear, laughter, and of course, tales" (Pande 17).

Is it some kind of an indoctrination that women undergo in the name of religion, tradition, myth, legend, ritual and worship? Are ordinary women to draw solace from the fact that even goddesses were not spared and hence whatever happens to them is justified? Or is there indeed a genuine feeling of remembering and respecting the extraordinary struggle the divine women put up with and triumphed on moral grounds? Is their courage, their suffering and their amazing sense of benevolence really being applauded? Are their stories constantly recalled so that women and even men learn lessons? Or are they simply "strategies of containment?" (Khan 18). Interpretations and implications galore: "A virtual ocean of such Devi tales surges around us; always full of random movement and mobile shadows. Much like the Goddess herself. It is entirely possible that as one longs to grab for one constant meaning, the tales shall move on, suddenly scattering the fragmented incidents like so many pieces of a broken mirror; or star-turds" (Pande 13-14).

As Devi turned sixteen, Pati became almost bed-ridden. Incapable of telling anymore myths and legends to the adolescent girl. The girl herself had grown weary of granny. Her mother's constant complains, that, Mahadevan's picture books and Pati's "feeble-minded stories of gods and goddesses" (45) were turning the girl surrealistic, seems to have triggered the detachment. It could also be a teenager's impatience with dictum and decorum. Anyhow the old rapport between grand-daughter and grandmother was now missing. The well of stories had dried up, so too the grandchild's love for the old woman. Pati, however, continued to love and long for her only grandchild till the end. It is to be noted that Pati was one of those rare old women who did not grudge having a granddaughter as 'heir' rather than a grandson. She never taunted or tortured Sita for not giving a male heir. She never resented Devi's presence. In fact, not only was she a supportive and sensitive mother-in-law but also a loving grandmother who cared little about the gender of her grandchild. Even though she was bed-ridden at the fag end of her life, she did not lose interest in her son's only heir—Devi. She saw beautiful dreams about her granddaughter and was anxious that she have a safe and secure future. She wanted Devi to imbibe the 'right' cultural values that she tried to elucidate and explain through myths. Till the last breath of her life she remained concerned about Devi.

Pati's death signaled the end of a phase of Devi's life that was never to return. Her world was never to be the same again. Devi's childhood was over. The time of fun and fabulous stories was to be a thing of the past. Little did Devi realize that Pati's death symbolized the end of some of the most joyous years of her life. Pati's death was the beginning of a chain of events that left a deep and dark impact on her family. Within a few years her father died. While she was sent away to America to pursue higher studies, her parents had proceeded to Africa for five years. Devi did not see her father alive again. He died of a heart—attack in his study bent over a paper he was preparing on African folklore and legend. This was the final lid on Devi's childhood, on her voyage to the marvelous and miraculous world of wild and weird myths and legends. Devi's guardianship went to her mother Sita who had little patience for illusionary tales about gods, goddesses, princes, princesses, kings and queens:

> Sita hated an illusion, however tantalizing a form it assumed. . . . Now the goddess she worshipped was no Veena—toting Sarasvati, all feminity and ambiguity; her god rode the most practical, the most tangible (and hence most ferocious) of chargers. (105)

It is not that Sita resented merely religious and royal stories. She was equally allergic to even 'human' stories, of past and present. In other words, she hated nostalgia either 'mythic' or 'real.' She did not like travelling back in time. She was all focused on the future. Past was a liability for her and the future a 'priority' for which she planned meticulously and often mercilessly and worked persistently. She told Devi not to get lost in the memories of her American sojourn. She showed little interest in the kind of life Devi led there. She was not at all inquisitive: "I had begun to tell her about America. She smiled gently and said, 'All that is over now. The important thing is that you are back, you are now in Madras. Why go over an old story again?'" (13)

At that time Devi had felt relieved that her mother respected her privacy or her right to reserve some facts; that she could "have some secrets" (13) of her own. However, it was only later that Devi realized that it was a calculated move. She did not want to probe too much and revive memories of America. She did not want to, in any way, encourage Devi's mental relapse into a world she had no intention to send her daughter back. She did not want Devi to be nostalgic, i.e., to have pangs of separation least she clamoured to return back to the life she might have begun to like. She was hastily eager to wipe America out of Devi's memory and plant in "grandmother stories of predestined husbands and idyllic marriages" (16). Devi was back to square one. The gods and goddesses, traditions and rituals that Devi had forgotten due to the deaths of Pati and Anna and because of Sita's pragmatism and abnormal fetish for 'planning,' came rushing back into her life.

Initially Sita had "banished all gods and goddesses to their rightful place, the little room with a chain of bright coloured bulbs that lit out all their mystery and seduction" (105) least Devi and Mahadevan got lost in "lying dreams of blood, paradisiacal palaces and women turning into men" (106). She had higher, more practical and tangible dreams for her husband and daughter. She took her husband Mahadevan "by the hand and led him from promotion to promotion" (104) till he won a prestigious overseas assignment in Africa. For daughter Devi too she was no less ambitious. The girl was held on a tight leash till she too was awarded with "a suitcase of gleaming certificates, an air ticket and a non-stop plane ride to a continent just distant enough: America" (106).

However Sita's task was not easy. Her reign did not always run a smooth course. There were little challenges in plenty. Both Devi and Mahadevan had grown into the sly, shifty-eyed accomplices of a mutiny that threatened to erupt through books, day—dreams, gods and goddesses, secret corners, the innocent (and therefore more dangerous) sensuality of a stranger like Annapurna. The wise, mature and shrewd strategist "quelled these phantoms of rebellion with master-strokes" (105) till her planning turned into concrete reality.

Sita's detachment from her past was clinical. Once when her

father-in-law cornered her about her duties as a wife and daughter-in-law, she broke the veena wires with vengeance and resolve. She did not visit her guru, parents or parental town least they reminded her about "a foolish young girl's dreams of genius and fame" (103). Wifehood and motherhood were to be the only two motives of her life. If as an artist her skill was exceptional, then as a housewife and mother too, she decided to become perfect—aiding and abetting the social, economic, official and academic interests of the husband and daughter duo with much planning and precision. Her exactitude left little scope for the 'unseen' and 'unforeseen.' The mind was not to get lost in 'delusions' and 'illusions' but concentrate strictly on the 'probable' and 'practical.'

Sita saw to it that neither her *dreamer* husband nor their secretive daughter got overwhelmed by "lying dreams of blood, paradisiacal palaces and women turning into men" (106). Hence she "banished all the gods and goddesses to their rightful place" (105). She also "sent away Annapurna, well—provided, her fascination blunted by her gratitude. Then she swept out dark corners, quiet afternoons, mystical books" (106), where Mahadevan and Devi had developed the habit of getting lost into.

Sita's assumption was that "the wholesome rays of a scientific, antiseptic" American experience will purge Devi's mind of "the darker monsters of the Brahmin World—the gods, the ambiguous myth" (106) that threatened to turn her into an emotional person content with feeling rather than hanker for 'concrete' achievements. She thought that Mahadevan too would forget the innocence of Annapurna in wide and wild Africa. She did achieve these targets but not without serious setbacks. Her husband did forget the naïve Annapurna only to get lost, fatally, in the weird tales of the dark continent. He died of a heart attack while preparing an essay on African folklore. Places changed but Mahadevan's love for cultural narratives remained. Sita, thus, could not completely kill his imaginative voyeurism.

The daughter, however, proved to be more pliable. Sita pulled the strings at will and Devi danced accordingly. Initially she resented Devi's proclivity for myths because she considered them purely recreational and regressive and therefore an impediment in the way of concrete achievements like academic excellence. However now that Devi was adequately accomplished, Sita slowly revived childhood memories. She waved the magic wand of maternal love to conjure up Pati's descriptions of *swayamwaras*, princesses and princes so as to mentally prepare Devi to co-operate in marriage negotiations:

> With the same eloquent hand, my mother prepared me for my swayamvara. When I was adept at wearing the right jewels and sari, the right smile; when I made the naïve and therefore innocent small talk suitable for a marriageable girl among her elders; she fed and stroked the rapidly returning memories of my grand-mother's stories of predestined husbands and idyllic marriages. (16)

Thus, Devi's mother first pushed her daughter away from the world of myths and legends that are full of traditional rules, regulations, codes of conduct and decorum lest they hampered Devi's growth in a world that values concrete achievements necessary for garnering financial and social benefits. Sita was scared that outdated ideas would turn Devi into an inhibited, dreamy girl with little grip on reality and scarce ability to compete with her contemporaries.

However when Devi was equipped with an impressive resume which included an American degree, Sita quickly set about encashing it in the marriage market so that she and her daughter did not become rootless in their own family, caste, society and country. The girl must come back to the roots and flower and flourish in the native soil. The blossoms must be visible to all. Devi must become a balanced and enviable combination of modernity and tradition, at ease with both. This was Sita's scheme and this was what she wanted to prove to the world. Her daughter was not an escapist emigrant rootless abroad nor was she uncomfortable at home without cultural moorings like an arranged marriage:

> With her mother's wisdom, Amma proved to them that she had not

> made a mistake in sending a young unmarried girl to America. "Your daughter will be lost to you, Sita"—they had shaken their heads and followed up their prediction with illustrative stories of boys and girls who never came back, married Americans, and forgot their ageing parents in India.
>
> See how I take risks, Amma's look said. She is different, she is special, but is just as pliant as your home-grown daughters. (14)

A modern day *swayamwara* commenced. Horoscopes were sought by Sita. Devi was transformed from a hip-hugging jeans clad girl to a sari-wrapped comely young woman polite and pleasant in bearing. Meetings were arranged with prospective grooms and their parents. After four or six such get-togethers, the dice was cast in favour of an executive working in a multinational company. His name was Mahesh and he lived in Bangalore. He seemed to possess probity. He was far more to the point than all the other young men or their parents whom had Devi met. Few of the boys seemed more interested in flirting with her than in wedding her. Mahesh, however, was different: "If I was going to play out a travesty of the myths that had filled my childhood, I would tear aside all pretence. I thought, I would be as matter-of-fact as Mahesh" (23).

Things turned out as Sita had planned. Devi was a dough of wet clay in the hands of her mother. A mother's "magnetic charm" of maternal love acted like magic and Devi played along. Sita banished or summoned the mythic world at will to get assistance in her schemes of 'arranging' Devi's life. First her education. Then her marriage. It never occurred to Sita that for a highly educated girl like Devi, career first would be better. A job first so that she would have something to fall back upon least things turned sour with husband and in-laws. Even if marriage proved to be a happy experience, a highly educated girl like Devi may get frustrated sitting at home all the time. It might be better if she was employed somewhere so as to break the monotony of a housewife's life. Devi might feel better thus. Her earnings might make her life and the life of her husband easier and that of their progeny secure.

These ideas never occurred to Sita. She simply seemed to be obsessed with Devi's marriage.

It is not that Devi was already too old and hence arranging her marriage was urgently necessary. Or was Sita genuinely eager to celebrate her daughter's marriage like all normal men and women who love to see their children wedded? The desire to see children settled professionally as well as in matrimony is natural to all parents. Devi, however, somehow did not feel this was the case with her mother. When her marriage fell apart, she looked back at her childhood and early youth only to feel that somehow her mother too was at fault for the fiasco.

The novel *The Thousand Faces of Night* actually gives vent to a daughter's resentment towards her apparently wise and well—meaning mother. It brings to the fore the misunderstanding that exists between different generations of women. It belongs to that class of fiction written by female novelists that focuses primarily on women's mutual relationship with rather than analyzing 'man-woman' relationship. It has made an attempt to study women's attitude towards one another and how they feel for each other. It brings to light the startling reality that sometimes women are more tough with each other than men are with women. Or that some women co-operate with men and conspire to ruin the happiness of those women who arouse their jealousy. The questions and realities that this novel raises and reveals are numerous. Men and women are 'allies' or 'enemies' depending upon what serves their vested interests at a particular point of time.

In the context of Devi an important issue is her career. It is a matter of mystery as to why Devi's career did not figure in Sita's scheme of things. Why did Sita educate Devi so much if she wanted her to become merely a homemaker? Simply to cash in on the qualifications in the marriage market? Why did Sita not visualize that a highly educated girl may feel frustrated sitting at home all the time? Was she in a hurry to wash her hands off Devi as soon as possible? Why did she repeat the mistake of her father-in-law with Devi? Was Sita scared that education coupled with employment would make Devi uncontrollable? Did she fear that she would lose her grip over Devi if she became self—reliant?

The novel provides the opportunity to study the psyche of elderly women and young girls in relation to each other. It also indirectly hints at the rapport that aged women have with men and menials in the context of young women whose life they want to master, manage and manipulate.

Why do the influential/connected/ married women desire to keep dependent/unmarried women under their thumb? Why are the matrons overeager or in hurry to pass the baton of control from their hands to a man of their choice? Do they wish to monitor even the married life of the women they feel threatened of? Is this the reason why they try to 'arrange' marriages with men who are in their good books, dependent on them in anyway or are at their beck and call? Do they want to keep girls demoralized as far as 'marriage' or 'husband's status' is concerned? Is 'status' of the prospective groom one of the factors why horoscopes of some girls are not matched intentionally? Do people with vested interests obstruct the marriage of certain girl because they do not want them to become wives of financially and professionally secure and sound grooms?

Why are girls treated like herds of sheep by elderly women? Why do women shoo girls like cattle? Do unmarried and educated girls pose threats to elderly women? Are mothers also fed-up and exasperated with the presence of opinionated young daughters who might like to live on their own terms? Why is there not much difference between the conduct of jealous men and some elderly women vis-à-vis young girls? Are men and elderly/influential ladies in connivance with each other as far as talented, young and unattached girls are concerned? Do they work in tandem to nip the girls in the bud? Are men and elderly well-placed women jealous of the opportunities that girls might avail if left unchecked? Are men and menials used by well-connected established women to harass girls who arouse their jealousy or threaten their monopoly anywhere?

These are some of the issues that need to be probed and highlighted so that shackles and chains are broken and nets and labyrinths are cut to save girls from the clutches of evil people. Something must be done to guard the interest of unsuspecting, inexperienced girls who are wise enough to led a conscientious life but not shrewd enough to guess the games being played behind their back by men and women with vested interests. The unholy network of such men and women must be exposed and opposed as vehemently as possible. Unfortunately sometimes even family members, relatives and even friends and acquaintances are in implicit connivance with such mischievous elements giving all information about the unsuspecting victims, manipulating facts and misquoting them with little regard for the victim's right to privacy and her right to live, learn, earn or marry as she wishes. Sometimes it is noticed that manipulative women even begin to offer sexual favours to men to farther their vested interest, i.e. get assistance in harming and hampering the progress of those naïve girls whom they are jealous of or dislike.

The question is why do the elderly or established women have this desire to control the lives of young women? Why do they oppose or try to curtail the social and professional mobility of women younger than them? Is it not an abnormal tendency? A clear case of jealousy? Not just the girl who arouses their resentment but her whole family is put under surveillance. The places they visit, the people they meet—all are surreptitiously watched. Even the goods or commodities or they purchase are noticed. They are indirectly or directly lectured or hinted by the jealous matrons or by their cronies not to forget their position and stay within limits. The victimized girl and her family are treated condescendingly and told to 'accept' what is 'given' and not exercise the 'freedom of choice.' Attempts are made to thrust things and decisions on them in personal as well professional matters. This is an ugly reality of the women's world that must be brought out in the open. Even psychological treatment through *tantric* rites is resorted to so as to hamper and hinder professional and personal growth.

Married female cousins, aunts or sisters manoeuvre and manipulate situations against their own female relatives out of sheer jealousy. Using their authority as wives or mothers, they instigate, coax or coerce their husbands and sons to harm or harass girls whom they dislike or resent.

A lot depends on the conscience of the men folk too. To what extent they will listen to their women folk vis-à-vis other (unrelated or related) females? Will they do the bidding of their female family members, female friends, superiors, subordinates or colleagues blindly and indiscriminately or use their sense of judgement to realize the difference between just and unjust? It has been noticed that sometimes women outdo men in harassing and humiliating each other. Is it not high time that before breathing down the neck of men, women must first put their own house in order? They do not have to become Mother Teresa or Mahatma Gandhi. They need to keep alive their conscience and exercise restrain instead of behaving like bitches and witches with each other. Healthy competition is valid but hounding competitors/rivals around and getting them harassed by male/female cronies is downright inhuman and criminal.

The Thousand Faces of Night provides opportunity to study a host of issues that confront women in real life. Devi was cajoled and convinced by Sita to get married as soon as possible. However in real life there are some instances when girls are under intense pressure 'not to' get married. Family members, relatives, acquaintances all work towards marriage proposals or negotiations getting thwarted. On the one hand, they co-operate covertly with each other to thwart marriage negotiations that are made traditionally. On the other, they keep tutoring the girls in question to take the matter of marriage in their own hands because a negotiated marriage is burdensome for their guardians. This process continues for years. The result is that girls are doomed to spinsterhood because many of them are not inclined towards scouting for husbands themselves. Moreover in Indian society the road to self—negotiated marriage is full of thorns and pitfalls. There are innumerable instances wherein the girl's efforts to convince boys to marry them has ended as cases of sexual exploitation with the boys in question refusing to tie the knot ultimately. Even girls of 'status' family have ruined themselves walking on the perilous path of 'self-negotiated' marriages via live-in relationships. Yet another piece of 'precious' advice given to female folks who are unattached is to dump the idea of matrimony altogether whether be it 'self-negotiated' or 'arranged.' They must instead lead a bon-homie life, wining and dining with every Tom, Dick and Harry. Surprisingly such advisers are not people unrelated to the family but often and almost always one's own close or distant kith and kin.

It has also been noticed that in Indian society and in almost all families people derive a strange kind of pleasure and satisfaction in seeing the faulty grooming of each other's daughters. If parents succeed in marrying off their daughters, they watch hawk eyed to see if she succeeds in establishing a good rapport with husband and his family. On the other hand, if a girl remains single then they eagerly wait for the news of her involvement with any man and if possible also elopement. These days there is an over-eagerness to see girls going in for inter-caste marriages or pre-marital affairs. Sometimes even married men are instigated towards unwed maid-ens primarily to damage her reputation. Kith and kin and acquaint-ances almost behave like touts instigating and cooperating with dubious men and women to entrap and ruin unsuspecting girls.

No wonder ordinary Indian men and women shudder at the thought of giving birth to girl child. Female infanticide has been in practice in this country primarily because parents are scared of the various social implications that entails a girl's birth. It is not just a financial issue. Even if a girl is ungrudgingly raised and ed-ucated, non-cooperation in the matter of matrimony or social and professional mobility breaks the courage of their parents. Life-time of effort is put to naught in the case of girls because of jeal-ousy, rivalry and lack of goodwill.

The Thousand Faces of Night, thus, is one of those novels

which gives a chance to think beyond the man-woman relationship. Unlike many other female oriented novels, this narrative does not restrict itself merely to studying how men and women behave or deal with each other. Rather it focusses on other equally important aspects and stages of a woman life, from childhood to old age, from being a daughter to a mother-in-law and a grandmother (especially of a girl child).

Githa Hariharan must be applauded for writing a book which is neither erotic nor evasive as far as women's life is concerned. Her work is, instead, a balanced account of women's life in which there are pleasures as well as pressures, smiles as well as tears, struggle as well as success that women receive at the hands of not just men but women too. The novelist brings under microscopic scrutiny her own gender instead of lambasting the male community. *The Thousand Faces of Night* is one of those novels which a mother or grandmother can gift to her daughter or granddaughter without any embarrassment or hesitation. It is a beautiful amalgamation of myth and reality, tradition and modernity thereby acquainting the readers and presenting a meaningful critique of them.

Devi, thus, was married with adequate fuss and fanfare. In the cacophony of celebration, Devi acted like a puppet. Sita pulled the strings and Devi danced to her tunes secretly apprehensive but amazingly compliant too. This was the state Devi was reduced to by a 'well-meaning' mother who would otherwise be analyzed as a manipulative and calculative individual as shrewd and cunning as any hard-boiled seasoned politician. Do home and hearth require these skills too? Can't women manage family matters without complicated maneuverings? Is home/ personal relationship a battle ground where cunningness has to be used? Are not good faith, frankness, sincere attachment, genuine concern vanishing qualities even in intimate blood ties? Do parents do 'politics' even with their own children?:

> Sita believed most in the power of her own magic. But like all good

> magicians, she knew when she needed a few carefully selected accomplices. She made discreet enquiries, collected horoscopes, more important, she conducted a thorough investigation of all the candidates she had short-listed. Horoscopes were all very well, but as far as Sita was concerned, they were useful props. The real decision, the choice was hers alone.
>
> The stage was set. The props and chorus were ready, awaiting the director's cue. What Devi, the innocent heroine who strayed unknowingly into Sita's script, do once the drama unfolded to reveal a life, a will of its own?
>
> Sita wisely gave the younger woman enough room to indulge in a few minor and token tantrums. (107)

Sita sent away daughter Devi with the sense of a task well accomplished. All her life she had "pruned and re-potted" Devi and Mahadevan's life as meticulously "as she did her plants" (107). Now she was looking forward to the harvest: Devi ensconced as an 'ideal' wife, daughter-in-law and finally a 'perfect' mother. All this would invariably go towards vindicating her as a successful house-wife, mother, mother-in-law and even a grandmother. This was the future Sita was looking forward to in the twilight of her life.

Sita had managed her own life as 'housewife' as carefully and single-mindedly as one pursues one's career. Much planning and pruning went into it. Not only did Sita held husband Mahadevan and daughter on a tight leash but set gruelling tasks for herself too: "Good housekeeping, good taste, hard work" (101). If she was tough with Mahadevan and Devi, then she was unsparing with herself too:

> Only Sita knew what relentless self-discipline had gone into the making of a perfect housekeeper, a blameless wife. . . .
>
> If there was one lesson Sita had mastered in her years of study, it was this: you did not get results with wishy-washy half-heartedness. . . .
>
> She plotted and planned with single-minded devotion, till years later, her schemes bore ripe, fulfilling fruit. (101-2)

Sita believed in the philosophy of *karma.* Her mentality was almost mathematical. Two plus two brings four. This was her logic. If she planned and played her cards well, she expected 'perfect' and 'expected' results. She had worked diligently, almost ruthlessly towards making her life as wife and mother faultless. Her parameters of success were the practical achievements of life such as promotions for husband, a nice house, a good education for Devi and a good marriage also. To achieve these targets she abandoned lethargy and worked round the clock. She also banished from her life and that of her husband and daughter all recreational (and also regressive) dreams, illusions, stories, myths and legends so as to remain focused like a hawk.

With Devi married to Mahesh, a man almost perfect from all practical angles, Sita anticipated nothing other than the best. In her opinion planning and persistency can never go wrong. However it is here that Sita erred. Human life is not pure mathematics wherein 'two' plus 'two' would always yield 'four.' Human beings are a bundle of emotions. Moreover, human life is unpredictable. Planning and precautions bear fruit only when multiple other factors too work in tandem. Devi's life did not turn out as Sita had planned, expected or visualized.

Mahesh was much akin to his mother-in-law Sita temperamentally. Practical, matter-of-fact, concerned with the fundamental 'realities,' that is, the 'basics' of life rather than the 'illusionary,' the 'superficial' or the 'ephemeral.' Mental excursions other than those directed to material achievements and mundane engagements exasperated him. Devi did adjust with him initially. She, in fact, was relieved that Mahesh was down-to-earth and more honest than all the other Indian men she had met during negotiations for matrimony. For Mahesh marriage was a task to get done and over with. He did not believe in prolonging or protracting a matter. He was not a person who would defer a decision unnecessarily. Hence he did not take much time in deciding whether he wanted to make Devi his wife or not. He was a man confident and in command of himself. Very sure about what he wanted or what he liked. He did not beat around the bush. His expressions and opinions were to the point. He talked clearly:

> 'I travel a great deal,' he tells me . . . 'I will be in Bangalore only ten days of the month,' Mahesh says. 'Are you ready to accept that? My father is there, of course, and our old maidservant, but you will be lonely sometimes. Have you thought of that?' . . .
>
> I liked Mahesh's frankness, his willingness to be fair, even if he did seem to be an unbending pillar of propriety and good sense. He is honest at least, I though, he admits to wanting a woman at home who will be a wife and a mother. (22-23)

Devi probably seemed to him a good blend of 'modernity' and 'tradition. A woman who would neither be a social embarrassment because of lack of education and grooming nor a social misfit whose short sojourn abroad went to her head and made her ill at ease in her native sociocultural milieu. Devi, indeed, was neither.

Devi was led to the matrimonial altar by her mother and in her husband's home she was received by her father-in-law 'Baba' and the family maid Mayamma. It was a house without a housewife. Mahesh's mother, as Mayamma later revealed to Devi, had one fine day abandoned house, husband and hearth quietly. Neither Baba nor Mahesh would talk or tell about the absentee lady of the house. Parvatiamma was never or rarely mentioned by them. Devi was, initially, more than relieved to find that she won't have a mother-in-law breathing down her neck. It was only later that she became inquisitive about her absentee mother-in-law. She began to empathize with the woman who abruptly abandoned husband, two good children and a prosperous household.

The young bride made appropriate manoeuvres to adjust in her new home and she was ably supported by husband and father-in-law. Her apprehensions and fears about marital "perversion, blind, bestial lust and impotence" (49) were put to rest by the reasonable conduct of Mahesh.

Devi's initiation into wifehood and domesticity was aided and abetted in another way apart from her own willingness or

Mahesh's balanced conduct. Her father-in-law did much to make her feel at home. The vacuum created by the death of Pati in childhood and of her father Mahadevan while a young girl, was filled by Baba. Like Pati, Baba too was a reservoir full of stories culled from Sanskrit literature that he had taught in college as professor. Saddled with a husband who was frequently on tours and a housemaid who was too efficient, Devi had ample time on her hands. She sought the company of Baba just as she used to reach out to Pati as a little child. Baba mixed 'music' and 'myth' to help Devi imbibe certain 'values' that would guide her and govern her life as 'wife' or 'woman.' Devi could not help comparing Pati and Baba:

> Baba's stories remind me of my grandmother's, but they are also different. They are less spectacular, they ramble less. Her stories were a prelude to my womanhood, an initiation into its subterranean possibilities. His defines the limits. His stories are for a woman who has already reached the goal that will determine the guise her virtue will wear. They make one point in concise terms: that the saints lived according to the laws of time-tested tradition. (52)

Thus, in her husband's house Devi got opportunity to interact with another story teller. This time the narrator was a 'man,' her own father-in-law. Devi got a chance to know the male perspective as far as 'myth' and 'history' is concerned. Pati did not exclude maidenhood, early youth, courtship or unwed love. Her heroines were primarily eligible princesses. Her stories were about how these young royal women got married or did not get married. Moreover she talked about not just Damayanti but also about Amba. Her choice of stories was, thus, wide including the blissful as well as beleaguered, happy as well sad. Baba's stance and selection was more or less static. His protagonists were not lovers or eligible princesses who had to be married. Rather his heroines were 'wives' and the stories elaborated their duties as such. The narration focused on the rules *of* and regulations as laid down by the scriptures that women/wives must observe. Pati's stories gave scope for revolt, escape and revenge. Baba's stories did not make room for these. His narratives were elaborations the rules of *Grihastaashram* as enshrined in *Manusmriti*. In Pati's case the rules and regulations were implicit. The focus was more on the story. Description was fundamental to Pati. She drew in detail the paraphernalia of Damayanti's *swayamwara*—the splendour and beauty of the venue. She described with palpable reality the encounter between Amba and Bheeshma when she met him with an entreaty to marry. Equally lively description was Gandhari's excitement and eagerness as a bride to see her husband. The description of garlands, marble palaces and seductive, supple youthful beauty were the stuff of her stories. The portrayal of human emotions—happiness, excitement, sadness, anger—constituted her narration. Baba's stories, however, were short and curt concentrating on the basic or the fundamental morals or messages that would help a woman or a wife in her vocation. He did not bother to describe or create 'environment.' He told in plain and simple manner the gist of the matter without any circumlocution: "His stories are never flabby with ambiguity, or even fantasy, a little magic perhaps, but nothing beyond the strictly functional. They always have for their centrepoint an exacting touchstone for a woman, a wife" (51).

Moreover Baba's narrative was medley of not just music and myth but also of Manusmriti and legends. If he talked about mythic Goddess Ambika, then he also mused about historic figures like Dikshitar, Jayadeva, Syama Sastri and Thyagaraja. He talked about the marital life of these saints and their encounter with mythic gods and goddesses. The purpose was to inform Devi about the different precedences set by the wives of these holy men in the matter of matrimony and household affairs.

Baba was a learned man. Hence he did not depend merely on the 'oral tradition' as in the case of Pati. He perused through the books of Sanskrit, he read Manusmriti and he went through the history of music. He tried to find out who were the creators of the different musical ragas. He took interest in the biographical details of the music maestros. He talked about music and matrimony in almost the same breath. If Devi liked music, then he used his musical discourses to drive home a moral for Devi to learn her lessons as woman, wife and mother.

Thus, Baba, as a father and father-in-law was overeager to see a successful married life of his son and daughter-in-law. He wanted to train the new bride in a manner that his son's married life would be without any hitch. He seemed to be a man trying to play both the 'father-in-law' and the 'mother-in-law'. His own wife had left him and his household abruptly at the twilight of life. He was saddled with the responsibility of not only getting his son married but also the daughter-in-law fully adjusted and at home. Mahesh married and brought Devi home. Baba's responsibility was not only to make her feel welcome but also to make her realize her 'duties' and 'responsibilities' as wife and daughter-in-law. Usually this is done by mothers-in-law who keep daughters-in-law on a tight lease by their advices, comments or taunts in Indian homes. Baba could not afford to be so crude, blunt or frank.

In Indian society, the mutual relationship of a father-in-law and daughter-in-law is one of great decorum and discretion. The two are mutually reticent, with either the husband, the grandchildren or mother-in-law acting as mediators. The father-in-law is looked upon as a father-figure but daughters-in-law usually do not take as much liberty with him as they would with their own father. They cannot rush to their fathers-in-law like little girls and hang on to their knees making 'this' or 'that' demand as girls often do with their fathers and brothers. If Indian men practice female infanticide, then they also on the other hand pamper daughters and sisters putting up with their incessant chattering and tantrums as patiently as possible. Baba, as father-in –law, had to extend moral support to her without pampering her. At the same time he had to teach her certain 'do's' and 'don'ts' without sounding like a dictator. He was placed in a delicate situation wherein he had to be a mother figure as well as a father figure, neither too lenient nor too strict.

Baba however handled the tricky situation with much grace and sensitively. Soon Devi began to look up to him as if he were not just Mahesh's father but her own. She was adequately reserve. At the same time she was frank too with the old man. He, on his part, made all efforts to assimilate her in the family. Perhaps he was anxious that Mahesh does not suffer a fate similar to his, that is, of having a wife who would abandon home and hearth for no rhyme or reason. Since Devi had a weakness for music, he quoted instances from the lives of music maestros too to show how their wives lived.

However it is worth noting that the examples that he cited were not one-sided, that is, emphasizing merely the 'duty' or 'devotion' of the wife. Rather he highlighted the mutual admiration of couples wherein the husbands openly acknowledged the virtues of their wives. They expressed gratitude for the contribution that their wives made. Unlike the stories selected by Pati wherein such reciprocal relationships were totally absent, Baba talked about husbands who were as devoted and respectful towards their wives as the wives were towards them:

> Then Krishna came to Padmavati, the wife of Jayadeva, his body smeared with oil, and in her husband's guise, he took the manuscript from her and restored the lines. When Jayadeva saw this miracle, he fell at Padmavali's feet. She had the fortune of seeing Krishna, a blessing he had been denied. (65)

Thus, the stories that Baba narrated to Devi were not just mythic but also, to some extent, realistic or historical. Since he happened to be a well-read person, he had a firm grip on not just the oral tradition but also on the scriptural and textual. He was a man well-versed in the language of the gods, that is, Sanskrit. He was equally knowledgeable about music. Hence he made an enthralling cocktail of myth, music, history and dharmic laws.

Baba told Devi about Jayadeva and wife Padamavati, about Syama Sastri and his wife, Purandara and Sarasvati Bai, Muthuswamy Dikshitar and his two wives, Narayana Tirtha and his wife,

Thyagaraja and his second wife. Baba's stories, thus, were invariably about couples. The focus was on devotion and wisdom of the wives as they carried on with their exceptional husbands. Devi's father-in-law tended to highlight marriages that included mutual admiration, adjustment and understanding. The affection and sincerity of the wives were reciprocated by their solicitous husbands. In many cases, he showed how the wives led their illustrious husbands to salvation.

Unlike Pati whose stories were about disgruntled princesses and wives married to incompatible husbands, Baba always talked about wives who gave unconditional support to their illustrious husbands so that they reached greater heights of glory. The wives, in the stories that Baba selected, exemplified the dictum, that behind every, successful man is a woman. Mahesh's father did not acknowledge the dark possibilities of matrimonial disharmony. Perhaps he considered it inauspicious to talk about mythic women like Amba, Gandhari, Kunti, Draupadi or Sita. These mythic women, in spite of being hailed in the annals of religion and mythology as great women, wives and goddesses; were invariably the victims of strange matrimonial decisions and denials. In fact, Baba did not even talk about his own wife Parvatimma who had left him all of a sudden. It seems he did not want either his son or his daughter-in-law to associate themselves even remotely with such sad mythic couples or with his own abruptly ended married life. He carefully and intentionally selected historic and mythic stories in which men and women had a long and happy innings of marriage.

Nonetheless, Devi's troubles were far from over. If Pati's stories horrified Devi in childhood, then Baba's sagas replete with idealism, weighed her down. She could barely breathe. She groped for a 'middle' path but could find none.

Devi realized the extremity of the stands that Pati and Baba took as far as women and marriage is concerned. Yet she could not help admit that ultimately it was she who would have to bear the burden of their beliefs. It was also true that Pati and Baba were better human beings than Sita or Mahesh or the boys whom she had met for marriage or that white American house owner whose tenant she was. Pati and Baba were good old traditional people who did not deny human emotional needs. They understood the need for emotional or mental nourishment. They knew that every activity does not have to be financially gainful. They did not believe in weighing everything on the scales of practical utility and practical results. They understood the human need for relaxation and reprieve. They were aware of the fact that not just the body but also the mind, the soul and the heart have their own share of certain rights. They too require rest and peace. They too have some cravings that are often emotional and spiritual and not merely material. It was because of this wholistic view of human beings that Pati and Baba seemed more agreeable to Devi than her mother and husband. No wonder when Baba died she felt orphaned and uprooted. Had Baba been alive perhaps Devi and Mahesh's marriage would not have broken. The relationship would not have deteriorated so fast. He might have convinced Mahesh to handle Devi gently and patiently rather than resenting her barrenness insultingly. An infertile woman needs sympathy and not crude reminders of her handicap. A barren woman already suffers enough on her own. Motherhood is often the cherished desire of almost all women. To be denied of this natural and normal right by nature is the biggest jolt for any woman. She does not need any more punishments or taunts to realize her inability. The physical inability to bear a child and to put up with the inability life-long is itself the biggest punishment that any woman can receive. Hence her husband or family or acquaintances do not really need to soil their hand or spit venom any further. The woman must be provided an environment in which either nature heals her body or medical science cures her. Natural healing process or medical procedures both require a positive bent of mind. In case both fail to bring forth desired result, human rights of dignified existence cannot be denied to her.

In Devi's case, however, Mahesh was not willing to give time for either of the recourses. He was a man in haste with harsh words to match. The air around Devi was thick with resentment and suppressed rage. No wonder Devi ran away from Mahesh soon after Baba died. There was nothing, neither husband's love nor Baba's dictums of traditional decorum to hold her back. There was no one to restrain Mahesh and convince him that he must give Devi some time. She too wanted to be a 'wife' and 'mother.' She had, in fact, almost fallen in love with Mahesh but he never realized this. He did not understand Devi at all. He misread her all the time and Devi could no longer put up with it. She was a sensitive girl hurt and bruised by the insensitivity of her husband. She did not take Mahesh lightly. Hence she could not cope with his resentment and rejection. She ran away and got involved with a man whose involvement with her and demands from her were superficial. Mahesh, on the other hand, was a serious man and he wanted to establish strong connections with Devi like making her the mother of his child rather than merely using her for vicarious pleasure. His sentiments were right but his method was wrong. He had made Devi his wife and now he wanted a child. Intentions all good but wrongly pursued. He almost pushed Devi towards Gopal. His indifference and misunderstanding made Gopal appear better and desirable to Devi. In fact married women in general do not really believe in the "rejection of ethics and family values" (Jaya Prasad 2005: 63). It is actually in the hands of the husbands and their family to treat wives and daughters-in-laws "in a manner that they would not be compelled to make such a rejection."

Mahesh was not a bad husband but like all men he could not imagine a barren marriage, that is, a marriage which wouldn't bring forth a child. Why did one marry after all if one could not start a family? The Hindu religious scriptures are very specific about the 'purpose' of marriage. The institution's primary function is not merely to provide 'companionship' to men and women but to ensure the perpetuation of the human race. Hence the very purpose of marriage is defeated if any marriage remains infertile. Moreover the raison d'etre of a woman's life too, according to the sacred scriptures, gets defeated if she does not give birth to children. The *Vedas* say that women have been created primarily to be 'mothers,' that is, to give birth to future generations of humanity through marriages to healthy men of good families:

> To be mothers were women created, and to be fathers men; therefore, the Vedas ordain that dharma must be practiced by a man together with his wife. Vivaha is one of the sarira samskaras (sacraments sanctifying the body) through each of which every man and woman must pass at the proper age and time. . . . He only is a perfect man, who consists of his wife, himself and his offspring. (149)

Hence Mahesh was not wrong in demanding a child from Devi. It was proper from religious point of view as also psychological. Just as all women want to become mothers, men too want to be fathers of their own flesh and blood. The weakness to have progeny is common to both the genders. The success of a marriage in today's Indian society still depends on whether a girl is fertile or not. Any problem on that front and the girl's marriage is on the rocks.

It is not that Mahesh forced 'motherhood' on Devi as soon as she stepped on the threshold of his house. He gave her one year to adjust in the new home. Now he wanted her to share his dreams too. The dream of having a child so that their tie would further be cemented and he would have someone to carry his name and legacy. So why delay it unnecessarily when children are what marriages are meant for:

> 'Let's have a baby,' Mahesh said. 'There is no reason to wait. I want you to have my baby,' he said. (74)

The intentions of Mahesh were noble, logical and even religious but Devi's physical health played spoil sport and tensions began to mount between the couple. Since the last one year both Mahesh and Devi had carried along with each other as tactfully and diplomatically as they could manage. They tried to adjust to each other's rhythm of life and mood swings. However this fragile peace agreement fell to pieces. Their temperamental incompatibility became too much for Devi to ignore and for Mahesh to swallow. Both of them were right in their own way but it was Devi who suffered more. She not only had to put up with own her physical inability but also Mahesh's desperation and frustration.

Mahesh was a practical man. He had a good job and a wife at home. A house well maintained by an old dependable maid. A sister married and away in America. A respected and learned father who died without too many health problems. No loans or liabilities. He saw no reason to complain or be unhappy. Hence he was irritated by his wife's long face and asked: "What is it you want?" (74) In a fit of frustration he observed: "This is what comes of educating a woman. Your grandmother was barely literate. Wasn't she a happier woman than you are?" (74)

Devi, on the other hand, was burdened by boredom. Baba's death further accentuated her emotional isolation and alienation from Mahesh and the house. An intellectual as well as emotional girl needed a soul mate more than material comforts. She was in need of a person to whom she could talk without hesitation and inhibitions. However the 'too perfect' and 'officious' conduct of Mahesh numbed her to silence. He was a man curt in his expressions and controlled in his reactions. This added to Devi's problems. Mahesh considered material comforts guarantee of happiness. He did not take cognizance of emotional needs. From the beginning of the marriage, Devi found her expressions and communications obstructed by Mahesh's pragmatism. She could not bring herself to talk her heart out or express her heart's desire. Mahesh's practical approach to life never gave her a chance.

Devi was undoubtedly impressed by this well-behaved and mature young man but she hungered for more. Perhaps she was waiting for a few sentences about herself and him. She muttered:

> I find I barely suppress my increasing longing to say, Yes, we have said enough about your work, your tours, your company. A marriage cannot be forced into suddenly being there, it must grow gradually, like a delicate but promising sapling. What about us? What kind of life will we make together? (49)

However the words died in her throat. She could not bring herself to ask such emotional questions from a man who seemed to be wise beyond his age. Totally at peace with himself and in control without any flicker of eagerness or excitement lightening up his face. His sagacious demeanour made Devi feel silly like a child: "It seems too foolish, too intense a question to ask of this reasonable stranger who had already carefully examined, experienced, dissected, and is now ready to file away as settled, something as fragile and newborn as our marriage." (49)

Mahesh's cool and mature conduct put to rest all of Devi's doubts. He was a well-behaved man. In fact too well behaved so much so that Devi found herself unable to express either her joys or pains freely and frankly. However consolations were galore. Mahesh was neither a pervert nor an impotent. Devi was relieved. She felt she "had escaped an axe by a hair's breadth" (49). What more could she ask for? Her husband was a well-groomed young man who did not even raise his voice. Hence Devi grew to like him. When Mahesh left for a tour the first time after their marriage, Devi felt miserable without him. As time flew, she too imagined raising his children in the calm house and playing around with them in the verdant garden.

Thus, it is not that Devi was averse to the idea of having a baby. The empty house, the idle hours, the vacant mind, the dull eyes—all, Devi knew, would come alive with the presence of a cute little bundle crying and smiling alternatively in her arms:

> Perhaps that is what I need. A cradle by my bed, lullabies that will soothe the knotted, discordant raga in my mind, all fragment and illusion. Something real to feel, to hold, to find me down with firmness of purpose. Something like Mahesh. (87)

However this pretty picture that Devi conjured up in her imagination did not turn into reality. Her body refused to play along. Mahesh's insistence and Devi's failure to conceive brought the schism between the husband and wife into the open. Mahesh failed to understand Devi's predicament. Her mind and body were not working in synchrony in spite of Devi's own desire to have a baby.

The husband, on the other hand, behaved as if Devi was unwilling and intentionally avoiding motherhood:

> 'Why are you looking at me like that?,' I asked.
>
> You look so fragile, so feminine, Mahesh said. 'It's hard to believe that you don't want a child.'
>
> Even as he says the words, I can feel myself diminishing.
>
> I feel myself getting blurred in Mahesh's eyes. The focus gets softer and softer, till everything but my stubborn, unrelenting womb. The game is over, just as I was beginning to learn the rules. (93)

A woman knows fully well her duties and responsibilities as 'woman' towards the man she marries, the family she marries into, and the humanity at large. It is the duty of a woman to nurture the human race through her children. It is indeed a woman's greatest desire as well as duty to bring forth the future generations of humanity but what can a woman do before her "stubborn, unrelenting womb?"

Perhaps a little sympathy, a little kindness would lessen the pain of barrenness and the sense of deprivation in women like Devi. Mahesh, however, almost accused his wife. He did not, as Devi herself disclosed, bring his hand down on her rebellious body but his terse observations hit her harder.

Devi could not help recall the dialogue between Yudhisthira and the water Yaksha who had struck to death his four brothers because they drank water before answering his questions. "The questions the Yaksha asks, and Yudhishthira's answers, constitute a brilliant dialogue, notable for its brevity, scope and philosophical depth" (Varma 21). In all, the Yaksha asked twenty-eight questions. The first few of them invariably revolved around primary human relationships:

> Who then is the friend given by the gods? demanded the invisible voice of Yudhishthira.
>
> It is the wife who is that friend and safe refuge, answered Yudhishthira.
>
> What is heavier than the earth? A mother.
>
> What is higher than heaven? A father. (86)

Pavan K. Verma has rightly observed: "Who can fully understand the chemistry of personal relationships?" (Varma 21). Devi was unable to jell with Mahesh and he with her but both vibed well with each other's parent. Mahesh had a good working relationship with mother-in-law Sita. He would frequently write letters to her to disclose and discuss his observations about Devi. Devi, on the other hand, was close to Baba. It was from Baba that she got emotional and moral support. It was he alone who made her feel at home. He filled the void that her own father's death had created. Sita, meanwhile, slipped into the place vacated by Parvatiamma in Mahesh's life. Yet the couple could not get along with each other. Neither Baba's advices about married life nor Sita's suggestions could reconcile Mahesh and Devi to each other. They remained close and frank with one another's parent but kept making mistakes in their mutual primary relationship.

In the context of both Mahadevan and Mahesh, neither Sita nor Devi proved to be the "friend and safe refuge" (86) that Yudhisthira had talked about to Yaksha. Mahadevan was reduced to carrying out the orders of Sita. He rose in profession more by her prodding and pushing than his own desire. Mahesh too did not get a friend in Devi. He could not make himself clear to Devi and Devi failed to view the world and their relationship from his perspective. The answer of Yudhisthira that "the wife . . . is . . . friend and safe refuge" (86) of a householder, indeed, turned out to be a myth. In fact, in the context of Mahesh, it was Sita, his mother-in-law, who was like a friend and safe refuge. It was to her that he would dash off letters in desperation over differences with Devi. It was to Sita that he disclosed his marital and domestic problems which Devi, his wife, was busy creating intentionally or unintentionally.

The same was the case with Devi. She was gradually becoming closer to her father-in-law than to her husband. Baba was like a friend who understood and appreciated her aesthetic interests. Till his death, he was a refuge for Devi when she was in search of succour and support. However Mahesh was luckier than Devi. Sita was there till the last to execute the catharsis. Baba left Devi abruptly and in the lurch. The buffer between Mahesh and Devi was gone. Devi did not take much time in abandoning Mahesh's home after Baba's death. Had Baba been alive he might have helped Devi to tide over the crisis but he was no more. There was no one to help Devi handle Mahesh. She could not manage him and his demands on her own. Hence she left. Baba's death snatched the only refuge that she had in her marital home. Thus, neither was Devi a wife who would come to her husband's rescue nor was Mahesh the safe haven in which his wife would lead a blissful life secure from all tensions and turmoil.

Yudhisthira had told the Yaksha that the mother was heavier than the earth and father higher than the sky. Implicit in this comparison is both a eulogy of both the figures and also a hint to the onerous responsibility that they bear. Another implication is that no matter what the children do they can never repay back the debt they owe to their parents. Thus, be it the *Ramayana* or the *Mahabharata* or the *Vedas*, the 'mother' and the 'father' remain figures next only to gods. Great importance is attached to these roles in every scripture.

While a well-groomed child would become an asset for family and society, a misguided one would be everyone's nemesis. Hence a lot depends on what mothers teach their children so that not only their future but everyone else's future remains secure. A mother, thereby, bears the burden of ensuring the well-being of not just her own children but society at large. A mother, thus, is answerable to everyone. The reply of Yudhisthira also alludes to the joys of parenthood and the unbridled love and affection that parents shower on their children. Mother's love is bountiful like earth's natural splendour and the father is the guarantor of fulfillment of every little desire of the child.

Devi could not help recalling this episode from the *Mahabharata*. All along she had loved the myths. Now she understood why her mother Sita had resented such religious as well as non-religious mythic stories. The beauty and romance of the myths gave impetus to expectations and dreams. They conditioned the mind in a certain way making it emotional and sensitive. The modern world, on the other hand, believes that success lies in curbing emotions and carrying on with life in a matter-of-fact manner. When neither she nor Mahesh could make themselves understood to each other, when motherhood seemed to be like a noose around her neck, Devi realized that myths were indeed illusory.

Her mother hardly cared for her. Sita was more interesting in scoring points over her relatives than bothering about what her daughter really wanted to do or felt like doing. Baba, too, was selfishly more interested in turning Devi into an ideal wife subservient to his son. Each was busy in his or her own plans regarding Devi. Devi, herself, as a person, hardly mattered. The pressure to become mother too was a pain and problem as heavy as the earth itself. She could not help but notice the contrast as well as convergence between myth and reality. While pains and problems of the myths did echo in real life, the joys were strangely missing. As a woman Devi was suffering like many of the mythic women but where was the ideal husband about whom Baba had read out from the book of scriptures?

Time and again the *Vedas* and the *Puranas* eulogize the figures of the mother and the father. They are emphatic that the primary function of the institution of marriage is to create families. However what about those men and women who are not so fortunate? What about people who are unable to either marry or procreate? Why are the scriptures so disparaging about women who are childless? There are very few women in this world who remain childless willingly. Some are doomed to this fate for no fault of theirs. God made them that way. In contemporary society, though medical science has made giant leaps in gynaecological matters, yet an infertile woman goes through hell if medical treatments too do not lead her to motherhood. Husbands may be sympathetic but the in-laws are hardly patient. The sword of divorce and husband's second marriage keeps dangling on the woman's head. On the other hand, if a man is impotent, the wife is expected to remain silent and put up with the curse of childlessness as gracefully as possible. No one suggests to her that she should dump the fellow, marry again and start a family. Why?

In Devi's case it was she who was at fault. Mahesh was an educated man. He did confirm facts before zeroing in on Devi. He got himself medically examined and emerged with a clean chit. He then thought of getting everything confirmed about his wife too before openly blaming her. Moreover he had faith on medical science. It was his belief that through proper treatment problems could be solved:

> 'I've been to the doctor,' Mahesh said, his eyes not meeting mine. 'He says I'm—I'm fine. I'll fix an appointment for you to see the gynaecologist. (89)

Devi understood well Mahesh's move. It was both a ploy to confirm his doubts and start the cure. She herself never had an inkling that she would face any problem on this front. She grew up like any other normal girl not very beautiful but presentable and healthy. Hence the new developments were hurtful to her too. She had not visualized this kind of a situation even in her wildest dreams. Moreover ever since childhood, she had not been averse to the idea of motherhood. She could not help but look back to that day when Pati had narrated the *myth of Ganga and King Shantanu*:

> When the Bharata King Shantanu rode alone near the Ganga, he met a woman who shimmered with beauty. . . . The King was smitten by Ganga, for that is whom the water-fresh goddess was, and he offered her his heart, wealth and the queen's throne.
>
> Ganga lowered her eyes with a smile of acceptance.
>
> Will you promise me not to ask me my name? Will you promise not to stop me from doing what I must do?
>
> He did not understand her cryptic conditions, so he hastily said, "Yes, yes, I promise."
>
> Every year Ganga bore the king a son. But for seven years, she threw the new born into the swirling open-armed water of the Ganga.
>
> This is for your own good, she said as she drowned each baby.

(88)

Pati was at the mid of this Mahabharata myth, when Devi got unnerved by the description of Ganga's apparently abnormal and heinous action. She could not put with the fact that a mother would drown her new born babies with her own hands. Even Krishna's natural mother *Devaki* had lost her new born babes but at least she did not kill them. It was their maternal uncle *Kansa* who committed the crime (and later paid for it heavily at Krishna's hands). In the Ganga myth, the offender was none other than the mother herself. It was too much for Devi to swallow and she began to resist hearing the rest of the Ganga-Shantanu story:

> 'I don't like the story,' I said. 'I don't want to hear it'.
> 'There is just a little more,' she said. 'It's for your own good, my precious.' (88)

Thus, the tender mother-instinct was very much alive in Devi's heart while she was still a girl. Even as a child she knew what and how a mother is to be. This is why she began to reject the story of an abnormal mother like Ganga who was busy drowning her babies each year.

In Indian society it is considered unbecoming of unmarried girls to talk about motherhood and things related to it in the open. The emphasis is, rather, on quietly grooming them for the responsibility. In good families, attention is paid to the health of the girls primarily with this objective. This was the reason why Pati brought up the topic of motherhood with Devi one fine day in her childhood. Devi was standing on the threshold of adolescence. She had to be educated with physical as well as emotional aspects of this role. As far as health was considered, Pati fed Devi with "the gooey, medicinal potions she brewed. She sprinkled it with powdered jaggery, and pretended it was sweet" (89). To tackle the emotional aspect of the matter Pati took the refuge of Shantanu and Goddess Ganga.

What Pati meant was that motherhood is not merely giving birth to a cute little baby. It is more than that. It is a life-long effort involving important issues such as morality, values, tradition etc. besides health and legacy. It involves being answerable to not just one's immediate family but society and humanity at large. It requires the ability to not just love the child but also to punish him or her for larger good. It requires the strength to be impartial and have the courage to admit the mistakes of one's children too. It requires a woman to understand that when she becomes a mother, she is the mother of not just her own children but of humanity at large. It is her responsibility to raise and groom her progeny in a manner that they do not become a Ravan, a Dushasana or a Putana. The responsibility of ensuring the well-being of the human world is actually the responsibility of each mother of this world. It is they who have to ensure that children imbibe right values so as to ensure a safe, secure and happy world. A mother must be tender as well as tough least her children go astray.

This is the reason why in Hindu religion female deities have twin personalities. They are kind as Parvati, Lakshmi and Saraswati but ferocious as Durga and Kali. As mother figures they shower blessings on devotees but do not hesitate in inflicting punishment when necessary. Pati tells Devi: "Devi, motherhood is more than the pretty picture you see of a tender woman bent over the baby she is feeding at her. A mother has to walk strange and tortuous paths." (88)

Devi did not actually become mother but her trial had already begun. Even before she could give birth to a child, life made her walk strange and tortuous paths. First of these shocks was the revelation that something was wrong with her and that her husband hated her for it. The second jolt was that she would have to allow people to peek in her personal life if she wanted medical assistance to solve the problem. Mahesh had no qualms about it but Devi felt uncomfortable in the midst of doctors and nurses asking objectionable questions and giving equally objectionable suggestions. Devi was basically reserved by nature. She was bewildered at the turn of events, hurt and shy. She was ashamed of herself, angry and saddened by Mahesh's decisions and offended by the probing of the medical experts.

Devi could not help but shed helpless tears at her plight. Her grandmother's confident assertion in childhood that she (Devi) "will be a mother" and that she too was well on the way to be "a woman" (88) was proving to be an illusion. She was turning out to be a kind of 'lesser' woman who could not even play her natural role of procreation. She was like a barren piece of land. Her husband, on the other hand, was becoming increasingly disappointed and desperate. Of what use was a wife to a man if she could not give him his heirs? The whole purpose of marriage got defeated and Devi was painfully realizing this.

Mahesh was not a man who would be happy with merely the company of his wife. He wanted not just a woman to be his wife but a wife who would be a mother too. Hence his frustration and impatience increased with each passing day. He even began to suspect the intentions of his moody and sullen wife whose grudge he could never understand. He had patiently put up with the long face of his wife with the vain hope that motherhood might make things better for both of them. Even this idea flopped and their relationship plumbed to greater depths. He still groped for solution and thought what nature couldn't do, medical science would. Hence he asked Devi to meet a lady doctor of repute. However Devi was more hurt than happy or hopeful. The medical procedures further alienated her from Mahesh. What she was looking for was time and patience on Mahesh's part but he was a man in hurry eager to ease out the problems by hook or crook. His clinical approach to a matter that was not merely medical but also emotional, hurt Devi more. He was eager to become a father and unhappy over the delay. However he did not try to understand how difficult it is for a woman to cope with her the reality of her own barrenness. His apathy made Devi search for a shoulder to cry on. Her search ended next door in the form of her neighbour's brother Gopal.

Before Devi's elopement with Gopal, Sita tried to reconcile Devi to the idea of motherhood. Both Sita and Mahesh thought that more than medical problems, it was Devi's mental block, probably her aversion to the idea of becoming a mother, that was responsible for the delay. It was ironical that Sita, with whom Devi could never connect as a daughter, was trying to reveal the joys of motherhood. Sita was suddenly talking of 'warmth' and 'softness' that Devi as her daughter never felt. Pati and Mahadevan pampered Devi; they were indulgent towards her. Where was her mother Sita? Why did not Devi ever feel the joy and tenderness that Sita claimed she had in heart for her child? Why did not those feelings descend from her heart to envelope Devi? Why did not she experience and feel the softness of Sita's love in childhood or even in youth? All she got was a strict supervision of her activities by Sita. Anyway Sita did try to make amends and make Mahesh's task easier by trying to convince Devi through 'right' words and phrases:

> All through the ages, my dear Devi, Amma wrote, women have sought the deep content that comes with motherhood. When I held you helpless in my protecting arms, when you first smiled at my face bent over yours, when you lisped that precious word Amma, what vistas of joy opened up before me! Mahesh writes that you are tired, depressed. Would you like to take a holiday in Madras? (86)

The effort to establish an easy rapport with Devi was too late. The snow refused to thaw. Devi knew that both Amma and Mahesh were temperamentally two sides of the same win. Measured even in the matter of love and affection with conditions attached. Devi, however, was fed-up with their demand of propriety. To hell with the norms. What she desperately wanted was unbridled and unconditional acceptance, love and affection. All her life she kept waiting in vain for her mother to understand this. She kept believing and trusting Sita. It was because of her persuasion that she agreed to marry. Till date she kept doing what her mother wanted or what her husband told her to do. What had she got in return? Mahesh's resentment and his apathy? Why were they not ever eager to find out what was Devi's wish? In fact Devi was never given time to realize what her wishes were. Bound by the chains of tradition she did what mother, father-in-law and husband said. She turned into an unhappy woman compelled to take a step immoral in search of succour and support.

A man called Gopal had already made his way into Devi's heart. If Mahesh was decent but mechanical, Gopal was gentle and desirous. Mahesh wanted a 'mother' Gopal needed just the 'woman' that Devi was. For Mahesh an infertile Devi was a liability. For the lover she was probably an asset. He seemed to be well aware of the situation in which Devi was and lost no time in making the most of it. It is clear that he was free from the desire of both marriage and parenthood because he was busy capitalizing on his spreading fame as a singer. However he was a man with his senses fully alive and he needed a woman who would reciprocate. Devi fitted the bill. She was soon dancing to his tunes. There was no risk in the relationship other than defamation. There won't be any child born of their affair. Gopal would easily have a fling without any fetters.

Mahesh, on the other hand, was desperately trying to somehow set things right. He was not yet ready to dump Devi. She was after all his wedded wife. He wanted to salvage the situation with medical help but Devi was no longer interested in wasting time and energy with him any longer. Mahesh's efforts did not move her. It, in fact, repelled her. The medical interference, for the sake of treatment, in her personal life was too much for her. She was hurt by the invasion of her privacy even if it was to cure her. She wanted motherhood to happen to her normally and naturally and at its own pace. Not in the manner Mahesh was going about it:

> I stood dumb, over-whelmed by this official reference to my sex life. Only a few years ago, I would have burst into laughter. But I seem to have lost, along with many other things, my sense of humour, even my girlish ability to giggle. I am someone else now. (91)

Devi tried to cooperate as best as she could. She even suggested 'adoption' as an alternative but Mahesh flatly refused. Any way Devi would have put with all the medical regimes and routines if only Mahesh had shown even an iota of love, sympathy and genuine concern for her mental and physical plight. He was, however, too mechanical and detached from Devi's inner feeling. He was not violent with her. He did not hit her but he was angry nevertheless and vented it through words. He was desperate for a child. Consequently he began to resent Devi for not being a normal woman like majority of the women folk who became mothers without any hassle:

> I felt myself getting blurred in Mahesh's eyes. The focus got softer and softer, till everything dissolves into nothingness, everything but my stubborn, unrelenting womb. . . .
>
> Is there no other way? 'Devi, Devi,' said Mayamma, when without warning I buried my face in her shoulder and wept. (93)

A well-accomplished woman was reduced to a bundle of nerves crying helplessly in her maid's arms. An able individual disabled by emotional jolts.

Devi's plight shows that education alone does not ensure a secure life for a girl. She also requires the courage to speak up and the ability to assert where she ought to. Modesty is right only up to the point where it is understood as courtesy and good manner. The moment it is taken as a manifestation of appeasement or weakness, steps must be taken to dispel the confusion. Devi was educated but if she did not get to use it, why did she not reflect it at least in the house and before family? She was, in fact, not much better than Mayamma or Gauri. Silently suffering and shedding copious tears like a helpless, illiterate woman getting bullied by parents, husband and in-laws. Devi herself observed: "My education has left me unprepared for the vast, yawning middle chapters of my womanhood" (54).

Devi, an America returned, modern, urbane twentieth-century woman, could have easily turned truculent and got away with it too. However she could not overlook the loneliness of her widowed mother. She couldn't bring herself to disobey her mother Sita. She was not excessively ambitious. She was full of sympathy and daughter's affection for her mother. She began to trust Sita and forgot the resentment that she had harboured. She agreed to marry a man selected by mother. After marriage she began to have tender feelings for Mahesh too. She was almost grateful for his decency. Devi began to respect father-in-law Baba and looked up to him for fatherly affection and encouragement. She did not try to dominate over the household and the menial staff like an authoritarian daughter-in-law. She did not try to make changes or disturb the family's way of life. Devi, thus, possessed a number of qualities enough to make her a likeable presence in the life of all.

Mahesh, however, lacked the eyes and the mind to gauge and appreciate the beauties of Devi's personality. He was blind to Devi's innate goodness. At the same time he was unwilling to make even the smallest of concessions. Devi couldn't have a job to kill boredom. She could not read the books she liked. She could not even sympathize with a sick maid. All this was denied to her. Mahesh rubbished all her suggestions. In his opinion he was more worldly-wise, hence, knew better. She must pursue what he suggested as a hobby. She must not be too sensitive towards the sick maid. He tried to teach Devi "how things work in real life" (55). This only added to Devi's disenchantment with him and the institution of marriage. He did not even pretend to like or love his wife. Marriage was a duty that he owed to himself, his family and society at large. A task to get done and over with. When Devi asked "why did you marry me?" he replied undiplomatically:

> 'Whatever people get married for. . . .' He peered into the mirror and readjusted the knot of his tie. 'Thank God we Indians are not obsessed with love.' (54-55)

Could he not say a sweet little lie so as not to hurt his wife? Or was he intentionally honest so as to hurt her and make it clear that she should not to expect any sentimentality from him? Had he been more thoughtful, Devi's myth about marriage and husbands would not have busted so soon. She would have lived on with the illusion that may be Mahesh did like her after all. He did need her in his life. He, however, turned to be very poor in the understanding of human psychology. Poor in human handling as far as his own wife was concerned. He made all the wrong moves and said all the wrong words at crucial junctures of his intimate personal relationship with Devi. He took Devi too casually. Devi could not bond with him even if she wanted to. He was too articulate in the expression of doubts or disdain. He did not allow confusions to linger and illusions to survive. He did not mince words thereby making adjustment or reconciliation all the more difficult:

> 'You look so fragile, so feminine, Mahesh said. 'It's hard to believe you don't want a child.'
>
> Even as he says the words, I can feel myself diminishing. I become a wispy, insubstantial cloud that can be blown out of sight, that can break apart when touched. (93)

While Mahesh was brutally frank about his feelings and blind to Devi's overtures, he himself expected a complete comprehension of his desires. Devi asked him: "Why do you want a baby?," Mahesh replied with amazement: "What kind of a question is this?" (57)

Devi was deeply hurt. She was not getting the emotional support that she desperately needed at this point of time. An educated and accomplished lady was reduced to being a helpless woman craving and crying for her husband's sympathy and support. Eager to express her own tender feelings for a husband whose decisions were based on hard reality than sentimentality. Devi had grown to love Mahesh but did he care to realize this? He never gave Devi an opportunity to express it. The feelings died a premature death buried by Mahesh's resentment over her barrenness. He never allowed something as trivial as 'love' to come in between them. It was sacrilegious to think about it, talk or express it. He was the first man of her life in true sense of the word. In a way not just her husband but also her first love but did Mahesh care? No, he didn't. "The despair and frustrations that comes from a relationship where one partner is stubbornly unaccomodative" (Jaya Prasad 2005: 72)," weighed heavily on Devi. She cried helplessly:

> The game is over, just as I was beginning to learn the rules. I will store them, but where? And for what use? The fingers ache to express their forbidden tenderness. They wrap and unwrap, obsessively, using the most delicate of tinsel, a package that is all rough edges. (93)

What could Devi do other than peep over the boundary walls of her house and search for reprieve outside? She did not run away with Gopal on her own. Mahesh, with his indifference, pushed her towards an illegitimate relationship. Many marriages break not because men or women do not believe in the institution but because the responsibility to make it work is not shared equally by the couple. In contemporary society, however, it is difficult to find people who would keep tolerating such a one-sided affair . In today's world it is not that all educated wives clamour for career and hence break homes and families because of ambition. It is not that all wives or husbands are morally bankrupt and enjoy having illicit relationships. More often than not, it is the misbehaviour of the wedded partner that creates space for the third party. In fact Devi "would have happily led" her life "within the confines of" her home if only Mahesh had "shown even a modicum of responsibility and sensitivity towards marital ties" (67). She ran away with the singer not because she "did not believe in marriage but because" Mahesh was indifferent towards her and she "could no longer put up with it" (67).

Had a child arrived, Devi would have reconciled herself to Mahesh. If they could not jell as husband and wife, may be as parents they would have got along well for the sake of their child. In Indian society, one of the important reasons behind stable marriages is the future of the children. Once a child is born, the priority of Indian men and women change. The focus shifts from marital ties to raising the child. The progeny acts like a glue keeping man and wife and the whole family together. In typical Indian families, men and women cease to be husband or wife. Rather they begin to live more as father and mother of a child who is the raison d'etre of their lives. They consider it shameful, unbecoming and inappropriate to behave like lovebirds or as lovelorn couples. Rather a shared sense of contentment, respect for each other and a shared sense of commitment towards their children creeps in. A woman's position becomes secure in her husband's life and within the in-laws' family once an heir is born. The birth of a child is actually a reiteration of their marriage vows, an occasion of repeating their religious, social, financial, emotional commitment to each other and each other's parental family. This is the reason why "the common features of religion for the majority of Indians lie in the worship of the mother goddess and the fertility cults" (Thapar 51).

Devi, however, was not such a fortunate woman. She could not depend on this traditional support system of 'motherhood' that Indian women have relied on since eternity to make their lives as women complete and to make secure their position in their husband's heart, house and family. God was not kind enough to bless her with a child who would wipe away all her tears with his/her mere presence or make her forget her personal frustrations with his/her toothless smiles, giggles and gurgles. Devi did not have the softness of a baby in her arms to forget the hardness of her husband's heart. Her own mother sounded too much like Mahesh. Hence she could not expect the kind of reprieve she badly needed. In despair she turned to Mayamma and cried her heart out. What could the poor maid do other than advice the distraught young woman to seek the refuge of the gods?:

> Pray, pray, Devi. Tell the beads till your fingers are calloused and numb with exhaustion. Sit between five fires in a grove of penance for the sake of your unborn son. Find Shashti's head, a smooth stone the size of a man's head that rests under a sanctified banyan tree. Offer the freshest, most luscious of fruits, flowers and rice to the rocky goddess. Drink the potion blessed by Jagammata, slit a goat's throat at Kali shrine. Only the goddess knows what knives of pain twist and turn in a woman's heart. (93-94)

Mayamma, in fact, was recounting her own experience. She too had been married for years and remained childless for long. Her mother-in-law was a witch incarnate. She often took the girl to task for it. Mayamma got beaten and tortured by the mother-in-law and son duo. Unlike Devi, she did not have the option of seeking modern medical assistance. She was dependent entirely on religious beliefs, folk remedies and superstition to tide over the crisis. There was no deity Mayamma did not pray to for fecundity. She tried to appease the forces of nature. She went scurrying to every pandit or tantric she could get hold off. She carried out the most repulsive of tantric rites to appease the malevolent forces. In other words, she left no stone unturned to be blessed with a child.

When the usual '*satvika*' style of worship fails to elicit divine benediction, people in desperation rush to '*tantra*.' Mayamma did the same. *Tantrism* is a form of worship alternative to the *satvika*. In *satvika* worship alcohol, meat, fish, parched grain and sex are eschewed. In *tantrism,* however, these *tamasika* elements are crucial and essential to the rituals. This is the reason why *tantrism* is not as popular and as respectable form of worship as the *satvika*.

It is the last resort of only those who are abnormally desperate either to gain something or mad in jealousy and resentment. If used in a benevolent manner, *tantric gurus* claim to cure mental and physical diseases, find lost articles and ward off witches and spirits or even rescue innocent individuals from the malevolent *tantric* charms of other *gurus*. *Tantrism* is also used to harm and harass opponents or rivals. It is because of the inclusion of *tamasika* elements, horrific and sensuous aspects of the deities, the tendency to aid even malevolent motives that tantrism is considered inauspicious, notorious, mysterious and fearsome. It is considered wise never to seek its assistance. Even people who are associated with it either as worshippers or as practitioner are looked at with apprehension. The practice of it and belief in it is commonly discouraged. However who can stop the desperados? Mayamma was one of them:

> A woman without a child, say the sages, goes to hell. Mayamma invoked the power of Pratyangira, the well-proportioned one, to stall this tortuous descent. She went in secret to the priest of Kali, the red-

> garbed who prays only at night. He promised her that a goat would be slaughtered the next moonless night; the flesh of the animal would be dipped in fuming liquor and then burnt. The body of Mayamma's enemy, the body that wished hers to be childless, would swell, putrefy, even as the flesh of the sacrifice swelled in the fire. (81)

It is unclear, whether the '*satavika*' puja or the *'tantric* rites did the trick but Mayamma was indeed blessed with a son. It is another matter that this son went astray early and died in youth. Hence she advised the same course of action to Devi.

Devi, who had always loved the myths of gods and goddesses, prince and princesses, suddenly found a new utility of them. Previously they were a ticket to a marvellous, mysterious and magical world she loved to listen, read or even recreate imaginatively. They were also the most interesting medium to get in touch with the cultural ethos of the Hindu religion and lifestyle. However, in Mahesh's house and in view of the given circumstances, Devi's equation with the mythic world changed. She approached the mythic figures not with girlish awe, admiration or curiosity but as a woman broken in spirit and mind making a last-ditch effort to redeem herself as a 'woman' in her husband's life, to become a mother and somehow gain some love or respect from him:

> I sat all evening in the dark room of Mayamma's gods. The light of the evening lamp cast a faint golden sheen on the face of the brass goddess. . . . I sat day after day in the airless room, the brass and stone pantheon surrounding me. (93-94)

As Neera Desai has rightly observed that more than men, it is women themselves who play pivotal role in "instituting patriarchal authority over the other female members" (75). Gender socialization of girls begins early and reaches its peak and bears fruit in the husband's house. In the course of her life a girl meets and interacts with a number of women who teach her a number of roles—from being an expert cook to a coy bride and sensuous seductress all directed towards pleasing the menfolk especially the husband and gaining control over their heart, mind, house and money. The sermons are invariably communicated by using religious and mythic figures. The women never say to each other that never suffer like Sita or struggle like Parvati or feel dejected for being dark like Haimavati. Rather they chant:

> Like Sati you must burn yourself to death, like Sati you must vindicate your husband's honour and manhood.
>
> Like Parvati you must stand neck-deep in cold turbulent waters, the hungry, predatory fish devouring your feet.
>
> Like Haimavati you must turn that black skin on your sinful body into golden sheen of light and beauty.
>
> Like Gauri you must reap the bountiful harvest that will be yours if you embrace the lingam on the sacrificial altar. (94)

Women who learn and internalize the patriarchal notions well, begin to 'master' the men. Women stoop but only to conquer. They fulfill the emotional and physical needs of men and gain control of their financial and social resources.

This is done either by the wives of the men or by their girlfriends. Since childhood girls are groomed in a manner that they grow up to be experts in managing men and, through the men, become powerful. This kind of socialization, however, is not always easy. Some women resent and suffocate at the pressure to appease, please or tease the opposite gender even if it is to make secure and stable their own position as wives or girlfriends. Even the mothers and mother-figures remain on tenterhooks till they are vindicated by daughters who make secure their position in husband's house and family. A woman's mothering and grooming skills is at stake till her daughter gets selected for marriage, love or arranged, and, through the passage of time, gain a firm control over her husband and his resources.

Devi, however, was a woman who would not understand the unspoken but understood politics and intricacies of her own gender vis-à-vis the men. She did not understand that while simple and perhaps foolish women slog like slaves following patriarchal norms, shrewd ones turn the tables on the men and make the men their slaves and not vice-versa. In history there are numerous instances of women who followed patriarchal notions to the hilt but only to tame the men and rule and live like queens. In fact, this feminine tactic, passed around as patriarchal expectations, is also a weapon that women use to outdo each other or eliminate each other from the race of winning, wooing and wedding a man. Thus, women are often caught between the devil and the deep sea—somehow keep the man in their life pleased and at the same time keep looking over the shoulder to check that there is not any other female contender coming up to challenge their monopoly over either the lover/ husband.

For naïve women like Devi the theory as well as practices of patriarchal beliefs were as difficult as understanding the power of femininity and feminism. She could not decide if she should adhere to the Sita-Savitri model or seek revenge like princess Amba. Examples from the real as well as the surreal world crowded oppressively in her mind and she felt caught in a tangle.

It is not that Devi was repelled by just the pressure to fit into "ideal moulds, impossibly ambitious" (27). The option to revolt, rant and ravage like Amba and Kali was equally burdensome. She felt equally tired of the second option. It was like swinging from one abnormality to another, from one extreme to another:

> Like Durga you shall be a beautiful, yellow-faced woman with ten arms and ride on a Himalayan lion. Despite your grace, you are born to kill. Take up your weapons then. The discus, the trident, the conch shell, the flaming dart, the bow, quiver and arrow, the iron rod, the thunderbolt, the club. A garland of snakes, and as a charger, the blood-streaked lion with the yawning red mouth.
>
> Ride into the dark night, disguised as a beautiful woman, and devour the demons, thirty to hundred at a mouthful. (94)

To Devi if the Sati-Savitri examples seemed regressive the Durga/ Kali type was repulsive. The violence inherent in the latter option, the ferociousness, the chameleon like ability to switch from bright to dark and vice-versa terrified Devi.

Devi was uncomfortable as she was caught between the 'docile' and the 'dominant.' She felt uneasy with both. She weighed the pros and cons of both stands but could not make up her mind. She felt constricted by the two polarities. She realized that both were a waste of a woman's life. Too predictable course of action with equally predictable results. She wondered if she couldn't do something different, that is, chart out a new path. Devi wanted to react and act according to her own will instead of copying or imitating set patterns. She realized that if patriarchy was a trap, the acceptance or rejection of it like mythic/archetypes of Amba, Durga or Kali was also another cage build up by society that compelled women to assume the mantle of a superwoman who was over and above all normal human cravings. Devi decided she would not do that: "I try endless variations on these themes, but even in my day-dreams they reek of cliché and platitude. No words then, no blood, no scenes" (95). Devi would indeed take the responsibility of setting things right in her own hands but not in the style of Durga or Kali. Rather she would play the game of life with new rules formulated by none other than herself. A new goddess would be born who would neither be 'this' or 'that' but equidistant from both. It would be a stance without any name or label. She would walk on in the forest of life making new ways to the river of contentment.

Gopal, the namesake of Lord Krishna, would be her companion. He did not promise home and hearth but gave his heart like Lord Krishna did with Radha and the milkmaids . Krishna did not make demands from Radha or the milkmaids. His love was unconditional. What alone mattered in the relationship of the flute playing god and his female devotees was their mutual spiritual commitment. Devi had wanted this kind of an understanding with Mahesh. Alas! he wouldn't accept her if she could not become an ideal home maker or the mother of his children. Her feelings of love were of no significance to Mahesh. She was useless if she could not be a perfect wife and a mother. Gopal, however, was different. Like his namesake Lord Krishna, he valued Devi for herself: "I can learn to be a woman at last. I will soar high on the crest of Gopal's wave of ragas, and what if I fall with a thud, alone, the morning after? I will walk on, seeking a goddess who is not yet made" (95).

Thus, Devi decided to remove all the mental blocks and look ahead to life with a new perspective. She was neither going to squeeze herself nor inflate to fit into moulds and cases created by other people. She rejected the option of either becoming, a 'goddess,' a 'heroine' or a 'she-devil.' All that she wanted to do now was to assert her selfhood and break loose of all bondages.

Later when she realized that even Gopal was a mirage, she abandoned him too. She returned to Sita to finally sort things out with her mother. She was finally going to talk to her mother and tell her what she would like to do with her life. At the end Devi emerged as one of those women to whom "neither the 'sacredness' of marriage nor the 'hypnotism' of love make . . . blind to what is wrong and what is more important" (Jaya Prasad 2005: 68). Devi realized that merely abandoning husband or lover is not enough. She would have to negotiate and coordinate with people of her own gender too (like her mother) because they are the ones who are the main agents of patriarchy, socializing girls in a way that often hurts and backfires.

Devi did try to fit into the traditional way of life. She did discharge her duties as a traditional daughter, daughter-in-law and wife. She showed, through her compliance, that education and modern lifestyle had not swollen her head and that she understood the value of cultural beliefs and narratives. She did not allow her academic excellence to turn her into an intellectual snob. It were, in fact, the agents of patriarchy who were at fault. Their rigidity and impatience ruined matters while a modern educated woman tried her best to cope and conform.

No woman wants to remain perpetually unmarried., Nor does a married woman wishes to remain childless forever. Why hammer such well-understood, well imbibed matters so much that a woman or girl begins to revolt and react? Homemaking is an inborn inclination of the female folks. Why turn it into an issue? Moreover why are women expected to become each other's or mythic women's copycat? The pressure to conform to 'this' or 'that' example is actually a denial of the individuality of each woman. It is an attempt to over-look the differences in the dispositions and personalities of women. It is high time people realized that women cannot be 'factory produced.' Each woman is unique in her own way. She is different from the other. This difference must be accepted and respected.

The novel *The Thousand Faces of Night* brings to the fore the ambivalent nature of myths. For Devi myths are a "retreat or escape" (Khan 60) from everyday life, a source of reprieve and recreation. It is also a method to connect with past and learn about cultural ethos. On the other hand, myths are restrictive too tying her down to set patterns of actions and reactions. In Devi's life myths operate in both ways and she experiences a desire to break loose and chart out a new course. She also realizes that some aspects of modernity are repackaging of patriarchal notions renamed differently to make them appear as novel. Hence modernity is not a panacea for all the ills befalling the women. Modernity is like a labyrinth and not liberation all the time.

Too much of liberty can also ruin a woman. Women can ignore this fact only at their own peril. *The Thousand Faces of Night*, thus, is a study of all the forces that operate in a woman's life today and how she attempts to cope. Githa Hariharan exposes the reality that humanity has tended to practice only those mythic/ religious beliefs that are regressive as far as women are concerned while the more progressive or egalitarian aspects of myth/ religion vis-à-vis the women have been conveniently and expediently ignored. What women need today is a balanced combination of 'tradition' as well as 'modernity' so that neither the emotional and moral nor practical aspects of their lives are ignored. Moreover, women need to be on guard against both 'modern' and 'traditional' myths. *The Thousand Faces of Night* is, thus, a novel written in the quest of "a goddess not yet made" (95), and a 'myth' that needs to be created by women for themselves.

Conclusion

Myth has provided Indian English authors insight, inspiration and stimulation for creative and critical endeavours. In art and literature "one can look anywhere for one's initial ideas" (Truzzi 2) and myth is one of such sources notwithstanding the controversy whether myth is an impediment or an impetus to individual and collective progress.

Myth caters to "some deeply felt inner need of human nature" (Nehru 26) that cannot be explained otherwise. It continues to be a part of life, art and literature because in spite of all modernity and technological advance "the ideals and objectives of yesterday are still the ideals of today" (Nehru 25). Arundhati Roy observes:

> The Great Stories are the ones you have heard and want to hear again. . . . You know how they end, yet you listen as though you don't. . . . In the Great Stories you know who lives, who dies, who finds love, who doesn't. And yet you want to know again.
>
> That is their mystery and their magic. (229)

Noted critics like Northrop Frye to Richard Chase, T.S. Eliot and P. Lal unanimously believe that the salvation of literature lies in myth. In their opinion myth is the breath and finer spirit of literature—a perennial source of all beauty, truth and technique. These critics and litterateurs point out that "myth has supplied most of the subject matter and atmosphere" (Malinowski 738) to the literature of all societies. In order to create any serious work of literature, the writer must have the knowledge of myth, that is, the past "in his bones. . . . We shall often find that not only the best, but the most individual parts of his work may be those in which the dead poets, his ancestors, assert their immortality most vigorously" (Eliot 294). Only then, believes Eliot, will a writer be able to proceed with his creative journey on a sound footing. "Without an absorption in the myths of the lands of one's forefathers it isn't even possible to live a meaningful life" (Lal 17) let alone create a meaningful work of art.

The novels that have been examined in this thesis are both in consonance with and contradiction to the views expressed by the literary critics. A writer like Lal Bihari Day has not overlooked the myths because at the time of writing 'The Bengal Peasant Life' (1874) myths were indeed a force to reckon with. He could not overlook the myths because myths were very much part and parcel of the rural peasantry about whom he was writing. For the Bengali peasantry of pre-independent India myths defined their "religious beliefs, historical traditions, cosmological speculation" (Frye 362). Hence Day retold the myths of the people as accurately as possible. In *The Bengal Peasant Life*, the reader comes face-to-face with the social function of myth.

Raja Rao in *The Serpent and the Rope* displays personal conviction, genuine faith and interest in the use of myth. He, like the critics quoted above and in the introductory chapter, believes that the salvation of man and of literature indeed lies in the mythic world view. Motivated by this belief he articulates and expresses, in mythic jargon a crisis that is essentially personal and also metaphysical. However his selection of myth is eclectic. Though profoundly impressed by the myth beliefs of Hinduism, he alludes to the myths of other cultures as well. In his opinion everyone, aliens and Indian alike, can ignore the myth and myth beliefs of their respective cultures only at the cost of jeopardizing their emotional, mental moral and spiritual health.

A different note is struck by the other two novelists. Mulk Raj Anand is openly critical of myth and myth values. He believes that myths with their discriminatory value systems have driven a wedge into the Indian society. Thanks largely to the religious myths Indian society is divided into antagonistic and mutually inimical castes of the 'blessed' and the 'oppressed,' the 'magnified' and the 'marginalized.' The myths have created an environment of mutual mistrust, non-cooperation and animosity that has been telling on the political, social and economic fibre of the country. While other nations of the world progress by leaps and bounds, India wastes her time and energy in trying to overcome the differences created by religious myths of all communities. Hence he openly calls for abandoning the baggage of the past, that is, the myths and mythologies and adopting in their place the mantra of 'humanism.'

Githa Hariharan almost concurs with this Marxian point of view. However, in *The Thousand Faces of Night* she is not blind to the positive elements in myth. None the less she too believes that myths of all types, primitive as well as modern, need to be constantly reinterpreted so that life becomes easier for women. Dalits and women have suffered a lot because of mythic values. Hence myths need to be reread, rewritten and recreated in a manner that they become sensitive and soft towards the marginalized castes and the marginalized gender of Indian society. Draconian dictums that "dhola gavara shudra pashu nari, sakal tarana ke adhikari" must give way to those religious or secular beliefs that are supportive of all the marginalized sections including women. As has been pointed out in the introductory chapter, "myths will always need retelling and reinterpreting, and the women's movement, feminist and post-feminist, has made striking contributions to this process" (Coupe 189). Women today are presenting some of the most interesting and incisive studies of myth.

The theories discussed in the introductory chapter make clear that myths contain '*archetypes*' and '*archetypal' patterns*. One encounters in the myths numerous characters and circumstances that help reveal "the two-sidedness of life, the deep and tragic division of the world" (Thorlby 71) the happy as well as the horrific. The issues that myths handle range from the 'acceptable' to the 'unacceptable.' In the myths one finds Ram and Sita, Nala and Damayanti, Adam and Eve, Goddess Kali, Kunti, Virgin Mary,

Shravan Kumar as also Yama and Yami, Brahma and Saraswati, Oedipus and Jocasta. It is with the help of these pious and problematic relationships and situations that myths of different cultures attempt to explain. "how the world was created what powers rule it, why men must behave in a certain way, and why they must die" (*Ibid.* 70).

Since myths tend to emphasis certain 'do's' and 'don'ts' it is commonly believed that myths are dogmatic and didactic. In the eagerness to draw lines and implement those lines in letter as well as in spirit, myths tend to become fanatical and fatalistic. There is even an element of barbarity in them. They do not recognize 'differences.' They, in fact, 'do not' tolerate differences. Myths are all about moral, social, political and religious 'certainties.' Roland Barthes (1915-1980) went to the extent of alleging that mythology is actually bourgeois ideology devoted to furthering bourgeois interests. In 'Mythologies' (1957) he described these stories as "conspiratorial aspects of bourgeois culture, binding us to the status-quo" (Coupe 171).

Critics of Barthes, however, point out that myth is actually "a disclosure rather than a dogma" (Coupe 197). Far from aspiring for uniformity it actually discloses the 'duality' of humanity and nature. Instead of attempting to erase the possibility of 'differences,' what myths do is show the presence of and probability of 'differences.' "Firstly, the myth recalls and projects an 'other' world. Secondly, the myth reminds us that there is always something else, something 'other' to be said or imagined. Thirdly, the myth, as a play of past paradigm and future possibility, gives expression to the 'other,' to those persons and causes excluded from the present hierarchy" (Coupe 196).

Since myths are essentially stories about 'duality' or 'opposites' they can be "both life-affirming and destructive. Our obligation is to be both receptive and vigilant" (Coupe 188). It is for the people to decide whether they want to accept, encourage and believe in the sober or the sinister. The only fault with myth is that it offers both the alternatives. Myth therefore "will always need retelling and reinterpreting" (Coupe 189). It will always require judicious selection and rejection. Myth tends to communicate life affirming and destructive truths through stories. Myth, in fact, are basically stories. The message is often not explicitly conveyed. It often has to be decoded from the fate that its characters suffer. The characters of these stories or myths are invariably either deities, devils, superheroes or superhumans or even legendary figures and the royalty. With the help of these characters myth brings to the fore either the duality of existence or it expresses "archetypal and fundamental human feelings . . . natural phenomena" (Clammer 111) or complex human relationships within a society.

Authors, thus, cannot give a realistic description of any society without taking cognizance of the myths that people believe in and live by. These myths, however, need not always be primitive or religious. Myths can be modern as well as secular. Sometimes primitive and contemporary myths co-exist in society exposing the reality that myth-making is not the prerogative of primitive man as had been thought by many. Each age creates its own myths, legends, tales, heroes and icons to keep itself intellectually engaged or to express its artistic aesthetic and emotional urges.

As mentioned already, humanity has at its disposal a repertoire of mythical archetypes that it has culled from its many mythologies and has used since eternity to express its fundamental fears, fervour or fantasy. It has used these archetypes to communicate its ideals, its rules and regulations of living and loving, winning and losing. It uses certain archetypal patterns to go about with life. It makes sense of human life and the world at large with the help of these archetypal symbols, patterns, heroes and heroines, demons and witches, gods and goddesses.

What writers and artists do is to borrow these archetypes in their works of art because, as T.S. Eliot believed, there is no better way of articulating the multiple complexes of modern life. While reviewing Joyce's novel Ulysses, Eliot observed: "Using myth, is simply a way of controlling, of ordering, of giving a shape and a significance to the immense panorama of fertility and anarchy which is contemporary history. Instead of the narrative method, we may now use the mythical method. It is, I seriously believe, a step towards making the modern world possible for art" (224).

In fact, the belief that mythology replenishes literature is widespread. Not just the litterateurs, mythologists but even historians, sociologists "and anthropologists have not failed to notice the nexus between . . . mythology and literature in art" (Jaya Prasad 2002: 34). Malinowski expressed similar views while reviewing 'The Mythologies of All Races' (Vol II) written by Uno Vdolmberg. The review was published in 1928, just five years after Eliot's review of Joyce's *Ulysses*. Malinowski opined: "Myth, clothing the brutal and naked beauty of primeval thought with the dignity of tradition and the majesty of sacredness, exerts a singular attraction upon the human mind, civilized and sophisticated, as well as simple and untutored. The mixture of incompatible extremes, of the shameful and the holy, the grateful and the raw, the fleshly and the spiritual, the tragic and the clownish, surround myth with an atmosphere of mystery and gives it a meaning which has always inspired the artist" (739).

P. Lal, writing in the late 1970s, went to the extent of advising Indian writers that they "should not commit pen to paper" until they have spent ten years of their adult life "carefully pondering the Indian classics, learning the Indian tradition, and absorbing the Indian myth" (18). According to him, a literature genuine of the Indian people would be produced only when "one's own myth values and structures are studied and loved and absorbed and used with creative and critical imagination" (16). This would not be imitation as Eliot had clarified. Rather deities, devils, heroes, ghosts, witches would be recalled so as to understand "the complexities of . . . feelings and activities" (18). Lal said: "The gods and goddesses are not out there, separated permanently from us; nor are the anti-gods and rakshasas. They populate the earth: to know them is really to know ourselves" (18).

In *The Serpent and the Rope* Rao has used myth primarily with this motive in view. He has constantly alluded to Ram and Krishna to understand himself better. Above all he has referred to the deities to realize what really is his duty—primarily to amuse his own self or to give 'purpose' and 'happiness' to others. In this novel myth has also been used to clear the complexities of human relationships. Savitri is someone else's fiancée. Rama someone else's husband. Yet there exists a bond between them. An illegitimate intimacy that cries out for acceptance and approval helpless as it is before spontaneous and involuntary surge of emotions on the one hand and social morals of the stringent variety on the other. Hence the author turns to the Radha and Krishna myth that allow of such attachments. Madeleine, Rama's French wife, too looks back to Greek gods and goddesses so as to console herself and gather strength to survive in the face of failure and unhappiness. When even gods and goddesses suffered, what to talk of human beings? This fact seems to, somehow, quieten the disturbed and perturbed souls of all—Rama, Savithri and Madeleine. They gather courage and move on in life.

In 'The Bengal Peasant Life' the problems are more or less social and financial rather than personal. In this novel one does not encounter archetypal symbols. Nor does the writer Lal Bihari Day establish mythic parallels between archetypes and his characters. At the same time it is also true that mythic entities are very much at the heart of this work. However, what this novel does is to exemplify Northrop Frye's theory of myth as "a structural organizing principle of literary form" (341). Frye co-related the different phases of human life with the seasonal cycle and then both of these to the four genres of literature.

According to Frye, the four main divisions of human life, of the seasonal cycle and indeed of literature are as follows:

1. The dawn, spring and birth phase: Myths of the birth of the hero, of creation, of the defeat of the powers of

darkness, winter and death—this phase corresponds in literature with the genre of romance and all rhapsodic poetry.

2. The zenith, summer, and marriage: Myths of marriage—the archetype of comedy, pastoral and idyllic.
3. The sunset, autumn and death phase: Myths of fall, of the dying god, of violent death and sacrifice, and of isolation of the hero—the archetype of tragedy and elegy.
4. The darkness, winter and dissolution phase: Myths of triumph of these powers, myths of flood or chaos and crisis, of the defeat of the hero—the archetype of the satire.

Lal Bihari Dey's *The Bengal Peasant Life* closely appropriates Frye's formula in its narrative structure. The novel opens with the birth of the protagonist in the style of the genre of romance. As his life runs its course the reader witnesses the unfolding of each genre and each myth associated with it. 'The Bengal Peasant Life' is nothing but a poignant unfolding of the archetypal pattern of human existence, a re-enactment of the birth, marriage, death and dissolution myth. Dealing as it is with the rural peasantry that subsists on agriculture, one comes face-to-face with the fundamental synchrony that exists between humanity and the world of nature. The seasonal phases—spring, summer, autumn and winter—are an expression and proof of this synchrony. They correspond with the birth, youth, adulthood and old age of man.

The Bengal Peasant Life opens with spring and ends on winter. It begins promisingly with romance but ends with tragedy. The protagonist is born amidst jubilation and celebration but, at the end of the novel, is broken by life's umpteen struggles and ultimately dies. He possesses the courage to fight back but is helpless before the much stronger malevolent powers. This further accentuates the element of tragedy and the myth of fall in the novel.

However apart from myth as a structural organizing principle of the narrative, one witnesses in this novel, myth as a potent force dominating and directing the characters as they go on with life.

Each phase of their life—the birth or the spring is again dominated by representative mythic figures. For example, if at the time of birth, *Govinda Samanta's* family worships *Shashthi* the goddess of fecundity, then at the fag end of the novel, when they have run out of luck, they face the wrath of *Agni*, the god of fire who consumes all their possessions and reduces them to penury.

Since Day's motive was to give a realistic account of the life of Bengali peasantry, he could not possible avoid any of the superstitions of the rural people or the myths that they believed in. "Any body of myths tries to give a comprehensive account of the world and of the people to whom it belongs" (Wiegel 10). The novel is peopled as much by the village folks as by their gods, goddess, witches and ghosts with Day describing these divine and supernatural entities as graphically as possible. Since the Bengali society is matriarchal, it is the mother goddesses in their varied forms who are given precedence. Of them it is the goddess of fecundity 'Shashthi' who is especially revered. Her blessings, believe the rural folks, is essential to ensure manpower (in the form of progeny) as also a good harvest of crops.

Day was a Hindu who later converted to Christianity. However in his narrative he displays amazing neutrality and diplomacy while dealing with his original religion Hinduism. It has been noticed that religious converts, in the eagerness to prove their allegiance to the new faith, begin to disparage their original religion. Day, however, did nothing of the sort. He has been very balanced in his analysis. He has not tried to insult the Hindu community and ridicule its beliefs. Nor has he overlooked the superstitions and social evils that have crept into the Hindu religion and its community. He makes explicit the ambivalent character of Hindu myths, Hindu religion and indeed of the whole Hindu society that both worships women as goddesses and also burns them alive in the funeral fires to get rid of them. These are the types of anomalies that Day has not overlooked in his well-written, truthful account of the Bengali peasantry.

Rao, the author of *The Serpent and the Rope*, on the other hand, is not such an impartial observer or analyst of the Hindu religion and Hindu myths. *The Serpent and the Rope* is the work of a man steeped in Hindu philosophy and in love with Hindu myths and legends. The only saving grace is that in his love for the Hindu religion and religious figures, he has not turned fanatical. He shows a healthy respect and understanding for all the other faiths of the world. He possesses as deep a knowledge about the other religions as he does about Hinduism. However what is noticeable that the more he studies other faiths, the more convinced he becomes of, the superiority of his own 'beloved' Hinduism. He seems to be mesmerized with Hindu mythic figures and is completely under the spell of Veda and Vedanta philosophy. His knowledge about Hinduism and his interpretation of the mythic figures is so superlative that some Hindu readers would feel ashamed about their meagre knowledge of their own faith and simplistic practices. Rao discusses Hindu beliefs, Hindu gods and goddess in such a manner and in such a language that a common Hindu would wonder if it is our own faith he is talking about. The book would, as a natural corollary, be all the more difficult for non-Indians and non-Hindus to comprehend. If the common Hindu gets daunted by the erudite Rao, how are naïve foreigners to understand him? His philosophizing is tiresome to say the least. His definition of Hindu mythic figures is too complex for ordinary readers to understand. Thankfully, he has spared the Greek gods and goddesses the same treatment.

The Serpent and the Rope is a novel fit for devout Hindus but only those who are learned. A religious Hindu woman living in an inconsequential village and visiting the village temple by the pond would hardly comprehend him or his logic. Hinduism and the mythic figures, as he has interpreted them, would be appreciated only by one who is as erudite as the writer. A sound knowledge of the *Sanskrit* would further add to the pleasures of reading this book.

Though literary critics may differ, but in the researcher's opinion Rao has used all the three techniques that Meenakshi Mukherjee has discussed in *The Twice Born Fiction*. Not only does Rao take recourse to the 'digressional technique' of using myth but also the 'structural parallel' and the 'reversal' of the mythic pattern in *The Serpent and the Rope*. In order to explain the concept of 'dharma' he digresses to the *Ramayana*. His hero compares himself to Ram, Shiva and Krishna and Savithri to Sita, Parvati and Radha. Around the end of the novel when Savithri leaves Rama finally to marry Pratap, it is clear that the Satyavana and Savitri myth has been turned upside down. Savithri rescues Rama from a life of mere senses and pseudo spiritualism. She pushes him towards self-realization. However she herself ends up marrying the 'Yama.' Savithri, as she reconciles herself to life with Pratap, dies an intellectual death. Rama was her paradise but Pratap was the Yama who finally claims her as his own. He takes her towards mundane life, the kingdom of death, instead of the metaphysical world in which Savithri wanted to live with Rama, the husband of Madeleine.

The Bengal Peasant Life and *The Serpent and the Rope*, thus, are in sharp contrast to each other. The first one is about the peasantry. The second novel about intellectuals and royalty. The former novel evokes the mother goddesses more. The later highlights mythic couples. It focuses on the relationship between the opposite genders of the celestial world and the terrestrial world. In Day's novel, each myth is described with its concomitant rituals. In Rao's novel rituals are largely absent. Even a layman can understand Day's work. The same cannot be said about Rao's novel. The Serpent and the Rope requires some education, some learning in its readers. Local myths and regional superstitions find mention in *The Bengal Peasant Life*. Moreover it concentrates merely on the life of Hindu peasants. Consequently only Hindu myths find space in it. The Serpent and the Rope, on the contrary, is, despite being permeated with Hindu myth and philosophy, a collocation of myths and legends of different cultures. Last but not the least, *The Bengal Peasant Life* is an impartial description of the Hindu way of life. *The Serpent and the Rope*, on the other hand, seems to be the work of a man who is fully convinced of the superiority of the Hindu faith, the Hindu philosophy, and of the Hindu myths and practices.

It seems the Nehruvian years had little impact on Raja Rao. Even Gandhi did not impress him much. Published in 1960, this novel bears little impact of either Nehru or Gandhi or even Karl Marx unlike his contemporaries R.K. Narayan and Mulk Raj Anand who were greatly influenced by the ideology of these political leaders. Rao was a secular intellectual no doubt but his secularism was very different from the kind that Gandhi or Nehru practiced. In the works of Narayan and Anand, religion was a marginal issue. In Rao's book, it had an overwhelming presence. Rao was not at all happy with the way the country was being managed after independence. He made this clear time and again through the character of Little Mother and Savithri in *The Serpent and the Rope*. He was probably not happy with the policy of industrialism that Nehru had embarked on. He probably felt the policy was being followed indiscriminately. He believed that progress did not lie in material achievements alone. He felt that native traditions and practices were being unfairly brushed aside and ignored. In his opinion, the best example of this phenomenon, the concrete urban rot, was northern India. *Rama's* step-mother and his lady-love are shown nauseated at it. They openly complain against the way things are going in the country. The two women seek refuge in the more traditional southern India and in the company of a philosophical man like *Rama.* No wonder Hindu myths and myths of all the other cultures crowd in this novel that has been written by a man who seems to hanker for old world charm and old-world values.

In sharp contrast to Day's novel and Rao's book, are the other two works that have been examined in this thesis. While Day was a neutral voice and Rao an espouser of the Hindu ideology who did not pretend diplomacy out of the fear of being politically incorrect, Mulk Raj Anand and Githa Hariharan are openly critical about myths and mythic values. Both the writers are amongst those "people who recognize and accept responsibility for their own culture's problems" (Brooks). They seem to agree that while "some cultures foster development . . . others retard it" (Brooks). Hence writers like Anand and Hariharan seek to either overhaul the whole value system as enshrined in religion and myth or "selectively reinterpret their own traditions to encourage modernization" (Brooks).

All through his life Anand protested against the hegemony of mythic values and religious rites on human life. He, however, did not protest merely for the sake of protesting. He was a keen observer who realized how religion becomes a tool in the hands of nefarious elements who loot gullible people. Not only do they take advantage of believers but also fan religious sentiments to ferment trouble for other religious communities making things difficult for the society at large. He, therefore, set down to expose the corruptions that have crept into religious institutions and highlight the anomalies inherent in religious practices especially in the context of women and the untouchables. It is precisely in this context that Anand questions mythic ideals and mythic values. Believing firmly in the principle of equality he protests against caste, class and gender discriminations and attacks those mythic/ religious believes that support caste/class/gender bias. Not religion but "the ideology of social change is the creative force behind" (Sati Prasad 5) his novels. Hence he writes to Lord Krishna in the 'Preface' to *Morning Face*: "You are really not the Krishna of the age of the gods. You cannot be, because the age of the gods is over" (vi). Even in the context of the art of narration, Anand did not want to take recourse to myths. While even the diehard critics of myths acknowledge that myths "illustrate essential principles of storytelling" (Frye 356). Anand observed in the 'Preface' to *Morning*

Face: "The novel is a good form for the troubled conscience without aspiring to the old epic myths, a rather formless form, to show the flow of sensibilities, thought-processes, and wills, in the love-hate relationships of human beings, relentlessly, pursued perchance they might connect" (viii).

Anand, therefore, turned upside down, in his novels, the value system and narrative pattern of myth. He exposes in 'The Big heart' the element of fanatism and barbarity that is inherent to myth and mythology. He, thereby, stresses the need for them to be tampered by rationality. He exposes, in this novel, the element of brutality and frenzy that is associated with primitive mythic figures and those who blindly believe in them. In Anand's hand "literature became essentially secular" and also a perfect medium "for raising voice against social injustices" (Sangeet Kumar 165) of all sorts.

As if taking cue from M.R. Anand, there has been an increasing number of women writers expressing similar opinions and sentiments. As already mentioned, right from Toru Dutt to Namita Gokhale, women have been writing about myths and mythic heroines. However, unlike Anand who was completely critical, the Indian-English women writers share a love-hate relationship with myths. This is clearly true of the novel that has been analyzed in the fourth chapter of this thesis.

The Thousand Faces of Night written by Githa Hariharan brings to the fore the ambivalent nature of the myths and indeed of her attitude towards them. In this work Hariharan cannot help acknowledge the recreational aspect of myths but she cannot also ignore their regressiveness. She exposes the fact that primitive myths tend to reincarnate themselves in modern avatars. Bottles change but the wine remains the same. Some women realize this while other don't. *Devi,* the protagonist of the novel, becomes aware of this startling reality rather painfully.

In this novel Hariharan has adopted the digressional technique. Since the work is specifically about women, only female mythic figures have been evoked. One comes across the diverse forms of the mother goddesses. Moreover, the mythic stories that Hariharan has selected have been borrowed from the *Mahabharata*. Unlike Day and Rao, Hariharan describes mythic figures with palpable realism. The goddess and the princesses, though purportly celestial, behave, react and act like humans. They are not remote, immobile stony statues who are only to be worshipped. In *The Thousand Faces of Night*, the princesses and queens from the great epic of *Vyas* are alive and electric. One begins to relate to them as human beings and realizes that life was no less tougher for these celestial and ethereal women.

Thus what Githa Hariharan has done is not to criticize outright the myths of Sita and Savitri as being the cause of all the ills that has befallen the female folks. Rather she has concentrated on what befell the mythic women who are blamed so much for setting "impossibly ambitious" (27) ways of living, loving and dying. She has concentrated as much on the pain and problem of contemporary women, women of the older generation as those immortal women about whom one reads in the *Ramayana*, the *Mahabharata* or the folktales and songs of the land. She empathizes as much with those unlucky goddesses and princesses as she does with contemporary women who are expected to replicate extraordinary examples from myth and human history.

The authors have drawn the myths both from the *'Great'* and *'Little Traditions.'* While *The Bengal Peasant Life* is peopled with local as well as Vedic gods and goddesses, witches and ghosts, *The Serpent and the Rope* includes, mythic heroes primarily from the *Ramayana* and the *Mahabharata*. Rao recalls Lord Ram and Sita, Yudhistar, Bheeshma, Arjun and Krishna as also Radha, Shiva, Parvati. Ganga too is an important mythic personage of the novel giving Rao the chance to indulge in a lot of philosophizing. Githa Hariharan, on the other hand, borrows mythic heroines primarily from the problematic epic the *Mahabharata* that has daunted many by the complexity of its narrative style, multiple themes and characters. Meenakshi Mukherjee observes "none of the Mahabharata characters has ever become everyday models of reference in Indian life as the characters of the *Ramayana* have" (165). She believed that "this total neglect of the Mahabharata as a source material for myths reveals what is part of the characteristic inability of Indo-Anglian fiction (perhaps Indian fiction in general) to face life in the harsh and unflinching light of reality, without softening it with idealism and sentiment" (166). According to her, since the *Mahabharata* deals "with evil in its various forms" the Indian English writers have refused to acknowledge it and deal with it.

Contemporary writers, however, have unhesitatingly either re-written the epic in their own unique style of satire, humour and poignant verse or taken one or the other *Mahabharata* personages to analyze threadbare their predicament. Shashi Tharoor does this in *The Great Indian Novel* (1989), Pavan K. Verma in *Yudheshtra and Draupadi* (1996) Githa Hariharan in *The Thousand Faces of Night* and Arundhati Roy in *The God of Small Things* (2000).

It must also be pointed out that Indian novelists have been fairly eclectic in the selection of myths and legends. Rao's choice varied from the Hindu and Greek to the Chinese. Contemporary writers like Arundhati Roy and Namita Gokhale too have talked about alien cultural and mythic heroes and heroines, gods and goddesses in their novels.

It must also be borne in mind that mythical characters are not all the time ahistorical or primitive. Similarly, mythologies are not always religious or hypothetical. It is possible to have secular or national mythologies. It is likely that myths would grow around contemporary legendary or iconic figures. It is probable that myths would get created about contemporary momentous events. For example if Christ, Mohammad and Ram are cultural heroes from the religious mythology of Christianity, Islam and Hinduism respectively then Benjamin Franklin, George Washington and Mahatma Gandhi are part of national mythologies of America and

India. They find mention in poems, dramas, novels etc.

These historical figures, because of their decisive role in shaping the destiny of their people for the better, have almost been deified. Thanks largely to this apotheosis, they have been accorded a mythic stature and a whole literature has been created around them. In the context of Indian English literature, there has been a steady flow of novels, poems, dramas with Gandhi as a character or as a creative force behind the work. Mulk Raj Anand's *Untouchable*, R.K. Narayan *Waiting for the Mahatma* and Rao's *Kanthapura* are examples of the apotheosis of Gandhi in the national and creative psyche of the Indian people.

The characters of Phantom, Superman, Spiderman etc. are the modern myths of contemporary society. Myths and mythologies, are growing by the day expressive of a people's aspirations, ambitions, ideals, expectations, fears, fun and fantasy.

Myth, thus, is a proof of man's "richly endowed imagination. . . . Richer, vaster, very beautiful and full of meaning" (Nehru 78). It is an artistic and literary endeavour to explain the social and religious world. Myth has been created by people who have contemplated society no matter how flawed their perception may seem to others.

Primitive myth and modern myth/story cycles have been, to say in the words of Shashi Tharoor "an unending source of metaphor for the rhetoric" of literary themes that are often both personal as in *The Serpent and the Rope* and national as in' The Great Indian Novel.' "No wonder . . . so many contemporary" Indian English poets, dramatists and writers "have found inspiration" from the myth and consequently have retold them "in a variety of ways" adding to each myth their own "unique personality and viewpoint." The adoption of myth in literature does not imply giving leverage to orthodox agendas. Rather it primarily means treating myth as a source of insight and trying to comprehend and critically examine an ideology that is not only sacred but also full of aesthetic, artistic and literary potentialities.

Appendix I

Archetypes

Some of the universal archetypes and their symbolic meanings are as follows:

(A) Images

1. Water: the mystery of creation; birth-death resurrection; purification and redemption; fertility and growth. According to Jung, water is also the commonest symbol for the unconscious.
    (a) The Sea: the mother of all life; spiritual mystery and infinity; death and rebirth; timelessness and eternity; the unconscious.
    (b) Rivers: death and rebirth (baptism); the flowing of time into eternity; transitional phases of the life cycle; incarnation of deities.
2. Sun (fire and sky are closely related): creative energy; law in nature; consciousness (thinking, enlightenment, wisdom, spiritual vision); father principal (moon and earth tend to be associated with female or mother principle); passage of time and life.
    (a) Rising sun: birth; creation; enlightenment.
    (b) Setting sun: death.
3. Colours
    (a) Red: blood; sacrifice, danger; violent passion; disorder.
    (b) Green: growth; sensation; hope; fertility; jealousy; death and decay (in negative context).
    (c) Blue: usually highly positive, associated with truth, religious feeling, security, spiritual purity (the colour of the Great Mother or Holy Mother).
    (d) Black (darkness): Chaos; mystery; the unknown;

death; primal wisdom; the unconscious; evil; melancholy.

(e) White: highly multivalent, signifying, in its positive aspects, light, purity, innocence, and timelessness; in its negative aspects, death, terror, the supernatural, and the blinding truth of an inscrutable cosmic mystery (as in Herman Melville's 'Moby Dick').

4. Circle (sphere): Wholeness, unity.

(a) Mandala (a geometrical figure based upon the squaring of a circle around a unifying centre as in the Shri—Yantra mandala): the desire for spiritual unity and psychic integration. In its classic Asian forms the mandala juxtaposes the triangle, the square, and the circle with their numerical equivalents of three, four and seven.

(b) Egg (oval): the mystery of life and the forces of generation.

(c) Yang-Yin: a Chinese symbol representing the union of the opposite forces of Yang (masculine principle, light, activity, the conscious mind) and the Yin (female principle, darkness, passivity, the unconscious).

(d) Ourboros: the ancient symbol of the snake biting its own tail, signifying the eternal cycle of life, primordial unconsciousness, the unity of opposite forces (cf. Yang-Yin).

5. Serpent (snake, worm): symbol of energy and pure force (cf. libido); evil, corruption and sensuality; destruction; mystery; wisdom; the unconscious.

6. Numbers:

(a) Three: light; spiritual awareness and unity (cf. the Holy Trinity); the male principle, animosity (rivalry in negative context).

   (b) Four: associated with the cycle, life cycle, four seasons; female principle, earth, nature; four elements (earth, air, fire, water).
   (c) Seven: the most potent of all symbolic numbers—signifying the union of 'three' and 'four,' the completion of a cycle, perfect order; also punishment or suffering in negative context.
7. The archetypal woman:
   (a) The Good Mother (positive aspects of the Earth Mother): associated with the life principle, birth, warmth, nourishment, protection, fertility, growth, abundance (for example Demeter, Ceres, Lakshmi, Parvati, Mary, Fatima).
   (b) The Terrible Mother (including the negative aspects of the Earth Mother): the witch, sorceress, siren, whore, femme fatale—associated with sensuality, sexual orgies, fear, danger, darkness, dismemberment, emasculation, death, the unconscious in its terrifying aspects.
   (c) The Soul Mate: the Sophia figure, Holy Mother, the princess or "beautiful lady"—incarnation of inspiration and spiritual fulfillment (cf. the Jungian anima).
8. The Wise Old Man (saviour, redeemer, guru): personification of the spiritual principal, representing "knowledge, reflection, insight, wisdom, cleverness and institution on the one hand, and on the other, moral qualities such as goodwill and readiness to help, which makes lies 'spiritual' character significantly plain. . . . Apart from his cleverness, wisdom and insight, the old man . . . is also notable for his moral qualities; what is more, he even tests the moral qualities of others and makes gifts dependent on this test. . . . The old man always appears when the hero is in a hopeless and desperate situation from which only profound reflection or a lucky idea . . . can extricate him.

But since, for internal and external reasons, the hero cannot accomplish this himself, the knowledge needed to compensate the deficiency comes in the form of a personified thought, i.e., in the shape of this sagacious and helpful old man" (Jung, 'The Archetypes and the Collective Unconscious' 217 ff).

9. The Trickster (joker, jester, clown, fool, fraud, prankster, picaro [rogue], poltergeist, confidence man ["con man"], medicine man [shaman], magician [sleight—of—hand—artist], "spirit Mercurius" [shape-shifter], simian dei ["the ape of God"], witch: The trickster appears to be the opposite of the wise old man because of his close affinity with the shadow archetype, however, he has a positive side and may even serve a healing function through his transformative influence. . . . Compensating for rigid or overly righteous collective attitudes, the image of the trickster or the clown functions collectively as a cathartic safety valve for pent-up social pressures, a reminder of humankind's primitive origins and the fallibility of its institutions.
10. Garden: paradise; innocence; unspoiled beauty (especially feminine); fertility.
11. Tree: life of the cosmos, consistence, growth, proliferation, generative and regenerative processes. Inexhaustible life, immortality.
12. Desert: spiritual aridity; death; nihilism, hopelessness.

(B) Archetypal Motifs or Patterns

1. Creation: perhaps the most fundamental of all archetypal motifs: virtually every mythology is built on some account of how the cosmos, nature and humankind were built into existence by some supernatural being or beings.
2. Immortality: another fundamental archetype, generally taking one of two basic narrative forms:
    (a) Escape from time: "return to paradise," the state of perfect, timeless bliss enjoyed by man and woman before their tragic fall into corruption and

mortality.

(b) Mystical submersion into cyclical time: the theme of endless death and regeneration—human beings achieve a kind of immortality by submitting to the vast, mysterious rhythm of Nature's eternal cycle, particularly the cycle of seasons.

3. Hero archetypes (archetypes of transformation and redemption):

   (a) The Quest: the hero (saviour, deliverer) undertakes some long journey during which he or she must perform impossible tasks, battles with monsters, solve unanswerable riddles, and overcome insurmountable obstacles in order to save the kingdom.

   (b) Initiation: The hero undergoes a series of excruciating ordeals in passing from ignorance and immaturity to social and spiritual adulthood, that is, achieving maturity and becoming a full-fledged member of his or her social group. The initiation most commonly consists of three distinct phases: (i) separation (ii) transformation, and (iii) rebirth. Like the quest, this is a variation of the death and rebirth archetype.

(C) Archetypes as Genres

Finally, in addition to appearing as images and motifs, archetypes may be found in even more complex combinations as genres or types of literature that conform with the major phases of the seasonal cycle. Northrop Frye, in his 'Anatomy of Criticism' indicates the correspondent genres for the four seasons as follows:

1. The mythos of spring	:	comedy
2. The mythos of summer	:	romance
3. The mythos of fall	:	tragedy
4. The mythos of winter	:	irony.

Source: Guerin et. al., *A Handbook of Critical Approaches to Literature*, pp. 161-67.

Appendix II

Types of Literature with Mythic Content

Some myths are also great pieces of literature. However all literatures are not myth, that is, related to religion or about gods, goddesses or cultural heroes and heroines. None the less it is probable that literary works of all types may contain mythic elements. Some examples of literature having mythic content but themselves not being myths are as follows:

1. Philosophical allegory
2. Sentimental or moral fable, parable or anecdote
3. Romance
4. Cultural propaganda
5. Heroic saga and epic
6. Realistic or satirical fiction
7. Narrative drama
8. Enriched history

Bibliography

Altekar, A.S. 1938; 2004, *The Position of Women in Hindu Civilization*, Delhi: Motilal Banarsidass.

Anand, Mulk Raj. 1945, *The Big Heart*, Bombay: Kutub Publishers.

_____. 1968, *Morning Face*, Bombay: Kutub Publishers.

_____. 1935; 1981, *Untouchable*, New Delhi: Arnold.

Barthes, Roland. 1957; 1973, *Mythologies*, London: Paladin.

Basham, A.L. 1954; 1989, *The Wonder That Was India*, Calcutta: Rupa.

Bradbury, Malcolm. 1977; 1990, *The Novel Today*, London: Fontana Press.

Brockington, J.L. 1981; 1998, *The Sacred Thread*, Edinburgh: Edinburgh University Press.

Brooks, David. "The Culture of Nations," *Sunday Times of India*, Patna, August 20, 2006.

Clammer, John R. 1983, *Modern Anthropological Theory*, New Delhi: Cosmos Publications.

Coote, Jeremy and Anthony Shelton, ed. 1992, *Anthropology Art and Aesthetics*, Oxford. Clarendon Press.

Coupe, Laurence. 1997, *Myth*, London: Routledge

Cuddon, J.A., ed. 1976; 1998, *A Dictionary of Literary Terms and Literary Theory*, Delhi: Doaba House.

Daiches, David, ed. *20th Century Literary Criticism.*

_____ and Anthony Thorlby, ed., 1972, *Literature and Western Civilization, The Classical World,* Vol. I.

Das, B. and J.M. Mohanty, ed. 1985, *Literary Criticism: A Reading*, Kolkata: Oxford University Press.

Day, Lal Bihari, 1874; 1908. *The Bengal Peasant Life*, London: Macmillan.

Deb, W.C., 1999, *Shastras*, Delhi: Progressive Publishers.

Desai, Neera & Usha Thakkar. 2001; 2004, *Women in Indian Society*, New Delhi: National Book Trust.

Deshpande, Shashi. 2000, *The Stone Women*, Calcutta: A Writers Workshop Greenbird Book.

_____. "Women's Complexities being lost," *The Indian Express*, 25 June 2001.

Dundes, Alan. 1965, *The Study of Folklore,* Englewood Cliffs, NJ: Prentice Hall.

Eliot, T.S. 1962. 'Tradition and Individual Talent," *English Critical Texts*, ed. D.J. Enright and Ernst De Chickera, 1991.

_____. "*Ulysses*, Order and Myth," *The Idea of Literature: The Foundation of*

English Criticism, Moscow Progress Publishers.

Elwin, Verrier. 1949; 1991, *Myths of Middle India*. Delhi: Vanya Prakashan.

Embree, Ainslie T., ed. 1958; 1992, *Sources of Indian Tradition*, New Delhi: Penguin.

Freud Sigmund. 1974. *"The Interpretation of Dreams," Complete Works*, 4 vols. London: Hogarth Press.

Frye, Northrop. 1957, *Anatomy of Criticism*, Princeton: Princeton University Press.

Frazer, J.G. 1922, *The Golden Bough*, London: Macmillan.

Gurrian, Wilfred L., et.al. 1966; 1999, *A Handbook of Critical Approaches to Literature*, Oxford: Oxford University Press.

Gunesekera, Romesh. "New Genealogies," *The Hindu*, May 7, 2005.

Hariharan, Githa. 1992, *The Thousand Faces of Night*, New Delhi: Penguin.

Hasnain, Nadeem. 1991; 1994, *Indian Anthropology*, Delhi: Palaka Prakashan.

International Encyclopadia of the Social Sciences, 9 & 10.

Iyengar, K.R. Srinivasa. 1962; 1994, *Indian Writing In English*, New Delhi: Sterling.

Iyer, N. Sharada. "Socialisation and Gender Construction in Shashi Deshpande's Novels," in Indra Mohan.

Jain, Jasbir. 2003, *Gendered Realities, Human Spaces*, Jaipur: Rawat.

Jenkins, Alan. 1979, *The Social Theory of Claude Levi-Strauss*, London: Macmillan.

Jung, Carl Gustava. 1968, *The Archetypes and the Collective Unconscious*, Princeton NJ: Princeton University Press.

_____. 1933, *Modern Man in Search of a Soul*, New York: Harcourt.

Karve, Irawati. 1969; 1994, *Yuganta*, Hyderabad: Orient Longman.

Khan, Fawzia Afzal. 1993, *Cultural Imperialism and the Indo-English Novel*, Pennsylvania: The Pennsylvania State U P.

King, Bruce, ed. 1966; 1998, *New National and Post-Colonial Literatures*, Oxford: Clarendon Press.

King, Elaine, 1998, *Tales & Legends of India*, New Delhi: New Editions Publishing House.

Kirk, G.S. 1970; 1971, *Myth*, Cambridge: Cambridge University Press.

Knappert, Jan. 1991; 1993, *Indian Mythology*, New Delhi: Harper Collins.

Kosambi, Damodar Dharmanand. 1962; 2000, *Myth and Reality*, Mumbai: Popular Prakashan.

Kumar, Sangeet. 2004, "Human Rights and the Indian Constitution," *Journal of Applied Research in Social Sciences and Humanities*, XIV & XV, 2003-2004.

_____. 2005, *Changing Role of the Caste System: A Critique*, Jaipur: Rawat.

Lal, P. 1962, *The Concept of an Indian Literature*, Calcutta: Writers Workshop.

Levi-Strauss, Claude. 1963; 1968, *Structural Anthropology*, London: Penguin.
Lewis, C.S. 1961, *An Experiment in Criticism*, Cambridge: Cambridge University Press.
Mackenzie, Donald A. 2000, *Indian Myth and Legend*, New Delhi: Smriti Books.
Mair, Lucy. 1965; 1983, *An Introduction to Social Anthropology*, London: Oxford University Press.
Malinowski, Bronislaw. 1963, *Sex, Culture, And Myth,* London: Rupert Hart Davis.
McKie, Robin. "*Ancient Legends Warn of Modern Disasters*," *The Hindu* December 5, 2005.
Mohan, Indra T.M.J, ed. 2004, *Shashi Deshpande*, New Delhi: Atlantic.
Morris, Brain. 1987, *Anthropological Studies of Religion*, Cambridge: Cambridge University Press.
Mukherjee, Meenakshi. 1971, *The Twice Born Fiction*, New Delhi: Heinemann.
Mukherjee, Prabhati. 1978, *Hindu Women*, Hyderabad: Orient Longman.
Naik, M.K. 1979, *Aspects of Indian Writing in English*, Delhi: Macmillan.
_____. 1982, A *History of Indian English Literature*, Delhi: Sahitya Akademi.
Narayan, R.K. 1964; 1999, *Gods Demons, & Others*, New Delhi: Vision Books.
Nehru, Jawaharlal. 1946; 1993, *The Discovery of India*, New Delhi: Oxford University Press.
Panov, Victor G. 1976; 1985, *Emotion, Myths and Theories*, Moscow: Progress Publishers.
Pande, Mrinal. 1996, *Devi*, New Delhi: Penguin.
Prabhu, H. Pandharinath. 1940; 2000, *Hindu Social Organisation*, Mumbai: Popular Prakashan.
Prasad, Jaya. 2002, "Myths an Expression of Ethnicity in English Literature," *Cyber Literature*, IX: 1, June.
_____. 2003, "Arundhati Roy and Her Concern for the Environment: In Her Novel and in Her Essays," *Indian Literature in English*, ed. C.L. Khatri, Jaipur: Book Enclave.
_____. 2005, "R.K. Narayan's Modern Heroines and the Dilemma of Men," *Cyber Literature*, XV & XVI, I & II, Jan.-Dec. 2005.
Prasad, Pratima, 2006, *Women in Nigerian and Indo-Anglian Fiction: A Comparative Study of Female Novelists*, Unpublished Thesis, Patna University, Patna.
Prasad, Shaileshwar Sati. 1994-95, "Myth and the African and the Indian Novel in English," *Swayamprva*, BMD College Magazine.
_____. 1997, *The Insulted and the Injured*, Patna: Janaki Prakashan.
Rajgopalachari, C. 1951; 2004, *Mahabharata*, Mumbai: Bharatiya Vidya Bhavan.
Rao, Raja, 1995, *The Serpent and the Rope*, Delhi: Orient Paperbacks, First Pub.

1960.

_____. 1938; 1996, *Kanthapura*, Delhi: Orient Paperbacks.

Roy, Arundhati. 1997, *The God of Small Things*, New Delhi: IndiaInk.

Sinha, Ila. 1995, *Myth in The Nigerian Novel: A Critical Study*, Unpublished Thesis, Patna University, Patna.

Singh, J.P., ed. 1996, *The Indian Women: Myth and Reality*, New Delhi: Gyan.

Tharoor, Shashi. 1989, *The Great Indian Novel*, New Delhi: Penguin.

_____. "Metaphor for Our Times," *The Hindu*, January 16, 2005.

Thapar, Romila. 1973, *The Past and Prejudice*, New Delhi: Publication Division, Government of India.

The New Encyclopaedia Britannica, Vol. 24.

Trivedi, Harish and Meenakshi Mukherjee, ed. 1996, *Interrogating Postcolonialism*, Shimla: Indian Institute of Advanced Study.

Truzzi, Marcello, ed. 1973, *The Humanities as Sociology*, Columbus, Ohio: Charles E. Merrill.

Tulsidas, *Shri Ramcharita Manas*, Gorakhapura: Gita Press.

Turner, Bryan S. 1996, *The Blackwell Companion to Social Theory*, Oxford: Blackwell.

Turner, Jonathan H. 1987 *The Structure of Sociological Theory*, Jaipur: Rawat (Indian Reprint).

Varma, Pavan K. 1996, *Yudhishtar & Draupadi*, New Delhi: Viking Penguin India.

Weigel, James, Jr. 1993, *Mythology*, Ludhiana: Kalyani Publishers.

Wimsatt, William K. and Cleanth Brooks. 1957, *Literary Criticism: A Short History*, Oxford: Oxford University Press.

Zimmer, Heinrich, 1946; 1990, *Myths and Symbols in Indian Art and Civilization,* Delhi: Motilal Banarsidass.